MILESTONES OF CHILD DEVELOPMENT

MILESTONES OF CHILD DEVELOPMENT

Maimun Nisha

Publications

KALPAZ PUBLICATIONS

DELHI-110052

Milestones of Child Development

Rs. 750

ISBN : 81-7835-498-5

Published in 2006 in India by
Kalpaz Publications
C-30, Satyawati Nagar, Delhi-110052
E-mail : kalpaz@hotmail. com

Laser Typesetting at : Master Computers, Delhi
Printed at : Salasar Imaging System, Delhi

Contents

Preface 9

1. **Physical Development of Child** 11
Child Development Basics • Concept • Stages of Physical Development • Positive Role in Child Development • Infants 0-6 Months • Infant Age between 0-12 Months • Toddlers Age about 2 Years • Toddlers Age about 3 Years • Pre-schooler Child Age between 3-5 Years • Nutritional Needs • Programme Included in Child Development • Principles of Physical Development • Factors Affecting in Physical Development.

2. **Motor Development** 35
Introduction • Development and Stage Theories • Motor Development in Infancy and Childhood • Fine Motor Development • Reaching and Grasping • Some Ideas • Bilateral Coordination • Simple Motor Activities • Developmental Delays • Stages of Motor Development • Toddler Development • Preschool Development • School Age Development • School Readiness • Studies of Motor Development • Who are the Children? • Enhancement of Motor Development • Motor Development Theories • Phases of Motor Development • Motor Development Stages • Classification of Motor Behaviour • Motor Development Stages of Children and Adults.

3. Social and Emotional Development **63**
Concept • Caring for Infants and Toddlers • Crying • Routine Care • Talking with Infants • Safe Exploration • Toddlers' Intense Feelings • Dealing with Feelings: Child • Feel What You Want, Control What You Do • Getting along Together: Children • Modeling Behaviour • Sharing from the Heart • Fairness • Co-operation Versus Competition • Theory Social and Emotional Development • Role of Nutrition • Positive Role in Social and Emotional Development • Physical Needs • Emotional Development • Characteristics of Childhood Emotion • Common Childhood Emotional Pattern • Common Childhood Behaviour Problems • Social Development • Factors Affecting Social Development.

4. Play Development **89**
Concept of Play • Stages of Play • What should Mother do? • Learning Milestones • What will Baby Learn? • Learning Through Play • Playtime in the 21st Century • Changes in Toys • How to Promote Creative Play • Play and its Role • Guidelines for Policymaking • Types of Play • Why are the Types of Play Important?

5. Intelligence Development **131**
Introduction • Definition on Intelligence • Concept of Intelligence • Nature of Intelligence • Types of Intelligence • Multiple Intelligences • Development of Intelligence Theory.

6. Intellectual Development **153**
Introduction • Jean Piaget—Intellectual development • Intellectual Development in

Children • The Preoperational Period (2-7 Years) • Period of Concrete Operation (7-11 Years) • Period of Formal Operation (11-15 Years) • Activity Intellectual Development • How Children Learn • Implications for Education • Intellectual Development and Diet.

7. **Creativity Development** 165
Introduction • Importance • Opportunities for Creativity • Varieties of Experience • Fostering the Creative Process • Creativity in Young Children • Encouraging Creativity through Teacher and Parents • Reality Behind Creativity • Barriers to Creativity • Creativity Develop Through Art • Role of Parent and Teacher • Characteristics of Creative Children • Developing Creativity Among Children • Suggestions for Creative in Thinking and Writing • Methods of Teaching Creativity • Enhance Creativity • Creative Play.

8. **Language Development** 181
Introduction • Stages of Language Development • How to Learn Child • Children's Literacy Development • Activities for Three and Four-Year-Olds • Principles of Language Teaching • Language Disorders • Defective Speech • Factors Affecting Language Development • Common Techniques to Improve the Language Development of Child • Communication • Communication Problem • Typical Communication Pattern • What is Language? What is Speech? • Definition of Speech and Language Disorders • Incidence • Characteristics of Language Development • Educational Implications • Articulation • Language-based Learning Disabilities • Role of Speech-Language Pathologist.

9. **Personality Development** 223
Introduction • Concept • Types of Personality • Temperament • Temperament Traits-9 Phases • Difficult or Easy to Raise Your Child • Adjust with Your Child's Personality • Role of Parents for Very Intense Children • Freud's Stages of Psychosexual Development • Freud's Structural and Topographical Models of Personality • Topographical Model • Ego Defence Mechanisms • Psychosocial Theory: Erikson • Ego Psychology • Zones, Modes, and Modalities • Erikson's Stages of Psychosocial Development.

10. **Moral Development** 247
Introduction • Moral Behaviour • Kohlberg and Piaget Theory • Interaction between Nature and Nurture • Moral Development Theory • Stages of Moral Development • Piaget's Stages of Moral Development • Kohlberg's Six Stages of Moral Development • Concept of Moral Development.

11. **Cognitive Development** 271
Positive Role in Child's Cognitive Development • Activities with Two-Years-Olds • Preschoolers Age between 3-5 Years • Role and Need of Nutrition in Child Development • Role of Nutrition • Nutrition for Cognitive Development • Piaget's Stages of Cognitive Development • Period of Concrete Operations (7-11 Years) • Period of Formal Operations (11-15 Years) • Stages of Cognitive Development • Brain Growth During the Third Year • Encouraging Interests.

Bibliography 289

Index 291

Preface

The growing interest in child study and development, as has been said in the proceeding ways, contributed to various perspectives embodied in the form of theories. Theories infant describe, explain and predict what will happen in a given situation.

Child psychology and child development deals with under finding of growth and development pattern and development of various characteristics in children.

Child development defined as a branch of knowledge concerned with the nature of development and regulation of significant functional and behavioural changes in children as they advanced in age and maturity. it deals with understanding the development of characteristics of children and the process through which development start.

I feel very happy in presenting the book to all universities students of home science, child study, psychology and other subjects. All the chapters are up to date study.

The author likes this opportunity to thank her well wishers and her publisher.

Maimun Nisha

1

Physical Development of Child

Child Development Basics

A child's growth is a continuous process, a gradual sequencing from one stage of physical and mental development to another. "Each child sits before he stands; he babbles before he talks" It's a marvelous process to watch and a marvelous opportunity for parents to foster and implement important periods of growth.

Babies and young children learn primarily through movement and their senses how to deal with gravity, to keep their balance, to move their body through space, about time and sequence of events.

Concept

The child development provides parents with information on physical, mental and emotional growth and development in children. The information helps parents to know what to expect from their children as they mature. Child development information can help parents know when they are expecting too much from a child as well as become aware of lags in development that may benefit from professional help. This chapter provide information on how to help children reach their full potential as they grow and develop.

Stages of Physical Development

From the start, babies want to explore their world. They are eager to move their eyes, their mouths, and their bodies toward the people and objects that comfort and interest them. They practice skills that let them not only move closer to desired objects, but also move desired objects closer to themselves. As they grow, children's determination to master mo child begins life as a being with little control of movement and progresses to one who can run, jump, laugh, sing, write with a pencil and control his own small and large muscles with growing confidence. This progression is physical development.

Although humans change physically throughout life, the changes which occur during the first four years are dramatic and eagerly awaited. Muscle skills development and maintaining a healthy body are especially important to future reading, writing, and math success.

There are individual differences in the area of physical development ranging from one month to four to six months for each particular skill.

Age	*Milestones*
The first year	A baby begins learning the basics of self-movement and begins to master the skills needed for hand-to-mouth coordination and holding objects.
Birth (0-3) months	Most infants begin to: • Raise head slightly when lying on stomach • Hold head up for a few seconds, when supported • Hold hand in a fist • Lift head and chest, while lying on stomach • Use sucking, grasping, and rooting (holding tongue to the roof of the mouth) reflexes • Touch, pull, and tug own hands with fascination • Repeat body movements, and enjoy doings—
3-6 months	Babies are quickly becoming stronger and more agile. Most begin to: • Roll over • Push body forward and pull body up by grabbing the edge of a crib • Reach for and touch objects

(Contd.)

Age	*Milestones*
	• Reach, grasp, and put objects in mouth • Make discoveries with objects (for example, a rattle makes noise when it is moved)
6-9 months	"Child-proofing" becomes important as babies get more mobile. During this time most begin to: • Crawl • Grasp and pull things toward self • Transfer objects between hands
9-12 months	By this time, most babies can: • Sit without support • Stand unaided • Walk with aid • Roll a ball • Throw objects • Pick things up with thumb and one finger • Drop and pick up toys
1-2 years	Walking and self-initiated movement become easier. Most children can: • Walk alone • Walk backwards • Pick up toys from a standing position • Push and pull objects • Seat self in a child's chair • Walk up and down stairs with aid • Move to music • Paint with whole arm movement • Balance improves and eye-hand coordination becomes more precise. Most children can: • Put rings on a peg • Turn two or three pages at a time • Scribble • Turn knobs • Grasp and hold a small ball; can use in combination with large motor skills to throw the ball • Shift marker or any drawing or painting tool from hand to hand and draw strokes
2-3 years	Children become more comfortable with motion, increasing speed, and coordination.

(Contd.)

Age	*Milestones*
	Most begin to: • Run forward • Jump in place with both feet together • Stand on one foot, with aid • Walk on tiptoe • Kick ball forward Children are able to manipulate small objects with increased control. Most can: • String large beads • Turn pages one by one • Hold crayon with thumb and fingers instead of fist • Draw a circle • Paint with wrist action, making dots and lines • Roll, pound, squeeze, and pull clay
3-4 years	Movement and balance improve. Most children can: • Run around obstacles • Walk on a line • Balance on one foot • Push, pull, and steer toys • Ride a tricycle • Use a slide without help • Throw and catch a ball Children's precision of motion improves significantly. Most are able to: • Build a tall tower of blocks • Drive pegs into holes • Draw crosses and circles • Manipulate clay by making balls, snakes, etc.
4-5 years	Children are now more confident, and most are able to: • Walk backwards • Jump forward many times without falling • Jump on one foot • Walk up and down stairs without assistance, alternating feet • Turn somersaults Children develop skills that will help them as they enter school and begin writing. Most can: • Use safety scissors • Cut on a line continuously • Copy squares and crosses • Print a few capital letters

Positive Role in Child Development

Child develop physically by feeding the child when he is hungry and by helping him exercise those developing muscles. Children develop from the top to the bottom. (First, the head muscles become strong, then the body, then the legs, then the feet.) They also develop from the inside to the outside. (First, the trunk of the body becomes strong, then the arms and legs, and then the hands and feet.)

Large muscles (those that control large movements like crawling, walking, hopping, throwing, catching, and balancing) develop before small muscles (those that control the wrist and hand in activities like drawing, cutting, stringing beads, building block towers).

Infants 0-6 Months

Large Muscle

Early on, infant will be able to turn his head to either side when lying on his back. At some point during the first two months, he will be able to raise his head and look around while lying on his tummy when his arms are out in front of him. The length of time he can do this will become longer and longer as his muscles strengthen. He can sit for short amounts of time propped up against the sofa cushions.

By three months, he will be able to keep his head controlled when he is in an upright position. He will grasp your fingers and pull to a sitting position. He can also roll from his tummy to his back. By five to six months, he will be able to roll from his back to his tummy. Around this time he will also be able to sit without support. At about eight months he will begin to crawl. However, if your child does not do each of these milestones at the time noted, it does not mean there is a problem.

Large Muscle

1. Move a light slowly across his field of vision from side to side so he will move his head to track the light. Try the same thing by moving the face.

2. Shake a rattle on one side and after he turns his head that direction, shake the rattle on the other side. Try the same thing with your voice.
3. Dangle objects for your three-month-old to reach out to grasp. Squeaky toys are popular with babies, too.
4. He will begin to smile and even laugh around four months. Laugh and smile right back at him. This is such a delightful time!
5. Exercise his legs gently at play time. Try singing a simple song or nursery rhyme as you exercise.
6. six-month-old will enjoy trying to remove a peg from a large pegboard.
7. Keep an unbreakable mirror around so he can see himself often.
8. Give him gentle body massages.

Small Muscle

Young infant can follow moving objects with his eyes. His best focusing distance is about 12", about the distance you are from him when you feed him. Right from the start you will notice that he is staring at you while he eats. He is forming the connection in his brain that you are his parent. He can move his arms and get his hands to his mouth but it is still somewhat random.

At three to four months, he will begin to try to grasp objects. He will also begin to touch the fingers of one hand with the other. At five months, he will begin to transfer toys from one hand to the other. By six months, his vision will be comparable to an adult's. Between six and eight months, his grasp will improve and he will begin to use wrist movements:

1. Give him rattles and squeaky toys to grasp when he is ready.
2. Teething rings are also handy because they are so easy to grasp.

3. As his grasp improves, begin to give him blocks to play with.
4. At seven months, give him small melt able finger foods like Cheerios to scoop up and eat. He will be trying hard to pick objects up with a pincer grasp (using his thumb and forefinger to hold a small object). As he becomes more accomplished, he'll be able to handle other finger foods. Remember he should always be seated and supervised while eating.
5. Begin using some simple gestures with him. He will pick them up and begin using them, too.
6. Roll a ball to him and encourage him to roll it back.
7. It's time for that rubber ducky to appear in the tub.

Infant Age between 6-12 Months

Large Muscle

Baby has become mobile. He is scooting and crawling! The world has opened up for him. He can even stand and take steps when helped. He can sit up all by himself. He can pull himself up to furniture and even walk holding on to the furniture.

When he is sitting, baby can turn the upper part of his body to the right or left. He can lean forward to pick up an object. Make sure that you have baby-proofed your house by now. . . baby will be exploring every inch of it!

1. Place toys at different places on the floor to encourage him to crawl and reach them.
2. Put toys on the sofa that he can see from the floor so he will want to pull up to get them.
3. Roll a ball back and forth with him.
4. Children this age love busy boxes to twist and push and honk. Play along with him.

5. He will enjoy some blocks to play with. He can bang them on the floor and carry them with him when he crawls.
6. Some cardboard books would be good to introduce. Just remember that everything will go into the mouth at one time or another.
7. Keep an unbreakable mirror around so he can see himself often.
8. Hold both of his hands and walk around the house together.

Small Muscle

The mobile infant is curious about everything. He will examine whatever is on his level. He loves to take things out of containers. He will try to put his nesting blocks back together but he won't care if only two or three are re-nested. Then he will laugh and dump them again. He will drop objects on purpose. This is especially fun to a child when he can drop objects off the side of his high chair. He now has a well-developed pincer grasp. He enjoys making noise by banging his toys together.

Small Muscle

1. Give him a toy telephone to play with. Pretend to call him and talk with him.
2. Play with him with some nesting toys. He will dump them. You can pick them up one at a time and try to make a stack with them. He will probably let you stack a few and then knock them all down. Talk to him as you play.
3. Invest in a few sturdy board books. Read to him daily and begin letting him turn the pages. Point out objects on the pages.
4. Give him small objects to pick up like small pieces of cheese when he is about 9 months of age and can chew and swallow it. Keep him seated and supervised during feeding.

5. Add some measuring cups to the bath so he can fill and pour while you bathe him.
6. Blow bubbles for him to watch and try to catch.
7. Give him a sponge to squeeze.

Toddlers Age about 2 Years

Large Muscle

This is a very exciting time for you and baby! baby is beginning to walk. He will be a little shaky at first, and will hold one or both arms out to the front or side for balance. He will want to walk all of the time. He may have trouble sleeping for the first week after he begins to walk. You may find him walking around in his bed when he should be sleeping. It is all so exciting to him that he finds it hard to take time out to sleep. He can stand up without holding onto furniture. He squats down to pick up objects or to play and then stands back up. By the end of the year, he will be able to jump up and down and he will be able to walk up stairs using a rail. He loves to pull or push a toy. Now he likes to put objects into a container. Give him his own kitchen cabinet with some plastic stacking cups and bowls and he will be happy moving them back and forth.

Large Muscle

1. Give him lots of time to practice his new skill. Try to keep him on a level surface as he learns to walk. After he has practiced enough, let him walk in the yard. He will be surprised when he falls down but he will quickly learn how to get around the little bumpy spots.
2. He will want to try stairs. Just stay beside him as he climbs. Work with him on a safe way to come down. A baby gate is an important safety device for those times when you can't be right there.
3. Play catch with him.
4. Take him for a walk and let him bring his pull toy.

5. Ask him to get his coat or shoes when you are going somewhere.
6. He will begin to walk faster when he wants to go in a different direction than you want. He will try to get around you and go his own way. Be friendly but firm in your guidance.
7. Play simple chase games with him. Blow bubbles to chase.

Small Muscle

Your toddler will begin to stack blocks. He will also be able to place two or three pegs in a pegboard before he gets tired of it. He has begun to enjoy scribbling. Later in the year, he will be able to make a circular scribble and a vertical line. He will also hold the crayon with his fingers instead of his fist. By the end of this year, he will favor one hand over the other. He has begun to use his finger to point to objects. He will be able to do a simple three piece knobbed puzzle.

Small Muscle

1. Use beanbags to throw at a target.
2. Let him help you fold clothes.
3. Play a body parts game where you name a part and he points to it.
4. Read books with him holding the book and turning the pages.
5. Let him explore with sidewalk chalk.
6. Have him push the buttons on a play telephone or on an activity toy.
7. Pack sand in a mold.
8. Provide age-appropriate toys like little cars with passengers that he can put in their seats.

Toddlers Age about 3 Years

Large Muscle

Two-year-old can run with good balance and even swing his arms when running like an adult does. At the beginning of the year he will walk up and down steps by putting both feet on each step but by the end of the year he will be walking up and down by having each foot step on an individual stair. He can catch a large ball at the beginning of the year but he will catch a small one by the end of the year. He can jump from a bottom step, walk on tiptoe, and ride a push strike. Later this year, he will begin to ride a bike with pedals. He will also be able to climb a jungle gym and will attempt to balance and hop on one foot.

Large Muscle

1. Take your child to a local park and encourage him to climb and slide.
2. Take walks with him and let him ride his tricycle.
3. Play chase games and hide-and-seek with him.
4. Play kicking and throwing games.
5. Play some copycat games where you tiptoe, walk backwards, jump, and hop.
6. Make an obstacle course and go through it together.
7. Fly a kite together.
8. Blow bubbles and chase them.
9. If you stay home with child, consider joining a Mother's Morning Out. This will give your child a chance to be active with other children.

Small Muscle

It's easy to see which hand child prefers. That's because he's using his hands all of the time, colouring, painting, and more. He is interested in using crayons and paint and he holds his crayon with a more adult grip. He can imitate strokes drawn by another person. He can make circles, vertical and horizontal lines, and draw a cross. Later in the year he will be able to cut on a line. He can screw and unscrew lids and string beads. He can stack up to 8 blocks in a tower. He can put on some clothes by himself and brush his own teeth with some encouragement.

Small Muscle

1. Let him use large pencils and crayons.
2. He can even try blunt-tipped safety scissors with supervision. Buy a quality pair of children's blunt-tip scissors so he will not get frustrated trying to cut. Local teacher's supply company can help you.
3. Begin counting small numbers of objects. Have him touch each item as he counts it.
4. Buy some simple six-piece puzzles and give him the advice needed to work a puzzle successfully.
5. Buy some blocks and play with them together. Build some zoos and castles and imagine what would happen there.
6. Make or buy some play dough and pound, squeeze, roll, and cut to your heart's content!

Preschooler Child Age between 3-5 Years

Losing the Baby Cubbies-Leaner and Proportional

It may have noticed that three-year-old or four-year-old has lost his chubby appearance. The growth of body fat slows and child looks much leaner. Average three-year-olds weigh about 32-34 pounds; four-year-olds, 36-38 pounds. Growth in height averages about two to three inches per year of age. Three-year-olds are, on the average 38-39 inches tall; four-year-olds, 40-42 inches. Variations in height are common. It's not unusual to find that four different four-year-olds are all of different heights. Your child's height is likely to be related to yours. His weight is affected by his genetics and environmental influences, such as nutrition and health care.

Child looks less "top heavy" because the head is more in proportion to the body. His facial features have changed, too. His eyes appear more widely spaced as the bridge of the nose has begun to form, and the lower jaw has filled out so that it is more proportional to the forehead. His fingers are longer and have lost their chubby appearance. His neck is longer so he doesn't look like his head is resting directly on his shoulders.

Large Muscle Skills

Large muscle or motor skills refer to your child's developing abilities to walk, run, jump, hop, throw, catch, and balance himself.

You are definitely noticing that your three-or four-year-old is nearly always in a state of constant physical motion. During the third and fourth year of life, child will acquire many basic motor skills. In fact, by the time he enters school, child will have acquired most of the basic motor skills that will later be improved upon and worked into more complex sequences of movement.

Just as you were amazed when he started to walk, which may just seem like yesterday, today your three-year-old can walk on his tiptoes, stand on one foot, and hop on both feet. He rides a tricycle, walks down a series of steps unsupported with both feet on one step, and jumps down from various locations such as the sofa or, perhaps, playground equipment at the park. He may even be able to do a forward somersault without your help. Your child's running is much quicker and more coordinated. And he can throw and kick a ball with some measure of accuracy.

Between four and five years of age, child continues to expand his motor skills. He can gallop; walk up and down steps unsupported using alternating feet, and may even perform tricks on his tricycle. You may see him hopping seven to nine times on one foot. Although not graceful in appearance, his hopping abilities are improving and with additional time and experience, he will be able to control his direction and coordination.

You may observe that three-year-old child practices many of the new skills over and over. As he becomes competent at these amazing feats, he will incorporate them into his play. For example, after riding his tricycle forward and backward and in circles many times, four-year-old child will pretend it is a race car zooming towards the finish line.

Small Muscle Skills

Small muscle skills are those budding abilities to feed and dress oneself, draw and paint, build with blocks, work puzzles, and use scissors.

At the time child is three or four years old, refrigerator is practically an art gallery, holding all of your child's artistic creations, each one cherished for its unique expression. In fact, you may notice that there is a shape or design appearing in the scribbles, and child may have told all about his drawing.

You may have noticed that three-year-old can draw a straight line and may even copy a circle if requested. He may create a more intricate pattern of loops and circles. If you watch carefully, you will see that he is holding his crayon in a more adult-like grasp. He will spend more time on his drawings. With great pride, he may say, "See what I made." For three-year-old, he wants you to notice the advancements he has made without hurrying him or pressuring him. These important strides in child's growth are remarkable. He views his creation "in process." For example, he begins drawing with no particular picture in his mind. As he creates, your child's drawing unfolds to him. These early scribbles are the foundation of later realistic drawings. Also, early scribbles are the basics of later writing and reading.

During the third year of life, child shows increasingly that he can eat by himself with few spills. You will still have to help him cut his food. He can dress himself and requires assistance with pullover shirts and some fasteners. He may tell you often, "I can do it by myself." He can brush his teeth by himself and he likes to brush his own hair.

Child may have watched you use scissors and shows an interest in trying to cut. His cuts may seem crude to you; however, his snips and cuts delight him immensely. Although he tries to hold the scissors as you do, child will sometimes put the wrong fingers in the holes and turn the scissors upside down. Before you know it, with experience and development of coordination, child will be cutting straight lines in his fourth year of life.

Between four and five years of age, child may be making letters in his name. These letters may show up randomly in his drawings at first. You may also see a person emerge in his drawings. Drawings of people are often the first recognizable pictures. Four-year-olds begin to use lines, shapes, and designs to represent reality. Once again it is important to remember that child's creation emerges in the process of doing, so he may not be able to tell what he is drawing. He may be more interested in the action of drawing and painting than in representing objects in his pictures.

Puzzles, bead stringing, and building are popular activities for three-and four-year-olds. Most three-year-olds can build a 9 or 10 block tower of blocks. Three and four-piece puzzles are workable by three-year-old child. A four-year-old can work ten-to twelve-piece puzzles.

Nutritional Needs

Three or four-year-old child requires more calorie intake per pound than you do as an adult. A child's stomach holds less food than the average adult's. Young children need to eat small amounts of food about every two hours. A good rule of thumb for serving sizes for young children is one level tablespoon per year of age for each food. That may sound like a small amount to you, but keep in mind child's small tummy capacity.

The daily diets of children should include three or more cups of milk or milk products; two or more servings of meat, poultry, fish, and eggs; five or more servings of vegetables and fruits (including at least one citrus fruit and one dark green or deep yellow vegetable); six or more servings of whole grain bread or whole grain cereal; and other foods as needed for energy. Fiber equal to the child's age plus five is also recommended. So a three-year-old should receive about 8 grams of fiber (3 years + 5) daily.

At mealtime, can encourage child to try new foods. Letting him serve himself encourages him to try new foods. foster good eating habits by showing child that, enjoy a variety of nutritious foods. Keeping family mealtimes relaxed and pleasant encourages child to eat healthily and enjoy the time.

By providing a pleasant experience at mealtime, help your child establish good nutritional patterns that will last a lifetime. Also, meeting the basic food needs of preschool child helps assure child will maintain her natural energy, curiosity, and abilities to learn.

Learning Activities–Help and Enhance Child's Development

You are your child's most important first teacher. There are many enjoyable activities that mother do together at home.

Large Muscle

1. Take a walk around the block.
2. Ride bikes together.
3. Encourage your child to help around the house-water the plants, vacuum the carpet, dust the table, and put away the groceries.
4. Turn on your favourite music-dance and march together to the rhythm of the music.
5. Act out your child's favourite storybook characters
6. Play hide and seek.
7. Play ball-throw, catch, and kick.
8. Do somersaults together.
9. Go to the park and play on the swings and slide.
10. Race to the nearest tree.
11. Throw beanbags at targets.
12. Crawl under the kitchen table.
13. Act out your child's favourite animals:
14. Place a piece of masking tape on the floor.
15. Swing on the monkey bars at the park.
16. Dig in the garden and plant a seed, plant, or tree.
17. Push a child's size shopping cart at the grocery store.

Small Muscle

1. Work a puzzle together.
2. Build a castle with blocks.
3. Construct a *Lego* car, spaceship, or building.
4. Provide lots of toys for the bath: various sizes of cups, containers, and sieves. Also, sponges for squeezing.
5. Paint a picture.
6. Read a book together.
7. Sort and stack laundry together, putting all like things together.
8. Set the table.
9. Help your child put his toys away.
10. Make a picture-provide plenty of different kinds of paper and writing materials (crayons, markers, chalk, pens, and pencils).
11. Provide stencils for tracing.
12. Wash dishes together.
13. Cut with children's safety scissors together—Play dough, pictures, newspapers.
14. Finger paint with shaving cream on a counter top.
15. Make a collage of your child's favourite foods.
16. String a necklace of large beads.
17. Brush your teeth together.
18. Let your child pour his favourite drink from a small pitcher.
19. Let your child set the table.
20. Sort large buttons and washers or other household items.
21. Have a stuffed animal or doll tea party. Let your child pour the drinks and set the table.
22. Add an appropriate computer game to your home computer.

Programme Included in Child Development

At School

The responsibility of the parent is twofold. Not only should proper emphasis be placed on movement and exercise in the home but whenever possible the school's approach to physical education should be monitored. A good program in elementary school ideally will offer three or four periods a week of 45-60 minutes' duration. The program need not necessarily be highly structured and should certainly not be highly competitive. Movement is the key, and that can include simple activities (running in place, jumping jacks) and games. The program should progress developmentally from grade to grade and should be designed to offer maximum benefit to every child, no matter how small or Late-maturing.

A word of caution: Parents must be careful of physical conditions that might limit a child's movements and participation. Most schools ask, for their records, that a medical report be on file at the school, but it is the parent's responsibility to see that the report is accurate and up to date and that everyone on the faculty who needs to be aware of the report knows about it.

In the Community

For youngsters who are interested in competitive sports, almost every community offers after-school and summer sports such as soccer, baseball, and football. But *these highly* organized activities can promote stress if emphasis is placed on winning rather than just enjoying the game. An observant parent can usually quickly tell if the child is paying a high emotional price rather than just having fun. And it should be noted that in some highly organized sports, the youngsters spend more time standing around and watching than actually participating.

The local YMCA and YWCA usually offer well-rounded pro-grams that include fitness exercises and swimming The fitness program may consist of carefully structured aerobics, and the swimming program is usually designed for individual mastery rather than competition.

At Home

Parents are enormously busy people-perhaps both parents work outside the family; perhaps there are several children in the family with differing needs and demands; perhaps it is a one-parent family. The activities that follow are offered with precisely those situations in mind. They are simple, inexpensive, enjoyable, arid can be adapted for groups (the whole family and/or friends) as well as for individual youngsters.

Caring by Parents for Infants and Toddlers

The first years are a wondrous time. As the months pass, parents are able to form deep, affectionate bonds with their babies and marvel at their rapid growth. Infants need a small, consistent group of people whom they can learn to know and trust. When babies are in childcare settings, it is important for group sizes to remain small (with at least one adult for every three infants) so that secure, meaningful relationships can form and each infant's needs for attention, affection and routine care can be met. Toddlers continue to need secure attachments and a great deal of individual attention.

Crying

Babies come into this world ready for relationships-each with a unique personality and style of communication. Babies tell about their feelings and needs through their facial expressions and body movements, as well as by cooing, babbling, and crying. Crying is one of the main ways babies communicate. They cry to tell us that they want or need something to happen-perhaps a diaper change, a bottle, a nap, or a hug.

Routine Care

Routine care, such as feeding a baby or changing a diaper, provides rich opportunities for one-to-one contact. Be sure to feed and change infants and put them down for naps based on their needs, not according to a schedule. Hold the baby during bottle-feeding in order to take advantage of this time for closeness and interaction. Keep in mind that too much stimulation, such as bright lights and constant noise, may overwhelm infants and cause them stress.

Infants' immunity to infectious disease is just beginning to build. Remember to wash your hands and take other sanitary precautions before and after feeding, diapering, and toileting. Keep sick children home so the infection or illness is not spread to other children and adults.

Talking with Infants

Even before they understand words, babies love to hear language and respond by cooing, babbling, and making sounds that gradually resemble adult speech. During the first two years of life, children understand much more than they can say. help children learn new words by noticing the things that catch their attention, naming them, and talking about them. Repeatedly using newly learned words will reinforce them and build child's vocabulary. By using the same words in different ways ("You have a face. And the clock has a face, too"), or finding different ways to say the same thing ("It's big, it's huge, it's gigantic") help children build a richer, more expressive vocabulary as they grow.

Safe Exploration

Infants need many opportunities to explore their world using all of their senses. As baby begins to crawl and then walk, a safe environment is essential. From child's perspective, if it's in view, it's interesting; and if it's in reach, it will be investigated. That's why it is important to "child proof" all settings where young children spend time. Potential dangers include unlocked cabinets, uncovered electrical outlets, medicines and cleaning supplies, and small objects that can be put into a child's mouth. prevent accidents with close supervision and frequent inspection to spot new dangers that crop up as children grow and develop.

Toddlers' Intense Feelings

Toddlers are very involved in learning about themselves in relation to the world around them Their day often involves conflict with siblings, playmates, and the adults around them.

Keep in mind that when a toddler wants something, she typically wants it intensely and immediately. If you are caring for more than one child, you can help reduce conflict by making sure there are enough toys and materials for all to share. It's also important that your toddler has enough time and space to fully explore her environment. Be sure she has plenty of opportunities to make real choices and decisions, like what snack food she prefers or which shirt she wants to wear.

When toddlers don't get what they want, tempers often flare. Children can be frightened by their own feelings and actions, and they rely on the adults around them to remain calm. In simple language, say what specific behaviors are expected and what will happen if the rules are not followed ("Stop throwing the crackers, or snack time will be over.") Let child know that you (or other caregivers) are there to help her work through her intense emotions.

An environment that encourages exploration and physical development is important for children of all ages. Be sure to allow your baby plenty of space for rolling, scooting and, eventually, crawling. Babies like to grasp and manipulate objects, so be sure you have rattles and other safe toys within easy reach. Make it a habit to wash the toys your baby puts in her mouth on a daily basis. Babies love to look at and reach for moving objects such as mobiles or streamers. Be sure to hang them safely.

Large Motor Skills

Play allows children to try out and practice new skills. children need opportunities to develop upper body strength by rolling balls and throwing bean bags, and later by pulling themselves up, hanging, and swinging. They need opportunities to strengthen their lower bodies by running, jumping and balancing. Encourage your children to try a variety of physical activities, involving large- and small-muscle skills, but try not to pressure or demand that they excel at every physical task. Remember that children need lots of time and space for energetic, noisy play.

Fine-Motor Skills

Using crayons, stringing beads, and doing puzzles are all good ways to help children develop fine-motor skills and eye-hand coordination. These kinds of activities can be tiring for young children, so don't expect them to work at such skills for long stretches.

Developing All Five Senses

Hands-on activities allow children to develop all their senses: sight, touch, hearing, smell, and taste. Encourage them to compare the way different objects look, sound, feel, or smell. As they grow, introduce new foods so they get used to a variety of tastes.

Safety Guidelines

As children become more physically active, it can be difficult to draw the line between taking sensible safety precautions and being overprotective. The goal is to maintain a high level of safety while allowing your children to experiment with mild risks that build feelings of competence as they are met and mastered. As child grows, experience will be your guide. A basic safety guideline is to avoid lifting child onto play equipment that he cannot climb onto by himself. Playgrounds should have soft surfaces (such as sand or rubber) to buffer falls.

Illness and Infection

Be sure that children's immunizations are up to date. Keep contagious children at home. Hand-washing is the single most effective way to avoid spreading disease. Children and adults should get used to washing hands before handling food and after diapering, toileting, or blowing their noses.

Principles of Physical Development

1. Physical Growth

Physical growth is sign of child's development. it follow two sequence cephalo caudal and proximodistal. These first principle refers to the growth and development proceed from head to feet. Growth starts from head to toe. The baby fist lift head than after moves arm, hand, shoulder etc. Second principles deals from axis to outward the periphery. Baby moves hand first than after fingers. Growth hamper by environmental condition, dietary intake, parental care, socio economic status, heredity, depression etc.

2. Changes in Body Proportion

Head and trunk are disproportionate at the time of birth. Growth of head is slow after the completion of fist year. Legs growth are more frequent than the trunk.

3. Changes in the Height

Boys are taller than the girls. Height rate increases during fist year of life. baby increase height between 6-7 inches during first 5 months. baby increases height at least 10-15 inches after completion of two years. Role of diet is essential part of growth of height.

4. Changes in Body Weight

Weight increases in rapid speed in first year of life. At birth baby is about 6-8 pounds. In first year baby doubles his weight. Body weights depend on age, sex, diet, fitness, heredity etc.

5. Nervous System

The growth of nervous system is very high during pre natal stage and after birth of 3-4 years. After 4 years the growth is very slow. brain development also in rapid speed during the age of 1-2 year.

6. Motor Development

Motor development is uniform developmental sequence of posture, prehension and loco motor. motor skill help the child to adjust with environment. It is an expression of emotion.

7. Postural Loco Motor Development

It occurs in between the age of 6 months to two years. Physical and motor development is very high in this age but brain development is little slower than the motor development. The child development maximum motor skill at between 2-15 months.

8. Prehension Development

Prehension involves coordination of sensory motor system, it is the ability to group object with fingers and thumb. It is not a continuous process. It decreases with increase in age. It starts from the 2 months when child wants to grasp things.

Factors Affecting in Physical Development

1. Sex gland—it influence the physical development of the child because it secrets hormone which are responsible for male and female characteristics.
2. Heredity—it has great affect on physical development, i.e., size, strength, appearance, metabolism etc.
3. Prenatal condition—that means maternal nutrition, infection during pregnancy, chronic diseases, birth injury, drugs, intoxication, X-ray, emotion also hamper the physical status of the child.
4. Socio economic status—it affects the health, nutrition, and stimulation of the child.
5. Nutrition-it influence body growth, deficiency and physical activity of the child.

2

Motor Development

Introduction

One of the most common concerns for a parent is whether or not her child is developing normally. The one area of development that tends to cause the most concern is gross motor development. Although many baby books provide lists of "what your baby should be doing" at various ages, few books explain just what "normal development" is and why there is a lot of room for variation.

To help parents understand development, it is important to know that the brain is fairly compartmentalized. The part of the brain that tells the shoulders to move is separate from the part the tells the right thumbs to move. The right side of the brain controls the movements on the left side of the body and vice versa. Therefore, movement of the right shoulder is controlled by a separate area of the brain from that part that controls the left shoulder. This part of the brain that controls muscle movement is called the "motor strip". The motor strip is separate from the part of the brain that interprets spoken speech, stores vocabulary words, recognizes symbols, signals the urge to breath, et cetera!

By the time a baby is born after nine months of pregnancy, the signaling from the brain is still immature. The part of the brain that controls basic functions like sucking and swallowing and breathing is pretty much ready to go, but the part that controls the neck muscles, arms, legs, etc is still under development. Furthermore, although the brain has to signal to the rest of the body, it is not the whole story when it comes to movement. Nerves receiving signals from the brain must also be in good working order. The nerves send chemicals from one to another as signals. For the signal to travel down the nerve (think electricity going down a wire), the nerve must also be properly insulated with a substance called myelin. Then the muscles that receive the signal must be able to respond. The whole process is extraordinarily complicated on a cellular level and it is a wonder the most of us do as well as we do!

The maturational process occurs fairly predictably from the top down. First head control is gained as the nerves supplying the neck muscles mature and the neck muscles gain strength. The shoulder, upper arms, and hand control improves. Upper body or trunk control is next, then the hips and pelvis, and finally the legs! Because hand movements are so complex, doctors track "fine motor" skills separately from gross motor skills. Balance and coordination are part of gross motor skills although they have more complex controlling systems than just the motor strip. Thus the familiar order of gross motor development: turning the head from side to side when lying prone (i.e., on the stomach) at two weeks, then lifting the head briefly when prone at two to three months, holding the head upright by four to five months, then raising up the shoulders and upper chest when four to five months. Arm movements also gain some control about age to four to five months as the infant can bring her hands to midline when lying on her back. After that, she can reach and grab an object and bring it to her mouth. She can hold an object in one hand and transfer it to another by six to seven months. Trunk control allows the baby to sit propped against her outstretched arms about six to seven months with independent sitting by eight to nine months. Finally, pulling up as the signals to the pelvis and thigh muscles increases followed by standing and then walking. After that, signaling continues to be refined and allows the child to run, climb, hop on two feet, then one foot, then skip by age five.

Because gross motor skills are so obvious, these are the ones that parents tend to notice the most. But remember, gross motor is only one part of development. If gross motor skills are associated with delays in the other areas of development, this is more concerning for the child's overall well-being. If gross motor skills are the only area that is lagging, this is usually not as concerning for long term well-being. There is large variability in the age at which children attain most gross motor milestones. If you have any concerns, always talk to your child's pediatrician or family practitioner.

Development and Stage Theories

When discussing any type of development, most theorists break it down into specific stages. These stages are typically progressive. In other words, you must pass through one stage before you can get to the next. Think about how you learned to run; first you had to learn to crawl, then you could learn to walk, and finally you could develop the skills needed to run. Without the first two stages, running would be an impossibility.

In this chapter we will discuss the most prominent stage theories in regard to motor development.

Motor Development in Infancy and Childhood

Most infants develop motor abilities in the same order and at approximately the same age. In this sense, most agree that these abilities are genetically preprogrammed within all infants. The environment does play a role in the development, with an enriched environment often reducing the learning time and an impoverished one doing the opposite.

The following chart delineates the development of infants in sequential order. The ages shown are averages and it is normal for these to vary by a month or two in either direction.

2 months–able to lift head up on his own

3 months–can roll over

4 months–can sit propped up without falling over

6 months–is able to sit up without support

7 months–begins to stand while holding on to things for support

9 months–can begin to walk, still using support

10 months–is able to momentarily stand on her own without support

11 months–can stand alone with more confidence

12 months–begin walking alone without support

14 months–can walk backward without support

17 months–can walk up steps with little or no support

18 months–able to manipulate objects with feet while walking, such as kicking a ball.

Fine Motor Development

Your baby's fine motor development is crucial. He/she needs to learn to use his/her hands well in order to manipulate toys and to acquire self-help skills such as feeding and dressing.

Babies who have good vision explore their environments from the very beginning by using their sight. They learn to coordinate their eye and hand movements so that they can soon manipulate a variety of toys and use their hands well. The beginning of "reaching" occurs with a baby's eyes. Babies who are blind or visually impaired must learn to coordinate the movements of their hands and arms with their hearing. They need to learn to use their hands in ways which will be functional, motivating and enjoyable. Your baby will need extra practice and many, many opportunities to learn to use his/her hands. Babies who do not use their hands for motivating and useful activities may begin to develop behaviors such as hand or finger flicking or tapping on a surface. Hands which are "busy" playing with toys are less likely to be used for self-stimulatory behaviours.

Play is a child's "work." Babies and young children need to have plenty of opportunities to play. Those who are blind or visually impaired need to be shown how to play with toys; they need to get satisfaction from their play so that they will be motivated to continue to explore and play. The goal is for them to get as much information as possible through their hands and to take that information and use it in meaningful ways.

All fine motor activities (i.e., Braille, writing, hand writing, eating, dressing, etc.) are built upon four important skills. These four skills must be learned before a child can go on to more complicated tasks. They are:

- Grasping objects
- Reaching out to objects
- Releasing objects deliberately
- Turning the wrist in various directions

The connection between weight bearing and learning to use one's hands is very important. Weight bearing gives the kind of feedback that makes the baby aware of his/her arms and hands, and shows him/her how he/she can use them. Weight bearing causes a baby to open his/her hands, straighten out his/her arms, and raise his/her head and trunk.

Reaching and Grasping

Grasping is the ability to hold on to objects and use them for specific purposes. Young babies have a reflexive grasp; their hands automatically close tightly when pressure or stimulation is applied to their palms. As a baby becomes more aware of his/her hands, he/she is able to open them voluntarily and develop a "true" grasp. The reflexive grasp is inhibited as a baby takes more and more weight on his/her hands. It is replaces by a series of different holding methods which, over time, involve more thumb participation. You cannot teach your child to grasp, but by observing the type of grasp your child shows, you can provide toys and activities that will help him/her move along to the next developmental step.

Some Ideas

- Give your child lots of opportunities for weight bearing on his/her hands (i.e., lying on his/her tummy and pushing up on his/her hands, rocking on hands and knees, crawling).

- Place various objects in his/her hands. Choose items which are about the size of his/her hands—the reflexive grasp will force him/her to hold the object, but his/her hands will be more open and less fisted. Examples are: rattles, foam hair curlers, pegs. Use a variety of textures, sizes, shapes and weights.
- Provide lots of dangling objects in the crib, in front of your baby's infant seat, from a hanger over the changing table, etc. Your baby will, at first, find them by accident and respond to them reflexively; when he/she is ready for deliberate grasping, he/she will expect to find dangling objects.
- Portable "bars" which can be placed in front of your baby's infant seat or on a blanket overhead are excellent for holding "dangling toys." Century makes "crib bars" Encourage your baby to bring his/her hands together and grasp his/her own hands. Gently stroke his/her hands, rub or pat them together, or pat his/her hand on yours.

Bilateral Coordination

Bilateral coordination is the ability to use both hands together to manipulate an object. This begins at an early age where an infant is observed to hold objects using two hands (in midline), progressing through transferring objects from hand to hand, to where each hand is used for different functions.

It is very important that children who are visually impaired or blind learn to manipulate toys well with their hands. When their hands are "busy" playing appropriately with toys, they are taking in a lot of information and learning from their environment. They are also less likely to use their hands for self-stimulatory behaviours such as eye poking or tapping. Following are some suggestions to help your child to use his/her two hands in a coordinated fashion:

- Clapping hands is often a good motivator for children who need practice with bilateral coordination. It stimulates the muscles in the hands and arms and can be practiced during songs, listening to music, and clapping games. When the child is able to hold a toy in each hand for a good period of time, begin banging games (using hand over hand if necessary).

- Use tactile exploration activities where two hands can work together:
  - — shaving cream
  - — water
  - — sand
  - — rice or macaroni
  - — finger paint

Make sure he/she gets both hands into the materials, and help him/her to use two hands to pick up lot of sand or to smear fingerpaint over the entire page.

- Try two-handed activities, where one hand holds, the other hand manipulates:
  - — hold container in one hand and put objects in other
  - — hold container in one hand and take objects out with other
  - — hold stick in one hand and put rings on with other
  - — hold stick in one hand and take rings off with other
  - — hold pegboard down when pulling pegs out
  - — stabilize ring stack to put rings on
  - — hold down paper with one hand and scribble with other
  - — thread toys using wooden dowel as needle
  - — wind jack-in-the-box
  - — pour water from one cup into another

- Try two-handed activities, where both hands move actively:
  - putting "jack" in the box
  - tinker toys
  - putting pop beads together
  - stringing large beads
  - screw kegs

Simple Motor Activities

Keep a simple record of child's physical development. Every year on his birthday, write down his weight and height. Find a convenient wall space, place a ruler on the child's head, draw a line, and date it. Children love to watch how much they have grown. While your child is standing in place, have him count the number of times he can go up and down on his toes.

Set aside time in the family schedule for a family walk, perhaps just 15 minutes, or a Saturday afternoon leisurely hike for an hour or more depending on the youngster's age and stamina. A family walk is a great way for parents and siblings to interact and chat-something that is often difficult to fit into the busy lifestyles of the nuclear family. Walks can also provide an in-depth look at changes in Mother Nature and the community during different seasons of the year.

And then there are the very simple motor activities: hopping, jumping, skipping, and climbing. All are important in a child's growth patterns. Each one calls upon various muscle groups to require extensive use.

Head and neck exercises. Turn head side to side, down and up, while standing, sitting, lying on the back and on the stomach.

Have the child walk across a fallen log or along a narrow curb. Have him repeat the walk, holding a bulky object in one hand, then the other hand, over his head. Repeat going backward and sideways.

Row a boat on dry land. The child must calculate which oat to use in order to turn a specific direction.

Water activities for pool, lake, or rub. Hold a ball and ask the child to hit it with his hands (right and left), elbows, knees, feet. If swimming lessons are available, enroll your youngster. The earlier, the better.

Just tossing a ball from parent to child is excellent for eye-hand coordination as well as large muscles. Don't let the activity get boring. Vary it by asking the child to kick the ball (using alternate feet) or batting it (with alternate hands). Ball size is important. Large enough for a success experience. Small enough for a challenging experience.

Differing chairs. The child sits down and gets up from chairs and stools of varying heights, descending and standing up slowly and without using his hands. The lower the chair, the more difficult the task.

Kangaroo hop. Have the child hold something (for example, a beanbag-or if you want to make it difficult, an apple or an orange) between his knees, then jump with feet together. Frontwards, backwards, sideways.

Wheel barrow. Hold the child's legs white he "walks", with his hands along a marked route.

Find a place where the child can see his shadow. Then see how creative you can be in directing his activities: "Make your shadow tall, short, wide, thin, make it jump, stand on one foot, touch its feet," etc.

Most of the activities that have been described can, for the most part, be done inside or out. It is important that they be done in a spirit of good fun and recreation. Once they become a chore, the child, either subtly or overtly, will decrease his effort and the sought after physical development will diminish. The secret probably ties in offering a variety of activities with an attitude of good cheer. And there may be a bonus-parents may discover that they, too, are in better shape!

Terms associated with child motor development, and movement.

Term	*Definition*
Abduction	Movement of an arm or leg away from the midline of the body.
Adaptive/Cognitive skills	Those skills associated with mental development. The skills that include how the child solves problems, anticipates an event, and interacts with his environment.
Adduction	Movement of an arm or leg towards the midline of the body.
Bilateral	Affecting both sides of the body.
Adjusted/calculated chronological age	Age of the child, taking into consideration the amount of pre maturity. An example: A child who was born on January 1, but was due on March 1 is two months premature. Therefore, on July 1, his CCA is 4 months.
Chronological Age	Actual age from your child's birth date.
Crawl	To move with arms and legs and tummy on the floor, "commando style".
Creep	To move with arms and legs, with the tummy off the floor.
Extension	The straightening of the trunk and limbs, the opposite of flexion.
Fine motor	The area of development concerned with using hands, eyes, and hands and eyes together, such as grasping, reaching. Refers to the small muscles.
Flexion	Decreasing the angle or bending of a joint, the opposite of extension.
Gross motor	The area of development concerned with how a child controls his larger body movements, such as head control, sitting, and walking.
Hypertonia	Increase tension of the muscles which can make movement difficult. Also referred to as increased muscle tone.
Hypotonia	Decrease tension of the muscles, making upright postures difficult to hold. Sometimes referred to "floppy" or decreased muscle tone. The opposite of hypertonia.
Prone	Lying on the stomach
Reaction	A reflex which appears in infancy or childhood which remains throughout life and are necessary for protection, balance and equilibrium.

(Contd.)

Term	*Definition*
Reflex	Activity performed automatically and without conscious volition. They are the raw material from which the central nervous system may build volitional movements.
Spasticity	Hyper tonicity that is velocity dependent, ie: the faster the movement the stronger the resistance.
Supine	Lying on the back
Tone	The state of muscle tension. Normal tone is that which is high enough to resist the effects of gravity in both posture and movement yet low enough to allow freedom of movement.
Within normal limits	Within the range of typical for that particular age child.

Developmental Delays

Parents are often have concerns about their children's development, especially when they see other children of the same age who have already attained a milestone that their child still hasn't met, causing them to think that their child is 'slow' or 'seems behind.' It is important to keep in mind that for each milestone, there is a range of ages during which a child will normally meet it. For example, some children may walk as early as 11 months, while others may not walk until they are 15 months old, and it is still concerned normal.

Developmental milestones are determined by the average age at which children attain each skill, therefore, statistically, about 3 per cent of children will not meet them on time, but only about 15-20 per cent of these children will actually have abnormal development. The rest will eventually develop normally over time, although a little later than expected.

Be sure to bring up any concerns that you have about your child's development with your Pediatrician, especially if he seems to be losing milestones, or not doing things that he was able to previously do.

A developmental delay occurs when your child has the delayed achievement of one or more of his milestones. This may affect child's speech and language, his fine and gross motor skills, and/or his personal and social skills.

Your Pediatrician should screen for delays at child's well child visits. This may consist of simple questions to see what child is able to do at different ages, or it may include a formal screening test, such as the Denver II Developmental Screening Test. The Denver test can look for delays in your child's social and personal skills, fine and gross motor skills and language.

Developmental delays, especially if they involve a language delay which may be secondary to a hearing loss, should be identified as early as possible.

A child with a global delay will have delays in all areas of development. It is usually caused by a static encephalopathy caused by a disorder before or near the time or birth. Causes of global delays include prematurity, cerebral malformations, chromosomal disorders, infections, and progressive encephalopathies.

Some signs that your infant may not be meeting his normal motor milestones include not being able to bring his hands together by 4 months, not rolling over by 6 months, having head lag when pulled to a sitting position after 6 months, not sitting by himself without support by 8 months, not crawling by 12 months, and not walking by 15 months. Remember that mild delays in motor development can be normal, and there is a range during which these milestones are usually met, so your child may not meet each one at the same time as other children. Delayed motor development, with normal language skills, can be caused by a neuromuscular disorder or mild cerebral palsy.

A delay in fine motor skills in older children may be manifested by not being able to use a spoon or fork, tie his shoes, button his clothes, write his name, draw shapes, color inside the lines, or hold a pencil correctly at the age appropriate time, or by having poor handwriting. A delay in gross motor skills in older children may include not being able to ride a tricycle or bicycle, being clumsy, or not walking correctly.

Stages of Motor Development

Infant Development Birth to 1 Month

By two weeks of age your baby will probably have regained most or all of the weight that he lost in his first week.

In the next few weeks you can expect your baby to look at your face, startle with loud noises, lift his head and begin to smile spontaneously. He may even begin to recognize familiar objects and sounds.

If using a pacifier, try and restrict its use to when your baby seems to need the self-comforting behaviour of sucking. Avoid using it every time your baby cries (it is usually better to pick and hold your baby to comfort him when he is crying) and to be safe, use a one-piece commercial pacifier and do not hang it around your baby's neck.

Remember that all babies are unique and they have different temperaments. Many are quite and calm and have an easy temperament. Others have a difficult temperament and may be very active and or sensitive and get fussy easily (and may need more structured and less stimulating environments to stay calm). Or your baby may have a temperament that is described as being slow to warm up, being quite and shy and slow to adapt to new things and he may need to be slowly introduced to new things. Try and keep your babies temperament in mind as you react to her needs.

Two Months

At this age you can expect your baby to smile, laugh and make noises, lift her head and chest up while lying on her stomach, turn toward sounds and to follow you around with her eyes. Over the next few months, developmental milestones will include rolling over, bearing weight on her legs, sitting with support and holding on to a rattle.

If using a pacifier, try and restrict its use to when your baby seems to need the self-comforting behaviour of sucking. Avoid using it every time your baby cries (it is usually better to pick and hold your baby to comfort him when she is crying) and to be safe, use a one-piece commercial pacifier and do not hang it around your baby's neck. After six months of age, you should restrict pacifier use to only when your baby is in her crib.

Remember that all babies are unique and they have different temperaments. Many are quite and calm, while others are very active and some are very sensitive and get fussy easily (and may need less stimulating environments to stay calm). Try and keep your babies temperament in mind as you react to her needs.

Four Months

At this age you can expect your baby to roll over (front to back), bear weight on her legs, sit with support, hold up her head and chest and support herself on her elbows if she is on her stomach, pull to a sitting position and hold on to a rattle. Over the next few months your baby will start to imitate speech sounds, reach for objects and sit without support.

If using a pacifier, try and restrict its use to when your baby seems to need the self-comforting behaviour of sucking. Avoid using it every time your baby cries and to be safe, use a one-piece commercial pacifier and do not hang it around your baby's neck. After six months of age, you should restrict pacifier use to when your baby is in his crib.

Most babies take at least two to three naps (length of naps are usually very variable between different children, but naps are usually 1 1/2-2 hours each) during the day at this age and are able to sleep for the majority of the night. If not, check to make sure that your baby has a good bedtime routine and has developed the proper sleep associations.

Six Months

Your baby has probably doubled her birth weight by now. At this age you can expect her to imitate speech sounds, reach for objects, roll over, and sit without support. Over the next few months she will start to stand holding on to things, pull to a stand, jabber and combine syllables, crawl and transfer things from hand to hand.

If using a pacifier, now is a good time to start restricting its use to only when your baby is in his crib. This will help to decrease his interest in it. Avoid giving your baby his pacifier every time he cries or allowing him to use it as a security object (offer other choices instead, such as a blanket).

Most babies take at least two naps during the day at this age (length of naps are usually very variable between different children, but naps are usually 1 1/2-2 hours each) and are able to sleep for the majority of the night (at least 10-11 hours). If not, check to make sure that your baby has a good bedtime routine and has developed the proper sleep associations.

Nine Months

At this age you can expect your baby to sit alone, pull to a stand, stand holding on to things, jabber and imitate sounds, crawl, wave bye-bye, and begin to show separation and stranger anxiety. Over the next few months your baby will start to combine syllables, say mama/dada, walk with her hands held, and bang objects together.

Your baby will now begin to explore how things work, enjoy playing peek-a-boo and pat-a-cake and being read to. It is important to give lots of praise and many opportunities for exploration. If using a pacifier, it is a good time to start restricting its use to only when your baby is in his crib, so that his interest in it will decrease.

Most babies take two naps during the day (length of naps are usually very variable between different children, but naps are usually 1-2 hours each) and are able to sleep for the majority of the night at this age. If not, check to make sure that your baby has a good bedtime routine and has developed the proper sleep associations.

Twelve Months

Your baby has probably tripled her birth weight. You can expect her to combine syllables, say mama/dada, walk while holding on to things, take a few steps alone, bang objects together, enjoy reading interactively, and point to pictures. Over the next few months she will start to walk well alone, say 3-6 words, understand simple commands, and begin to use a spoon or fork.

This is also a time that your child will begin to explore and try and figure out how things work and will enjoy playtime. It is important to give lots of praise and many opportunities for exploration. If using a pacifier, it is a good time to start restricting its use to only when your baby is in his crib, so that his interest in it will decrease.

Most babies take two naps during the day at this age (length of naps are usually very variable between different children, but naps are usually 1-1 1/2 hours each) and are able to sleep for the majority of the night (at least 11 hours). If not, check to make sure that your baby has a good bedtime routine and has developed the proper sleep associations.

Toddler Development

Fifteen Months

Your baby has probably tripled her birth weight. Developmental milestones you can expect her to meet include starting to combine syllables, say mama/dada, walk alone, bang objects together, enjoy reading interactively, and point to pictures. Over the next few months she will start to say 3-6 words, understand simple commands, and begin to use a spoon or fork.

This is also a time that your child will begin to explore and try and figure out how things work and will enjoy playtime. It is important to give lots of praise and many opportunities for exploration. If using a pacifier, it is a good time to start restricting its use to only when your baby is in his crib, so that his interest in it will decrease.

Most babies take two naps (length of naps are usually very variable between different children, but naps are usually 1-1 1/2 hours each) during the day at this age and are able to sleep for the majority of the night (at least 11 hours). If not, check to make sure that your baby has a good bedtime routine and has developed the proper sleep associations.

Eighteen Months

At this age you can expect your child to walk backwards, walk up steps with her hand held, kick a ball, say 10 to 25 words, name 3 body parts, turn pages of a book and stack two blocks together. Over the next few months your child will learn new words, start to throw a ball overhand, use two word combinations, and remove clothing.

He may begin to play around other children, but it will be 'parallel play.' Children at this age are very self-centered and may play alongside each other, but it will be some time before they actually start playing together. Your child will probably not want to share his things and he may be very possessive. It is important to closely supervise children that are playing together at this age and reassure them that the other child will not keep his toys. Keep a few of his favourite items separate and not available for sharing so that he feels he has some control over things.

This is also a time that your child will begin to explore and try and figure out how things work and will enjoy playtime. It is important to give lots of praise and many opportunities for exploration. If using a pacifier, it is a good time to start restricting its use to only when your baby is in his crib, so that his interest in it will decrease.

Most children take at least one nap (length of naps are usually very variable between different children, but naps are usually 1-1 1/2 hours each) during the day at this age and are able to sleep all night (for 11-12 hours). If not, check to make sure that your baby has a good bedtime routine and has developed the proper sleep associations.

Two Years

At this age you can expect your child to put on clothing, brush his teeth with help, stack 4-6 blocks, combine words, know over 50 words, use pronouns (I, me, you, mine), follow two step commands, know his body parts, walk up steps, kick a ball, jump up, throw a ball overhead, and his speech should be half understandable. Over the next year his speech will become more understandable, and he will be able to name pictures and colors. If using a pacifier, it is a good time to start restricting its use to only when your baby is in his crib, so that his interest in it will decrease.

He may begin to play around other children, but it will be 'parallel play.' Children at this age are very self-centered and may play alongside each other, but it will be some time before they actually start playing together. Your child will probably not want to share his things and he may be very possessive. It is important to closely supervise children that are playing together at this age and reassure them that the other child will not keep his toys. Keep a few of his favourite items separate and not available for sharing so that he feels he has some control over things.

Most children take at least one nap during the day at this age (length of naps are usually very variable between different children, but naps are usually 1-1 1/2 hours each) and are able to sleep all night (for 11-12 hours). If not, check to make sure that your baby has a good bedtime routine and has developed the proper sleep associations

Three Years

At this age your child is becoming more independent and you can expect him to dress himself and button clothes, brush his teeth with help, stack 9-10 blocks, draw circles and squares, use scissors, walk up steps by alternating his feet, jump from a step, hop, walk on his toes, pedal a tricycle, play with imaginary friends, have a very large vocabulary and use 3-4 word sentences and his speech should be 3/4 understandable. Over the next year his speech will become fully understandable.

Your child will now begin to ask 'why' questions, tell stories, remember nursery rhymes, appreciate special events, and understand daily routines.

Your three year old will now begin to play cooperatively with other children in small groups, share his toys and develop friendships. Playtime will include structured games and fantasy activities.

Most children take at least one naps during the day at this age (length of naps are usually very variable between different children, but naps are usually 1-1 1/2 hours each) and are able to sleep all night (at least 11 hours). If not, check to make sure that your baby has a good bedtime routine and has developed the proper sleep associations.

Preschool Development

Three Years

At this age your child is becoming more independent and you can expect him to dress himself and button clothes, brush his teeth with help, stack 9-10 blocks, draw circles and squares, use scissors, walk up steps by alternating his feet, jump from a step, hop, walk on his toes, pedal a tricycle, play with imaginary friends, have a very large vocabulary and use 3-4 word sentences and his speech should be 3/4 understandable. Over the next year his speech will become fully understandable.

Other developmental milestones include beginning to ask 'why' questions, telling stories, remembering nursery rhymes, appreciating special events, and understanding daily routines.

Your three year old will now begin to play cooperatively with other children in small groups, share his toys and develop friendships. Playtime will include structured games and fantasy activities.

Most children take one nap during the afternoon of about 1 hour in length (he will give up taking naps between 3-6 years of age) at this age and are able to sleep all night for at least eleven and a half hours. If not, check to make sure that your baby has a good bedtime routine and has developed the proper sleep associations.

Four Years

At this age you can expect your child to dress himself, brush his teeth without help, play board and card games and follow simple rules, name 4 colors, hop, walk down stairs alternating feet, talk in 4-5 word sentences, sing songs, listen to stories, shares things spontaneously, count to 4, and his speech should be fully understandable. Over the next few years he will be able to count to ten, recognize letters of the alphabet, and be able to learn his phone number and address.

Most children take one nap during the afternoon of about 1 hour in length (he will give up this nap between 3-6 years of age) at this age and are able to sleep all night for at least eleven and a half hours. If not, check to make sure that your baby has a good bedtime routine and has developed the proper sleep associations.

Five Years

At this age you can expect your child to dress himself, brush his teeth without help, play cooperatively with other children, play board and card games and follow the rules, name colors, hop, walk down stairs alternating feet, skip, talk in 4-5 word sentences, sing songs, listen to stories, shares things spontaneously, recognize letters of the alphabet, print letters, know his phone number and address and his speech should be fully understandable.

This is a time of growing independence and children at this age want to be considered more responsible. To help foster this sense of responsibility, now is a good time to begin giving your child an allowance. The amount is not very important, but is usually 50£ to $1.00 per year in age and should be used for special things that your child wants. Managing an allowance will help to teach your child about the value of money and the importance of saving. While it is also important that your child begin to have regular age appropriate chores (setting or clearing the table, taking out the garbage, cleaning their room, etc.) around the house, these should probably not be tied to their allowance. Positive reinforcement is important for completed chores, and failure to complete chores can be punished by loss of a privilege (TV, videogames, etc.). Allowing your child to have a choice of which chore to do sometimes helps with compliance.

Encourage self esteem and a positive self image in your child by using positive reinforcement and frequent praise for things that he has accomplished. Encourage your child to be curious, explore and take on new challenges.

School Age Development

Six Years

Developmental milestones at this age you can expect your child to dress himself, brush his teeth without help, play board and card games and follow the rules, name colors, hop, walk down stairs alternating feet, skip, talk in complete sentences, sing songs, listen to stories, shares things spontaneously, read age appropriate books, print letters, know his phone number and address and his speech should be fully understandable. He will also be able to ride a bike, play team sports and develop better coordination while running, jumping or throwing things. He will develop stronger friendships, although usually still of the same sex children, and learn the difference between right and wrong behaviours.

This is a time of growing independence and children at this age want to be considered more responsible. Positive reinforcement is important for completed chores, and failure to complete chores can be punished by loss of a privilege (TV, videogames, etc.). Allowing your child to have a choice of which chore to do and alternating undesirable chores among your children sometimes helps with compliance.

Encourage self esteem and a positive self image in your child by using positive reinforcement and frequent praise for things that he has accomplished. Encourage your child to be curious, explore and take on new challenges.

School Readiness

The skills that your child will need to be ready to start first grade include knowing the names of colours, identifying all letters, writing their name, counting items, playing cooperatively with others, following two to three part commands, paying attention and concentrating, sitting for long periods of time, and fitting into the daily routine of the school day. Your child should also be able to read a few simple words, listen to and understand simple stories, spend extended time away from parents, dress himself, verbally communicate his needs and wants, and be enthusiastic and curious about new activities.

Not all children are ready for school at the same time. If your child is very immature or shy, you can take some steps to help prepare him for starting school, such as spending time with and playing with other children (especially children who will be in his class), taking him to see his classroom and meet his teacher beforehand, or allowing him to take something special to which he is attached with him to school. If you feel that your child is still not ready to start school, you can discuss the problem with his teacher and school to see if accommodations can be made and to discuss the pros and cons of retaining him for a year.

Eight to Twelve Years

The middle to late school age years are a time of great change in your child. In addition to starting puberty, his mind will also grow to understand logical and abstract thinking and he will develop the moral standards by which he will live his life. You can also expect him to begin to move away from the family as he develops his own identity and also become more influenced by his friends. Fortunately, this influence is usually limited to outward things, such as hair and clothing styles.

Encourage self esteem and a positive self image in your child by using positive reinforcement and frequent praise for things that he has accomplished. Encourage your child to be curious, explore and take on new challenges.

Studies of Motor Development

The study of motor development involves the study of the characteristics of motor behaviour as these characteristics change over time as the result of maturation and experience. The study of motor development may also change in different environmental situations as the demands for motor control change. For example a throwing task may become easier or more difficult if the size of the target changes.

Who are the Children?

When working with children's motor development, you are not working with children in general.

Instead, you are working with particular children in particular situations.

It is essential that we look at and learn to see what is happening when a child moves, not just when "children" move.

We need to find out where a child is in his development and try to determine where he could be.

Enhancement of Motor Development

We need to recognize that not all children will necessarily progress to a mature level of movement control unless we provide opportunity and guidance in movement experiences for them.

We need to recognize that not all children will necessarily progress to a mature level of movement control unless we provide opportunity and guidance in movement experiences for them.

Motor Development Theories

Most theories on development and motor development in particular, combine two points of view:

Some aspects of development are innate (nature) Some aspects of development are learned and developed by practice (nurture).

According to Gallahue 1982-motor development.

"A progressive change in motor control and motor behaviour brought about by the interaction of both maturation and experience."

Phases of Motor Development

The development of a child's motor behaviour is a sequential process. This development starts with simple reflexes to the learning of postural movements, to loco motor responses, and finally, fine manipulative movements.

Four phases of development are usually identified.

Phase 1

From reflexes to rudimentary movements such as sitting, crawling, creeping, standing, and walking.

Phase 2

Running, climbing, jumping, balancing, catching and throwing are developed. These are sometimes labeled as the fundamental skills. These fundamental skills are common to all healthy children and normally develop in the same order as all children.

Phase 3

During late childhood, more specific movement skills will appear, while the general fundamental skills become more refined and will appear more fluid and are more automatic.

Phase 4

During adolescence the specific movements develop further and can be called specialized. This process depends o the amount of practice an individual has with specific skills, which is influenced by talent, motivation and stimulation as well as success and failure.

Motor Development Stages

Stages are used to describe qualitative differences in overall motor behaviour within a selected motor skill.

The major characteristic of a stage is qualitative change that is, a stage contains new motor behaviour.

Example of a new motor development stage:

Moves forward or backward to catch a ball. Previously the child stood only in one place to catch a ball. Bends arms to prevent contacted ball from bouncing away. Previously the child contacted the ball with stiff arms.

Catching

Ideally, objects are caught in the hands so they can be manipulate.

Beginning Catching

Children initially position the arms and hands rigidly and sometimes trap the ball against their chests.

Children sometimes turn their head away or close their eyes.

Proficient Catching

Hands "give" with the ball to gradually absorb force. Catcher moves side to side or forward and back to intercept the ball. Fingers are pointed up on high balls and down on low balls.

Developmental Changes in Catching

Task constraints greatly affect the difficulty of catching.

Arm Action

1. Little response
2. Hugging
3. Scooping
4. Arms "give"

Hand Action

1. Palms up
2. Palms in
3. Palms adjusted

Body Action

1. No adjustment
2. Awkward adjustment
3. Proper adjustment

Classification of Motor Behaviour

The classification of a child's motor behaviour requires the child to have the ability to do the motor skill.

This sequence of illustrations shows the inability of the very young child (17 months) to jump from the elevation.

The child is stepping from the elevation.

The child is not jumping off the elevation because they always have foot contact with either the elevation or the floor.

The classification of this child's motor behaviour (jumping) can be done because the child is able to perform a primitive jump.

This sequence of illustration shows a very primitive jump as indicated by the momentary suspension during a jump make at 18 months.

Neither foot is touching the step or the floor.

The classification of a child's motor behaviour for a jump at age 21 months can be completed since the child is able to perform a jump.

Motor Development Stages of Children and Adults

Normal children will use all or most of fundamental motor patterns which they are capable.

Most normal children do not attain a mature form of these skills by age eight or nine.

Most adults never achieve the mature form of fundamental skills, and therefore remain at a very primitive stage of motor development.

Running has a required flight phase.

Most adults never achieve the mature form of fundamental skills, and therefore remain at a very primitive stage of motor development.

Running has a required flight phase.

Motor Development Stages, Adults

Most adults never achieve the mature form of fundamental skills, and therefore remain at a very primitive stage of motor development. For example, the overhand throw pattern frequently used by poorly skilled college girls fits Wild's description of the throwing stage generally characteristic of four or five old children.

In this stage, foot opposition is not yet established and forward rotation of the trunk occurs as a whole with little or no differentiation between pelvic and spinal rotation.

The result is a very ineffective throw, which in turn discourages the girls from taking part in activities demanding its use.

Another example of the failure of the adult performer to achieve a mature movement pattern is illustration by Craig's investigation of the standing broad jump.

In this study, most of the poor female college jumpers used one foot take-off.

They swung one leg ahead similar to the pattern of a child of less than 32 months.

A physical education teacher will see examples of poor fundamental skills each time they teach.

Unfortunately this incomplete motor development is not recognized early enough.

Also this incomplete motor development is hard to recognize, because of the lack of information on how movement patterns develop.

3

Social and Emotional Development

During the first three years of life, child will develop crucial intellectual, emotional and social abilities, learn to give and accept love, to be confident and secure, to show empathy, to be curious and persistent—all abilities that will enable your child to learn, relate well to others and lead a happy and productive life. This is an exciting period in your child's life!

Each child grows and develops differently. This gives you general information about what a child from birth to age five might be doing at a certain age.

Concept

Social and emotional milestones are often harder to pinpoint than signs of physical development. This area emphasizes many skills that increase self-awareness and self-regulation. Research shows that social skills and emotional development (reflected in the ability to pay attention, make transitions from one activity to another, and cooperate with others) are a very important part of school readiness.

Age	*Milestones*
The first year	From the start, babies eagerly explore their world-and that includes themselves and other people.
Birth to 3 months	Babies spend a lot of time getting to know their own bodies. They:

(Contd.)

(Contd. Table)

Age	*Milestones*
	• Suck their own fingers • Observe their own hands • Look at the place on the body that is being touched • Begin to realize she is a separate person from others and learn how body parts, like arms and legs, are attached Infants are interested in other people and learn to recognize primary caregivers. Most infants: • Can be comforted by a familiar adult • Respond positively to touch • Interact best when in an alert state or in an inactive and attentive state • Benefit from short, frequent interactions more than long, infrequent ones • Smile and show pleasure in response to social stimulation
3 to 6 Months	Babies are more likely to initiate social interaction. They begin to: • Play peek-a-boo • Pay attention to own name • Smile spontaneously • Laugh aloud
6 to 9 Months	Babies show a wider emotional range and stronger preferences for familiar people. Most can: • Express several clearly differentiated emotions • Distinguish friends from strangers • Respond actively to language and gestures • Show displeasure at the loss of a toy
9 to 12 Months	As they near age one, imitation and self-regulation gain importance. Most babies can: • Feed themselves finger foods • Hold a cup with two hands and drink with assistance • Hold out arms and legs while being dressed • Mimic simple actions • Show anxiety when separated from primary caregiver
1-2 years	Children become more aware of themselves and their ability to make things happen. They express a wider range of emotions and are more likely to

(Contd.)

(Contd. Table)

Age	*Milestones*
	initiate interaction with other people. At this stage, most children: • Recognize themselves in pictures or the mirror and smile or make faces at themselves • Show intense feelings for parents and show affection for other familiar people • Play by themselves and initiate their own play • Express negative feelings • Show pride and pleasure at new accomplishments • Imitate adult behaviors in play • Show a strong sense of self through assertiveness, directing others • Begin to be helpful, such as by helping to put things away
2-3 years	Children begin to experience themselves as more powerful, creative "doers." They explore everything, show a stronger sense of self and expand their range of self-help skills. Self-regulation is a big challenge. Two-year-olds are likely to: • Show awareness of gender identity • Indicate toileting needs • Help to dress and undress themselves • Be assertive about their preferences and say no to adult requests • Begin self-evaluation and develop notions of themselves as good, bad, attractive, etc. • Show awareness of their own feelings and those of others, and talk about feelings • Experience rapid mood shifts and show increased fearfulness (for example, fear of the dark, or certain objects) • Display aggressive feelings and behaviors Children enjoy parallel play, engaging in solitary activities near other children. They are likely to: • Watch other children and briefly join in play • Defend their possessions • Begin to play house • Use objects symbolically in play

(Contd.)

(Contd. Table)

Age	*Milestones*
	• Participate in simple group activities, such as singing clapping or dancing • Know gender identity
3-4 years	As their dexterity and self-help skills improve, 3-year-olds become more independent. Most can: • Follow a series of simple directions • Complete simple tasks with food without assistance, such as spreading soft butter with a dull knife and pouring from a small pitcher • Wash hands unassisted and blow nose when reminded Children become more interested in other children. They are now more likely to: • Share toys, taking turns with assistance • Initiate or join in play with other children and make up games • Begin dramatic play, acting out whole scenes (such as traveling, pretending to be animals)
4-5 years	At this age, children are more aware of themselves as individuals. They: • Show some understanding of moral reasoning (exploring ideas about fairness and good or bad behaviour) • Compare themselves with others 4-year-olds are very interested in relationships with other children. They: • Develop friendships • Express more awareness of other people's feelings • Show interest in exploring sex differences • Enjoy imaginative play with other children, like dress up or house • Bring dramatic play closer to reality by paying attention to detail, time, and space

Caring for Infants and Toddlers

The first years are a wondrous time. As the months pass, parents are able to form deep, affectionate bonds with their babies and marvel at their rapid growth. Infants need a small, consistent group of people whom they can learn to know and trust. When babies are in childcare settings, it is important for group sizes to remain small (with at least one adult for every three infants) so that secure, meaningful relationships can form and each infant's needs for attention, affection and routine care can be met. Toddlers continue to need secure attachments and a great deal of individual attention.

Crying

Babies come into this world ready for relationships—each with a unique personality and style of communication. Babies tell us about their feelings and needs through their facial expressions and body movements, as well as by cooing, babbling, and crying. Crying is one of the main ways babies communicate. They cry to tell us that they want or need something to happen-perhaps a diaper change, a bottle, a nap, or a hug.

Routine Care

Routine care, such as feeding a baby or changing a diaper, provides rich opportunities for one-to-one contact. Be sure to feed and change infants and put them down for naps based on their needs, not according to a schedule. Hold baby during bottle-feeding in order to take advantage of this time for closeness and interaction. Keep in mind that too much stimulation, such as bright lights and constant noise, may overwhelm infants and cause them stress.

Infants' immunity to infectious disease is just beginning to build. Remember to wash your hands and take other sanitary precautions before and after feeding, diapering, and toileting. Keep sick children home so the infection or illness is not spread to other children and adults.

Talking with Infants

Even before they understand words, babies love to hear language and respond by cooing, babbling, and making sounds that gradually resemble adult speech. During the first two years of life, children understand much more than they can say. You can help children learn new words by noticing the things that catch their attention, naming them, and talking about them. Repeatedly using newly learned words will reinforce them and build your child's vocabulary. By using the same words in different ways ("You have a face. And the clock has a face, too"), or finding different ways to say the same thing ("It's big, it's huge, it's gigantic") you can help children build a richer, more expressive vocabulary as they grow.

Safe Exploration

Infants need many opportunities to explore their world using all of their senses. As your baby begins to crawl and then walk, a safe environment is essential. From child's perspective, if it's in view, it's interesting; and if it's in reach, it will be investigated. That's why it is important to "child proof" all settings where young children spend time. Potential dangers include unlocked cabinets, uncovered electrical outlets, medicines and cleaning supplies, and small objects that can be put into a child's mouth. You can prevent accidents with close supervision and frequent inspection to spot new dangers that crop up as children grow and develop.

Toddlers' Intense Feelings

Toddlers are very involved in learning about themselves in relation to the world around them Their day often involves conflict with siblings, playmates, and the adults around them. Keep in mind that when a toddler wants something, she typically wants it intensely and immediately. If you are caring for more than one child, you can help reduce conflict by making sure there are enough toys and materials for all to share. It's also important that your toddler has enough time and space to fully explore her environment. Be sure she has plenty of opportunities to make real choices and decisions, like what snack food she prefers or which shirt she wants to wear.

When toddlers don't get what they want, tempers often flare. Children can be frightened by their own feelings and actions, and they rely on the adults around them to remain calm. In simple language, say what specific behaviours are expected and what will happen if the rules are not followed ("Stop throwing the crackers, or snack time will be over.") Let your child know that you (or other caregivers) are there to help her work through her intense emotions.

Dealing with Feelings: Child

Emotional Health

It takes a lot of patience combined with good judgment and warm, nurturing relationships to raise emotionally healthy, comfortable and cheerful children. But no matter what you do, children are still going to feel sad, afraid, anxious, and angry from time to time. Your challenge, as a parent, is to learn how to help children cope with their feelings and express them in socially acceptable ways that don't harm others and that are appropriate to their age and abilities.

Importance of Trust

The most important factor in fostering mental health in child is the quality of the relationship you have with her. Without the presence of trust in this relationship, it's impossible for your child to feel safe, close, or comfortable. Trust has its roots in infancy, when babies gain confidence that they can depend on adults around them to meet their basic needs. From your baby's perspective, reasonably prompt and consistent care is an essential ingredient in developing trust. When her needs are responded to, baby develops trust and confidence, and feels valued and important.

It's also important to maintain that trustful feeling as child continues to grow. One of the easiest ways to build trust is by maintaining an orderly routine throughout the day so child can predict what's going to happen next. Consistent rules that your child understands also add to his sense of trust. Adults who maintain their self-control encourage children to trust them. Then children can predict what their responses will be and this breeds confidence in the relationship. It's also important for rules and tasks to be appropriate for the child's age and abilities.

Trust between you and child's other caregivers is also essential. This connection is important for all children, but especially for children with disabilities.

Choices and Limits

The toddler's drive toward independence and self-assertion is an important stage of emotional development. Maintain limits when necessary and independence when it's possible. Avoid confrontations, insist on doing things your way when necessary, and provide as many choices for child as possible. There are many choices that you can offer, but they are limited choices: not "do you want to put on a sweatshirt?" but "which sweatshirt?" not "do you want any vegetables on your plate?" but "do you want carrots or beans?" You can also give children choices about their play and activities When children are expected to choose for themselves what they want to do, they have endless opportunities for making decisions.

Older children of 4 or 5 years need to reach out to the world around them, to be a part of and connected to the group. Try to encourage children of this age to think things up and try things out. It's important for them to feel the emotional satisfaction that comes from experiences of exploring, acting and doing new things together with friends.

When children don't have opportunities to make choices, endless struggles result with a spirited child and a loss of self-confidence in less spirited children. But not everything is a choice and sometimes the answer is "no." Learning how to cope with disappointments, delays, and setbacks is also a critical part of developing a healthy, balanced mental attitude. Try to reduce the level and frequency of disappointments and frustrations in order to avoid unnecessary battles.

Feel What You Want, Control What You Do

One of the most valuable skills you can teach children is how to express strong emotions without hurting themselves, others, or damaging property. Help r children learn to feel what they want, but control what they do. Begin by communicating to child in a non-judgmental way, showing him you understand how he feels. Encourage child to say his feelings out loud and to tell the other person how he feels. If the child's too young or inexperienced to know what to say, model a simple sentence for him to copy. The important thing to remember is that the same rule applies to you: feel what you want, but control what you do.

Emotional Health

Here are some ways that can help you decide if child is doing all right:

- Is child working on emotional tasks that are appropriate for her age and ability? For example, if she's two and a half, is she asserting herself from time to time?
- Is child able to separate from you without undue stress and form an attachment with at least one other adult?
- Is child learning to conform to routines at school without too much trouble?
- Is child able to involve himself deeply in play?
- Can child settle down and concentrate?
- Is child aware of all her feelings and can she express them without harming herself or others?

Getting along Together: Children

Developing Social Competence in Young Children

Childhood is a time for children to learn about the world-and that includes learning how to get along with others. Parents play a crucial role in helping children figure out how to form satisfying relationships and develop into socially competent people. Social competence allows children to be cooperative and generous, express their feelings, and empathize with others.

Modeling Behaviour

Modeling the behaviour you want to encourage is the best way to help children develop socially. Every time you say "please" or lend a helping hand, you are showing children how you would like them to act. Ask for your children's help with daily tasks, and accept their offers of help. Look for the things children are doing right and find opportunities to comment on them. Praise can reinforce good behaviour, but it is equally important to help children recognize the sense of satisfaction that comes from within when they act on a generous impulse or get along well with others.

Sharing from the Heart

Good feelings about oneself and others is the root of social competency. Try to create a climate of kindness and generosity so that children can help each other and begin to take responsibility for each other naturally. In this way they will begin to share "from the heart"-not just because you want them to.

Talk with children about being generous with each other. Point out that sharing and being considerate of feelings makes other people feel happy and makes them feel good too. You can encourage acts of generosity throughout the day and be generous yourself by providing enough satisfying experiences and materials for your children. In group settings, try to let young children use toys and materials until they feel ready to pass them on to someone else. Point out when a playmate has waited a long time to have a turn. Reward generous acts with words of praise.

Empathy, the ability to imagine what another person is feeling, is a very important concept for children to understand. You can foster empathy by talking about your own feelings

("That story made me sad"); helping children express their own feelings ("How did you feel when it started to rain and we had to leave the park?"); and encouraging them to listen to other people's feelings Responding to the needs of children who have disabilities provides excellent opportunities for children to share from the heart. Keep in mind that the kindest thing children can do is to simply include others in their play.

Fairness

Children know from their own experiences that words can hurt, and that name-calling, teasing, or excluding others affects how people feel. Children want to be treated fairly, but they don't always understand how to treat others the same way. One way to teach fairness is to explain a rule to child, pointing out that it applies to him as well as to others.

Children have the right to have their feelings and choices respected and you can model this throughout the day. Be sure to acknowledge and respect your child's feelings, never insisting that she stop crying if she is sad or say she's sorry when she isn't. At the same time, you can help her understand what may have gone wrong in the situation.

Cooperation Versus Competition

Provide plenty of opportunities for children to play together cooperatively. Play is one of the most important ways children learn how to relate to other people. As they play, young children will find cooperation less frustrating and more satisfying than competition. When children compete, only one person or team wins; everyone else loses. Children will have plenty of opportunities to express their competitive spirit later on.

You can help children learn problem-solving skills that can be used in challenging social situations. As they interact with siblings and other peers, children can be helped to negotiate, "bargain," and compromise with each other. Most children love it when an adult has a problem and everyone is encouraged to pitch in their ideas and help solve it.

Theory Social and Emotional Development

When two four-year-olds are playing together in a sandbox, sharing the sand toys, that's social development—the ability to get along with others in a group.

When one of the four-year-olds takes a toy from her friend, and offers her another toy in its place, that's emotional development—the process of learning to control your emotions and having empathy and respect for others

Role of Nutrition

You don't just feed child. You love and nurture her at the same time. The act of loving and feeding a child creates a bond that sets the stage for the child's entire developmental future. Forming that parent-child bond begins the process of developing self-esteem in baby, which is critical for all future development.

Child depends on you to meet all of her needs. By meeting all her basic needs for food, clean diapers, sleep, and nurturance, you are helping her grow and develop a sense of trust in you.

Infant becomes a toddler, good nutrition helps her develop properly. Like many toddlers, your child may become a very picky eater during the early years. She might prefer carrot cake to carrots. It may be a real challenge for parents to find foods their toddler likes, while also providing the vitamins, protein, and other nutrients necessary to sustain her rapid growth and development.

Positive Role in Social and Emotional Development

Remember, you are child's first and favourite role model. You can send a positive message to her that she is capable of doing many things. Start by being supportive. Take pleasure in your child's accomplishments and let her know it.

Love child and show your affection for her. Hug her, cuddle with her, read to her, and talk to her throughout the day.

Encourage child to try new things and to believe in her abilities. As she becomes a toddler, give her opportunities to play with other children her age. She will watch and imitate these new friends to learn new skills.

Establish daily routines so your child will feel secure within a schedule. Don't be afraid to alter the schedule occasionally for special activities.

From the moment she is born, child is developing a sense of self. She is working toward being attached to, but separate from, you. The first step in this development is learning to trust. When you meet baby's physical and emotional needs, you are helping her trust herself and feel secure in the world.

Physical Needs

1. Feed baby when she is hungry and change her when she is soiled or wet.
    - Hold and talk to your baby as you feed her. Make eye contact, smile often, and speak in a soothing voice.
    - Talk to baby about what you are doing as you change her. Sing little songs or nursery rhymes. You will be bonding and helping her hear the rhythm of language.
2. Put baby down to sleep when she is tired.
    - Speak soothingly to her as you lay her down.
    - Play soft music or sing to lull her to sleep.
3. Give her variety in her day.
    - During alert times, occasionally alter baby's physical position to give her a different view of her surroundings.
    - Carry her around with you when possible.
    - Alternate quiet activities with more vigorous ones such as taking your baby for a walk.

Emotional Needs

1. All children need to be comforted when they are upset. Hold child. Speak soothingly and calmly. She will let you know when she is feeling okay again.
2. Spend time with child and help her explore her world and get to know the people in it.
3. Young children need consistent routines. Have a few routines and stick to them. This helps child make sense of the world and become confident that events happen in an orderly fashion.
4. Be attuned to child. Let her see you happy or sad when she is. She will learn that you can share the same emotions she has. This will help her learn to have empathy for others.
5. Children pass through many stages in social and emotional development. Some of their progress depends on nature (genetics) and some on nurture (the many loving and supportive things we do to help our children develop). Often, a child will temporarily slide back into a previous stage. This is only temporary and you will probably know of a recent upsetting event that caused this regression. For instance, your two-year-old starts asking for a bottle again. Maybe she has seen the attention a new baby nephew with a bottle is receiving from the family. With patience and love, your child will soon be back on track.

Children usually progress socially and emotionally in the following areas :

1. Become interested in their immediate surroundings
2. Develop a sense of self and of belonging to a family
3. Develop trust
4. Develop a communication system with their parents
5. Learn to separate from their parents

6. Develop ways to show their emotions
7. Watch other children play from a distance
8. Play near other children but not with them—often imitating the actions of others
9. Play with other children
10. State their desires and wants
11. Share and take turns
12. Use words to solve conflicts and develop control of their emotions
13. Learn that it is okay to make a mistake
14. Develop self-confidence and self-respect
15. Develop respect for others and feelings of empathy

Infant Age between 0-12 Months

Socially, infant is fascinated by her immediate surroundings. She'll spend some months taking in information and learning how to deal with it in her own way. She is learning how to calm, comfort, and reassure herself. She is developing a sense of trust in those closest to her.

By about four months, your baby will begin to smile, laugh, and really enjoy being with others. It is so exciting to hear her laugh out loud, especially when you hear that first real "belly" laugh.

Infants are in love with life. They're also in love with their parents-the people they know will meet their every need. Your eight-month-old baby is learning to communicate with you about her needs. She will let you know when she's ready for play time, quiet time, and nap time.

By 10 months, baby is the star of her world. She is developing confidence in her abilities and she needs for you to acknowledge them by showing your excitement. Let her lead your play. Observe and follow her lead. Her confidence will grow daily

Activities

1. Make feeding time a learning and bonding time. Talk to infant as you feed her. Smile at her and gaze into her eyes. Hold her close and cuddle her. Eating is a social activity.
2. Put face close (about one foot) to her as you interact. This is the best distance for her to see you.
3. Use her name when talking to her.
4. Use mirrors so your child will see herself and begin to develop self-identity.
5. Move her feet and legs while singing a cheerful song.
6. Play music of many varieties for her to listen to, "sing" along, and move with.
7. Read to her several times a day. Use colourful books with simple illustrations. Begin buying board, cloth, and vinyl books for her to hold and look at on her own.
8. For young infants, crib mobiles hung just out of reach are excellent for developing the visual skill of tracking moving objects.
9. For older infants, use a floor gym with a smiley face for her to bat and grasp with her hands.
10. When infant looks away after a play period, she just needs a little time to "take in" or absorb what you have been doing together. Give her that time alone to regroup.

Toddler Infant Age between 1-2 Years

Toddler is curious about everything. She wants to explore physical objects and also her own feelings. Help her express these feelings. This is part of her emotional growth. If her expressions of her feelings become too aggressive, help her find acceptable ways to express these feelings without hurting others. Toddlers are developing feelings of empathy. They do not fully realize how much they can hurt others. Show affection for other members of the family throughout the day and she will begin to imitate you.

Along with a sense of empathy, child is also developing self-regulation. She needs to have space to assert herself and she needs to be allowed to state her opinion about things. She also needs to be allowed and encouraged to accomplish tasks on her own. She will return to the security of your lap or to get a hug often. She loves you madly but she is becoming her own person. She is also very interested in having a predictable routine. She will know her routine and what is likely to happen next.

By the end of the year, toddler has a sense of self. She calls herself by her own name. She recognizes herself in the mirror or in a picture. She imitates your actions. She will often play by herself. She believes everything belongs to her

Activities

1. Toddler is beginning to pick up words. Say the words for objects in your home and outdoors. Look at her as you pronounce words so she can see how you pronounce them. She is a great imitator. Encourage her to use words.
2. Read to her every day. Begin reading some predictable books so that she can "read" them to herself.
3. Play "Hide and Seek" games.
4. Give her stacking toys and play with them beside her.
5. Let her use the computer mouse with the games and activities on this website. This will help her coordination skills and it is a good opportunity for you to notice her abilities.
6. Use the mirror to make faces and to name body parts.

7. Play simple chase games with her. You will be building muscles and laughing together at the same time.
8. Go on walks and talk about the neighbourhood.
9. Let her choose her clothes from among two or three choices.
10. Share toys, books, snacks with her. Hold out your hand for her to share with you.

Toddlers Age between-2 Years

Two-year-old, who once considered you her favourite playmate, is now beginning to enjoy playing near other children. She is watching and learning from them. She will sing and dance with others. She jealously guards her possessions. She is beginning to engage in very simple dramatic play involving the home. She has learned to imitate her mother's behavicur. She loves the word "no" and uses it often. She is confident in her actions and she can complete tasks. She dominates her world and when those around her don't do as she likes, she can be very stubborn. Avoid power struggles. They will leave both of you exhausted and unhappy. Offer choices instead. The choices you offer can be controlled by you. Set some common sense limits. Once you have set limits, be consistent in enforcing them.

Two year-old likes to watch other children play and may join briefly in their play, then withdraw to watch again. This is all very normal. She is learning about the world around her and the social skills she'll need to be a part of it, by watching others. This is also a great time to begin to teach child to use her words to solve conflicts rather than hitting, or throwing a tantrum.

Children at this age can be easily distracted. Do not force her to keep on doing an activity when you can tell she has lost interest. You can try the activity again another day.

Activities

1. Encourage her to talk about her family. Answer any questions she may have.
2. Do things together as a family. Make your family life warm and nurturing.
3. Play "choosing" games where your child chooses her favourite picture from a group and tells you a story about it.
4. Play games where you both imitate the pose or actions on a card or the computer screen.
5. Take turns brushing your teeth or choosing a book or saying silly words.
6. Go on an outing to the park where she can watch other children and interact when she is ready.
7. Provide some materials like play dough or water play that she can use to work out her frustrations when she is really upset.
8. Read simple picture books with repetition. Soon she will begin to "read" those favourite books to you.
9. Play pretend games with her. Children this age like to use dolls and play house. She will change roles often during her play. You will notice that she acts just like you when she plays your role!
10. She can work simple computer roll-overs and predict how the object will change before she does the rollover.

Toddlers Age between-3 Years

Three year-old no longer hesitates when she sees a group of children at play. Instead, she jumps right in, ready to play, too. She loves pretend play. She has enough language to make herself understood and she is ready and eager to use it. She is learning that other people have feelings and she tries to be nice to everyone. She is even learning to wait for her turn. She wants to be everybody's friend. She is actually beginning to share. Three-year-olds will use "please" and "thank you" if they have heard it from you at home.

She's learning that it is okay to make a mistake. She is eager to please you and wants to do things right. Three-year-olds love to be praised and to show off all of their accomplishments. Give lots of hugs and encouragement! She loves it when you have time to play with her and she is even beginning to ask for help when she needs it.

If you send child to a preschool or to a child care programme, she may have problems with separation for a few weeks. She is so close to you that it will be hard for her to be away from you for so long. At this age, life is so interesting to children that it probably won't be long until she eagerly looks forward to being with her friends each day. If you do not send your child to preschool, consider taking her to a playgroup twice a week. The experience she will gain in playing with others will help prepare her for kindergarten.

Activities

1. Eat meals together as often as you can. Make it a priority and make it a pleasant get-together. Conversational, social, and cognitive skills all develop at this important meeting place.
2. Ask her opinion often and respect her answers.
3. Encourage child to try again when she makes a mistake. Let her see you make mistakes, too.
4. Give child some simple chores to do like picking up her toys and carrying her own dishes to the sink after meals. Let her dust when you are cleaning. This gives her a sense of contributing to the family.
5. Find pictures of various related items. Ask child which one she likes best and why (for example: a picture of a cat, a dog, and a bird).
6. Provide opportunities for child to play with other children. Take her to a park or join a play group if

she does not go to a day care center or attend a preschool.

7. Cook with child. Make it something simple and let her do some of the measuring and stirring. Keep a child-sized wooden spoon ready just for her.
8. Take child to the grocery store. Talk about where the foods came from. After you get home, let her help you sort, name, and put away the groceries.
9. Tell child stories about herself as a baby. Also, at the end of the day, go over her day with her. This helps build her memory and it will also allow her to bring up any unanswered questions she had during the day.
10. Let child choose her own clothes to wear. Talk about why she made the choices she did.

Preschoolers Age between 4 Years

Whether it's at a tea party, or a t-ball game, four-year-old has learned to play well with other children. She changes friends often. She may be jealous of a new child who tries to enter her group. She is often boastful. She shares well and is getting better at using words to solve her problems. Encourage her self-discipline. She loves to play dress-up and pretend that disasters are happening. She is learning to use words to solve her conflicts. She is often very silly. She is beginning to truly feel empathy for others.

Four-year-olds have strong likes and dislikes. They hate to lose games. They hate for things to be unfair. They love fantasy play and reality-based play. They love simple board games. They love their parents and their teachers. They are trying to learn all they can about their parents. Often, your four-year-old will choose one parent to study and imitate and leave out the other. Later, she will decide to study the other parent and exclude the one she has just been totally absorbed with. Just give her time and she will pass through this stage and be loving and friendly to both of you again.

Four-year-olds are also very interested in their gender identity. This is one of the reasons they study each parent individually. They are establishing in their own minds what it means to be a boy or a girl. child may benefit from preschool or a playgroup this year. She'll develop the social skills she'll need to succeed in kindergarten.

Activities

1. Read to child each day and let her pretend to read to you. If she has fears, ask librarian for children's books that will help her learn to deal with those fears.
2. Have her draw pictures of each family member and talk about them.
3. Spend time alone with your child each day. Do something that you both enjoy. Show affection for her.
4. Play charades and perform the actions of a community worker.
5. Talk to child about her day at preschool. Keep a daily journal and have her dictate to you. Read parts of it back to her occasionally.
6. Give child chores to do. She is old enough to keep her own room picked up. With help, she can make her bed. She can help set the table each night. Talk to her as she sets the table about numbers of forks needed and about the food you will be sharing.
7. Cook with child. She will be very interested in having a part in preparing the food she will eat. At the table, give her credit for her contribution.
8. Talk about feelings. Ask her how she would feel in different situations. Ask her how a friend would feel in those same situations.
9. Play board games that require taking turns. Tell her how happy you are that she knows how to wait for a turn.

10. Set up the rules of the house together. You will be surprised at some of the rules child will come up with.

Emotional Development

Definition

Emotions means organize behaviour, energize behaviour and disrupt behaviour. It is a conscious process involving bodily changes. It adds to pleasure of everyday experience, serves as a motive to action and determine the characteristics pattern of adjustment of life. Child's emotions are first diffused and not very clear cut.

Characteristics of Childhood Emotion

There are certain characteristics features of children's emotion.

1. Children's emotions are for short term and brief, it last for few minute.
2. Children's emotions are very intense.
3. Children's emotion arise in minor situation.
4. Children's emotions are transitory.
5. Children's emotions re not changeable.
6. Children's emotions appear frequently.
7. Children's emotions grows with increase in age.
8. Children's emotional responses are different.
9. Children's emotions are identified from the symptoms of behaviour.
10. Children's emotion change in strength.
11. Children's emotions are shows with expression change.

Common Childhood Emotional Pattern

1. *Fear:* Fear start in infancy because of organic pain, loss of support, sudden change in visual

presentation, deep voices, masked faces, strange faces, animal bark. Fear change with change in age.

2. *Anxiety:* Anxiety is an internal fear. It may arise out of conflicts, critics, denial.

   Anxiety is a painful uneasiness of mind concerning apprehended ill or danger.

   Anxiety can be reduced by discussion, self analysis and relaxation therapy.

3. *Anger:* Anger is a more frequent emotional response in childhood than fear. anger increases with age when fear decreases. Anger attract others toward self and fulfill desires.

4. *Jealousy:* It arises out of a social cause. It is expressed in mild annoyance and well as in extreme hostility. Jealousy is normal response to loss of affection. It is expresses in an outburst to anger or temper.

5. *Joy and delight:* Pleasant emotions appear from physical well being, cooing, babbling, standing, walking, running, comics etc.

Common Childhood Behaviour Problems

1. *Thumb sucking:* It is a problem for children, it arise when something is wrong.
2. *Behaviour problems:* Child refuses to eat solid food after arrival of a new baby is using this to attract the attention.
3. *Eating problems:* Keep the child in humor and see that he eats rather than forcing him to eat something.
4. *Sleep:* These problems are seen because of reluctance of leave the family, fear of darkness, nightmares, etc.
5. *Discipline problems:* These arise as a reaction against over strict discipline.

6. *Betwetting:* These arise due to emotional disturbances. It reduced in relaxed home, normal activity of child.
7. *Sex problems:* It arise due to attitude of parents. If they strongly disapprove the normal curiosity of the child, they may both increase his curiosity and drive underground.

Social Development

Socialization is the process of presenting alternate channels for individual behaviour together with positive and negative sanctions emphasizes the influence social groups, formal and informal upon the personality of the individual. it involves three processes:

1. Child behaves according to the norms of his own group.
2. Child plays appropriate sex roles and other roles and defined by the group, parents, and children etc.
3. Child develops proper social attitudes.

Social development is a slow process. There are periods of development. It is quite rapid at first. Social development follows a pattern. Social development is predictable.

Factors Affecting Social Development

1. *Home:* It is the first place which influence on the socialization of the child. The culture of the home, language of family members, the behaviors displayed by parents and elders slowly but surely become a part of the child's personality and socialization. So these influence the socialization.
2. *Socio economic status:* The child from low economic status face a lot of problems in his day to day life. A poor child cannot adjust with a high economic status child.

3. *Relationship:* It also play a vital role in social development. Parental relationship, children relationship, father-son and mother-daughter relationship which influence the social life.
4. *Culture:* It is powerful socializing agent in the life of an individual. Ancient society differ from modern society. A good culture makes a individual perfect but a bad culture makes a child delinquent.
5. *Peer groups:* Child behaviour influenced by peer group, they give approval and attention, affection and child imitate the behaviour of the peer groups.
6. *Adult:* Child influenced by adults, when he enter to school he learn negative thing from senior and follow the attitude of the senior child.
7. *Twins:* They spend maximum time together, have more interests in common in outside companionships as compared to other siblings. They imitate each other and display same feeling.
8. *Family size:* Small family secure greater economic advantage they do produce problems of over protection and occasional tensions in the child. Joint family provide less economic advantage.
9. *Education and occupation of parents:* They provide models for observation and imitation. working both of parent effects on child development.
10. *Urbanization and modernization:* It provide greater stimulation at the same time greater diversion for undesirable habits, insecurity, lost of identity.

4

Play Development

Concept of Play

Newborn may not seem to be ready to learn and play, but all of his senses are working, and he's taking in the sensations, sounds, sights, and scents of his world. Since you comprise most of your newborn's world, teach him that it is a safe and loving one: fill his senses with lots of smiles, soothing sounds, and gentle caresses.

Stages of Play

First Baby Learn

A parent's face is a newborn's first and most wonderful "toy." Baby will love to fixate on face, and it will be all the entertainment he needs for now. Provide plenty of smiles, and talk to him so he becomes familiar with voice.

Baby is curious about noises he hears, but none more so than voice. He will learn very quickly to associate voice with the things he needs: food, warmth, touch. He will listen carefully when you talk to him. If mother react enthusiastically to the little noises he makes, he'll learn that mother want him to express himself.

Parents will learn to recognize when the baby is alert and ready to learn and play and when he'd rather be left alone. Sometimes baby will need to protect himself from over stimulation by "shutting down" for a bit.

What should Mother do?

Newborn loves attention. Talk to him, read to him, stroke and cuddle him, and cover him with kisses to promote bonding and recognition.

Even infants enjoy music and enjoy being read to. In fact, it seems that some babies actually remember songs and stories they heard repeatedly while still in the womb! But even if the song or story is not familiar to baby, he will find it soothing.

Give newborn simple toys that appeal to his sight, hearing, and touch. These include unbreakable crib mirrors, rattles, textured toys and musical toys. Choose toys and mobiles with contrasting colors and patterns; red and black patterns seem to appeal to newborns. A newborn's eyesight isn't very well developed, and strong contrasts will help him focus on his surroundings and keep his interest longer. Don't go overboard, though—offer your baby one plaything at a time. Too many can lead to confusion and over stimulation.

Play is not "play" to babies and children; play is how they learn about the world. Here are some ways to play with your newborn, but be sure to invent your own ways:

Dancing: Put on some music with a beat. Hold the baby's face close, and gently sway and move to the tune. Feel free to sing softly.

Name game: Touch and name all the parts of baby's body as he watches you. Make a game out of it by jumping from foot to foot or hand to hand.

Cuddling: Cradle baby in your lap and gently stroke him in different rhythmic patterns.

Should Mother be Concerned?

Any questions about newborn's ability to see or hear, should bring them to doctor's attention immediately. Even newborns can be tested using sophisticated equipment, if necessary. The sooner a potential problem is caught, the better it can be treated.

Learning Play (Infant 1-3 Month Old)

1-3 month old is more alert and aware of her surroundings than she was as a newborn. She already recognizes her parents' voices and faces, and she might be ready to respond to them with smiles. Your baby is ready to be an active participant in play.

What will Baby Learn?

The baby will carefully watch facial expressions and listen voice. By listening, she is learning the importance of speech before she understands or repeats any words herself. She'll also learn during this period that she has the ability to vocalize, too; make sure to answer her coos and gurgles with own sounds, and she will be more willing to express herself.

Now that baby's hands are open (and she's discovered them), she'll begin to use them to learn about the world. She'll play with her fingers, bring her hands to her mouth, and try to swing at things within view. In this way, she is learning hand-eye coordination. When lying down, she'll stretch out her arms and legs—soon she will learn to grasp and kick!

Learn to recognize when baby is alert and ready to learn and play and when she'd rather be left alone. Sometimes the baby will need to protect herself from over stimulation by "shutting down" for a bit.

What should Mother Do?

Remember that play is not just "play" to babies and children. Play is how they learn, so be enthusiastic when baby shows interest in playing. Take every opportunity to interact with her-provided she's in the mood. Don't over stimulate her with too many activities at once, and let her tell you when she's bored.

Baby will enjoy listening to music, the sounds her toys make, and singing—and she won't care whether or not you're any good. Her eyesight is improving, so she'll be fascinated by brightly colored pictures in books and the mobile above her crib. And she won't be able to take her eyes off herself if she has an unbreakable crib mirror.

As baby's hands open, offer her a rattle to hold, and watch her search for the source of the rattle's sounds. Give her safe objects of different textures, shapes, sizes, colors, and weights to hold. Dangle objects above your baby and let her swat at them. To get her hands moving, clap them together. Move her legs like a bicycle with your hands. These body games will help her learn to control her movements.

Once baby can hold her head up, introduce these classic games, or make up your own:

Elevator: Lie on your back and lift your baby up over you. Say, "I'm going to kiss you!" while you lower her down and give her a kiss.

Bouncing Rides: Place your baby on your lap and hold her under her arms. Move forward until you're at the edge of the seat, then raise and lower your heels to give her a gentle bounce. Reciting rhymes while you do this will add to the fun and encourage language development.

Learning Milestones

Here are some milestones to look for during this period. By the end of three months, most babies:

- Smile at the sound of a parent's voice
- Smile at others
- Reach for, grasp, and hold objects
- Support their heads well
- Make babbling sounds
- Bring objects to their mouths

Babies develop at different rates, and there is a wide range of normal development. It is usually not a cause for concern when a baby misses a developmental milestone, but talk to your pediatrician if your baby seems behind.

Learning Play (Infant 4-7 Month Old)

4-7 month old knows his name? You're probably right! His memory and attention span are increasing, and he's learning all sorts of things, even at this tender age.

Repetition is the name of the game for learning and play. Be prepared to play games, sing songs, and repeat actions over and over—you may be bored, but baby is excited and stimulated!

What will Baby Learn?

Baby is now beginning to understand the fundamentals of language. He's starting to pick out the components of speech. He can hear and understand the different sounds make and the way words form sentences. During this period, baby will probably recognize and respond to his name-and it won't be long before he's learned to ignore the word "no"!

Babies generally begin to grasp the principle of cause-and—effect during this stage: he learns that his actions cause reactions and that he has the ability to make things happen. He will explore this concept by doing things—dropping an object, kicking his crib, yelling-over and over (and over) again. Although this may be frustrating, it is the way your baby is learning the effects his actions may have. He is not throwing his pacifier on the floor over and over in order to upset you. He is doing it in order to see if it appears before him again.

Baby is beginning to realize that his actions have an effect on you, he will enjoy playing copycat games where you mimic what he says. He may also make the discovery that whenever he cries, he grabs your attention. This is mostly a good thing, but he will also use it on occasion when he is bored or frustrated. Rather than punish him for this, give him extra attention once he stops crying or fussing.

Baby will learn a great deal about the properties of objects with his hands and mouth. He will struggle to reach objects and learn to transfer them from hand to hand. Every object he manages to reach will go in his mouth, so watch him carefully, and make sure the objects he can reach do not pose a choking hazard.

What should Mother Do?

The baby gives him a chance to observe the way you talk and mimic the sounds you make. If the book has bright pictures, all the better. Be sure to show them to baby and describe them. Books that will withstand some mouthing and chewing are best.

With baby's more sophisticated motor skills, he is probably ready for toys that he can activate himself. Toys that make sounds when shaken are good, as are toys that teach cause-and-effect, such as pop-up toys. Puppets and other toys with finger holds will allow your baby to practice hand control. Be sure to read toy packages, and stick to the age guidelines suggested by the manufacturers.

Allow baby to use his toys other than for their intended purpose. This stimulates his creativity and curiosity and encourages him to experiment.

Baby is now beginning to understand the idea of object and person permanence, which means that objects and people continue to exist when they are out of sight. To demonstrate the principle of object permanence to the baby, try hiding a rattle, ball, or other toy under a towel or washcloth. See if he forgets all about the toy, or if he seems to grasp that the toy is simply hidden.

Captivate baby with these simple games, and introduce your own:

Food Painting

Place some purified food on baby's highchair tray, and let him "finger paint" with it. It's messy, but it's a lot of fun for the baby.

Peekaboo

This old standby will delight baby, with his budding understanding of object and person permanence. Cover your face with your hands, then remove your hands and say: "Peekaboo, I see you!"

Hide-and-Seek

Hide one of baby's toys-but don't hide it very well-and encourage him to find it.

Sometimes baby won't be in the mood to play, especially if he's tired, hungry, or cranky. The best thing to do is accept it and try again later.

Learning Milestones

By the end of this period, most babies will have learned to:

- Find an object that you have hidden
- Explore objects with their hands and mouths

Keep in mind, though, that there's a wide range of what's normal for babies. Some develop slower and some faster than others. If child is a little behind what is considered normal, check with your pediatrician, but there's usually no cause for alarm.

Learning Play (Toddlers 1-2 Year Old)

The majority of a child's social skills come as a result of play. During this stage, through play, toddler will learn to form relationships and will begin to imitate adult actions and experiment with social activities. Play with your toddler as often as you can, and introduce him to a playmate or two.

What will Baby Learn?

Something that surprises many new parents is that babies do not learn steadily, but rather in spurts. They latch onto new ideas or skills quickly and practice them over and over, often seeming to forget much of what they've already learned. When they feel comfortable with the new skills, the old ones will be brought out and employed again. If child enjoys an activity, don't hesitate to repeat it while also introducing him to new ones.

Most babies say their first words by 12 months to 14 months, though some start sooner and some put it off for a while they focus on walking. Between 15 and 18 months, your baby will enjoy language games that ask him to identify things, such as: "Where's your ear?" and "Where is Mommy?" Vocabulary will grow quickly, but pronunciation likely won't keep pace. Be patient and resist the temptation to correct your baby's pronunciation; instead, emphasize the correct pronunciation in your response. Soon he'll try to form sentences and questions with a combination of words and gestures.

At this age, baby will begin symbolic play for the first time-he'll imitate things he sees you do, and he'll use objects for their intended purpose. He'll attempt to brush his own hair with a hairbrush, or he'll use the phone to "talk".

Child may fluctuate between wanting independence and wanting to cling. This is absolutely normal-children this age are learning about their separateness from you but are still very dependent on you for comfort and reassurance. Give child as much freedom as you safely can, and be there when he needs to be a "baby" for a while.

What should Mother Do?

Remember that safety is responsibility. baby may be learning how things work and what things do, but that doesn't mean he understands what is harmful or dangerous. Take a look at house from you toddler's point of view, and periodically check your childproofing efforts.

"Lessons" should be in the form of games to keep your child's interest, and they should be stopped at the first sign of boredom. Removing the pressure from a lesson or playtime will teach your baby that learning is fun, and he'll look forward to the activity in the future.

Toddler will be very interested in experimenting with social activities and imitating adult actions in make-believe play. Give him toys that encourage symbolic play, such as kitchen sets, dolls, and dress-up clothes. Allow him to "shadow" you as you do chores or everyday activities, and give him some "chores" to do, such as brushing his teeth or putting on his shoes.

Great toys for exploring and experimenting include trains, play garden tools, outdoor toys (swing sets, slides), blocks, large crayons, baskets, and pots and pans. Shape sorters, pegboards, nesting toys and simple puzzles allow baby to enhance his analytical skills. As always, read to the child. He will now follow along with the story and point out objects and people in the picture.

Toddler will be fascinated with other children at this age. One or two playmates at a time is plenty. Don't expect your toddler to "play" with other children in a cooperative way or to be enthusiastic about sharing toys; he's not mature enough yet. You'll need to be there at all times to diffuse conflict. Nevertheless, children this age can learn a lot from each other by imitation.

Enthusiasm and applause can be two very powerful tools for stimulating child to learn. Pay attention to his successes, no matter how small, and he'll be encouraged to try for more.

Learning Milestones

Although babies develop at different rates, most babies this age:

- Engage in symbolic play
- Speak at least 15 words by 18 months and use two-word sentences by age 2
- Imitate your expressions and actions and follow your instructions
- Attempt more independent activity

Learning Through Play

Play is one of the most powerful vehicles children have for trying out and mastering new skills, concepts, and experiences. Play can help children develop the knowledge they need to connect in meaningful ways to the challenges they encounter in school. Play also contributes to how children view themselves as learners. As they play, they resolve confusing social, emotional, and intellectual issues by coming up with new solutions and ideas. They experience the sense of power that comes from being in control and figuring things out on their own (something children often do not get to do in real life). This helps them develop a positive attitude toward learning.

Playtime in the 21st Century

Many of the changes in childhood that have occurred in recent years are undermining the quality of children's play. "Playtime" is being shortchanged in school as more emphasis is placed on teaching "the basics" at younger and younger ages. Today's children and parents have busy lives so there is less free time outside of school. For safety and economic reasons, the culture of neighbourhood kids playing after school is becoming a thing of the past. When children do have playtime, they often choose to watch TV instead—an average of four hours a day—not to mention the additional time they spend watching videos or playing videogames. But of all the factors affecting play today, few have a more worrisome impact than the recent changes in toys.

Changes in Toys

The kinds of toys that are multi-purpose and unstructured, like clay, blocks, generic toy figures, and baby dolls, encourage play that children can control and shape to meet their individual needs over time. Unfortunately, most of today's best-selling toys promote highly-structured play. They're usually action figures or video games linked to TV programs or movies. They "tell" children how to play and can channel them into merely using the toys to try to imitate what they see on TV or in the movies.

How to Promote Creative Play

Do a lot of to help child develop play that supports her social, emotional, and intellectual development. Here are some suggestions:

- Encourage and value play that is appropriate to the age and individual interests and needs of child.
- Help child bring his own experiences into his play. Children's play is usually more creative and less imitative when it grows out of their daily lives. For instance, providing empty food cartons and a simple toy cash register after a trip to the supermarket can help child start recreating his experience through play.
- Watch child as she plays to see what she is working on and what interests her. This can help provide ideas about what play materials and other input might further develop her play.
- Choose new toys carefully. Toys that can be used in many ways usually promote the most valuable play. They give children many opportunities to invent new uses for them over time. Too many toys, or a constant barrage of new ones, can prevent children from doing this.
- Find ways to interact regularly (but not always) with your child as she plays. Getting involved with kids as they play—as long as you're not interrupting or taking over—shows them that adults value play.
- Try to have regular, uninterrupted playtime in child's life. This tells him that play is important. It also helps him develop the skills he needs over time to become involved in meaningful and satisfying play. For children who are heavily dependent on

television, develop this routine gradually and help children figure out how to begin their play.

- Work to counteract the gender, racial, and cultural stereotypes and violence that characterize many toys. Stereotypes limit children from developing their full potential. Children sort out who they and other people are through their play. Keep this in mind when choosing new toys and try openly talking with child about these issues when they come up.
- When child does engage in violent, imitative play based on TV shows, movies or toys, help her bring in her own creativity and imagination. However you view this kind of play, the more you can help your child's play become creative, the less violent it will be.
- Make thoughtful choices about the role of media in your child's life. What and how much children see in the media can have an enormous impact on their play. TV takes time away from play activities and media content greatly influences play. So, try to develop rules-for example, about screen time and screen content

Play and its Role

In speaking of play and its role in the preschooler's development, we are concerned with two fundamental questions: first, how play itself arises in development–its origin and genesis; second, the role of this developmental activity, which we call play, as a form of development in the child of preschool age.

Is play the leading form of activity for a child of this age, or is it simply the most frequently encountered form?

It seems that from the point of view of development, play is not the predominant form of activity, but is, in a certain sense, the leading source of development in preschool years. Let us now consider the problem of play itself. We know that a definition of play based on the pleasure it gives the child is not correct for two reasons–first, because we deal with a number of activities that give the child much keener experiences of pleasure than play.

For example, the pleasure principle applies equally well to the sucking process, in that the child derives functional pleasure from sucking a pacifier even when he is not being satiated.

On the other hand games in which the activity itself does not afford pleasure–games that predominate at the end of the preschool and the beginning of school age and that give pleasure only if the child finds the result interesting. These include, for example, sporting games (not just athletic sports but also games with an outcome, games with results). They are very often accompanied by a keen sense of displeasure when the outcome is unfavourable to the child.

Thus, defining play on the basis of pleasure can certainly not be regarded as correct.

Nonetheless, it seems that to refuse to approach the problem of play from the standpoint of fulfillment of the child's needs, his incentives to act, and his affective aspirations would result in a terrible intellectualization of play. The trouble with a number of theories of play lies in their tendency to intellectualize the problem.

Describe a child's development as the development of his intellectual functions, i.e., every child stands before us as a theoretical being who, according to the higher or lower level of his intellectual development, moves from one age period to another.

Without a consideration of the child's needs, inclinations, incentives, and motives to act–as research has demonstrated–there will never be any advance from one stage to the next. I think that an analysis of play should start with an examination of these particular aspects.

It seems that every advance from one age period to another is connected with an abrupt change in motives and incentives to act.

What is of the greatest interest to the infant has almost ceased to interest the toddler. This maturing of new needs and new motives for action is, of course, the dominant factor, especially as it is impossible to ignore the fact that a child satisfies certain needs and incentives in play; and without understanding the special nature of these incentives, we cannot imagine the uniqueness of that type of activity we call play.

At preschool age special needs and incentives arise that are very important for the whole of the child's development and that are spontaneously expressed in play. In essence, there arise in a child of this age many unrealizable tendencies and immediately unrealizable desires. A very young child tends to gratify his desires at once. Any delay in fulfilling them is hard for him and is acceptable only within certain narrow limits; no one has met a child under three who wanted to do something a few days hence. Ordinarily, the interval between the motive and its realization is extremely short. I think that if there were no development in preschool years of needs that cannot be realized immediately, there would be no play. Experiments show that the development of play is arrested both in intellectually underdeveloped children and in those who are affectively immature.

From the viewpoint of the affective sphere, it seems that play is invented at the point when unrealizable tendencies appear in development. This is the way a very young child behaves: he wants a thing and must have it at once. If he cannot have it, either he throws a temper tantrum, lies on the floor and kicks his legs, or he is refused, pacified, and does not get it.

His unsatisfied desires have their own particular modes of substitution, rejection, etc. Toward the beginning of preschool age, unsatisfied desires and tendencies that cannot be realized immediately make their appearance, while the tendency to immediate fulfillment of desires, characteristic of the preceding stage, is retained. For example, the child wants to be in his mother's place, or wants to be a rider on a horse. This desire cannot be fulfilled right now. What does the very young child do if he sees a passing cab and wants to ride in it no matter what may happen? If he is a spoiled and capricious child, he will demand that his mother put him in the cab at any cost, or he may throw himself on the ground right there in the street, etc. If he is an obedient child, used to renouncing his desires, he will turn away, or his mother will offer him some candy, or simply distract him with some stronger affect, and he will renounce his immediate desire.

In contrast to this, a child over three will show his own particular conflicting tendencies; on the one hand, many long-lasting needs and desires will appear that cannot be met at once but that nevertheless are not passed over like whims; on the other hand, the tendency toward immediate realization of desires is almost completely retained.

Henceforth play is such that the explanation for it must always be that it is the imaginary, illusory realization of unrealizable desires. Imagination is a new formation that is not present in the consciousness of the very young child, is totally absent in animals, and represents a specifically human form of conscious activity. Like all functions of consciousness, it originally arises from action. The old adage that children's play is imagination in action can be reversed: we can say that imagination in adolescents and schoolchildren is play without action.

It is difficult to imagine that an incentive compelling a child to play is really just the same kind of affective incentive as sucking a pacifier is for an infant.

It is hard to accept that pleasure derived from preschool play is conditioned by the same affective mechanism as simple sucking of a pacifier. This simply does not fit our notions of preschool development.

All of this is not to say that play occurs as the result of each and every unsatisfied desire: a child wants to ride in a cab, the wish is not immediately gratified, so the child goes into his room and begins to play cabs. It never happens just this way. Here we are concerned with the fact that the child has not only individual, affective reactions to separate phenomena but generalized, unpre designated, affective tendencies. Let us take the example of a micro encephalic child suffering from an acute inferiority complex: he is unable to participate in children's groups; he has been so teased that he smashes every mirror and pane of glass showing his reflection. But when he was very young, it had been very different; then, every time he was teased there was a separate affective reaction for each separate occasion, which had not yet become generalized. At preschool age the child generalizes his affective relation to the phenomenon regardless of the actual concrete situation because the affective relation is connected with the meaning of the phenomenon in that it continually reveals his inferiority complex.

Play is essentially wish fulfillment–not, however, isolated wishes, but generalized affects. A child at this age is conscious of his relationships with adults, and reacts to them affectively; unlike in early childhood, he now generalizes these affective reactions (he respects adult authority in general, etc.).

The presence of such generalized affects in play does not mean that the child himself understands the motives that give rise to a game or that he does it consciously. He plays without realizing the motives of the play activity. In this, play differs substantially from work and other forms of activity. On the whole it can be said that motives, actions, and incentives belong to a more abstract sphere and become accessible to consciousness only at the transitional age. Only an adolescent can clearly determine for himself the reason he does this or that.

Finding criteria for distinguishing a child's play activity from his other general forms of activity it must be accepted that in play a child creates an imaginary situation. This is possible on the basis of the separation of the fields of vision and meaning that occurs in the preschool period.

This is not a new idea, in the sense that imaginary situations in play have always been recognized; but they have always been regarded as one of the groups of play activities. Thus the imaginary situation has always been classified as a secondary symptom. In the view of earlier writers, the imaginary situation was not the criteria attribute of play in general, but only an attribute of a given group of play activities.

There are three main flaws in this argument.

First, there is the danger of an intellectualistic approach to play. If play is to be understood as symbolic, there is the danger that it may turn into a kind of activity akin to algebra in action; it may be transformed into a system of signs generalizing actual reality. Here we find nothing specific in play, and look upon the child as an unsuccessful algebraist who cannot yet write the symbols on paper, but depicts them in action. It is essential to show the connection with incentives in play, since play itself, in my view, is never symbolic action, in the proper sense of the term.

Second, this idea presents play as a cognitive process. It stresses the importance of the cognitive process while neglecting not only the affective situation but also the circumstances of the child's activity.

Third, it is vital to discover exactly what this activity does for development, i.e., how the imaginary situation can assist in the child's development.

Let us begin with the second question, as already briefly touched on the problem of the connection with affective incentives. We observed that in the affective incentives leading to play there are the beginnings not of symbols, but of the necessity for an imaginary situation; for if play is really developed from unsatisfied desires, if ultimately it is the realization in play form of tendencies that cannot be realized at the moment, then elements of imaginary situations will involuntarily be included in the affective nature of play itself.

Let us take the second instance first–the child's activity in play. What does a child's behaviour in an imaginary situation mean? We know that there is a form of play, distinguished long ago and relating to the late preschool period, considered to develop mainly at school age, namely, the development of games with rules. A number of investigators, although not at all belonging to the camp of dialectical materialists, have approached this area along the lines recommended by Marx when he said that "the anatomy of man is the key to the anatomy of the ape." They have begun their examination of early play in the light of later rule-based play and have concluded from this that play involving an imaginary situation is, in fact, rule-based play. It seems to me that one can go even further and propose that there is no such thing as play without rules and the child's particular attitude toward them.

Let us expand on this idea. Take any form of play with an imaginary situation. The imaginary situation already contains rules of behaviour, although this is not a game with formulated rules laid down in advance. The child imagines herself to be the mother and the doll a child, so she must obey the rules of maternal behaviour. This was very well demonstrated by a researcher in an ingenious experiment based on Sully's famous observations. The latter described play as remarkable in that children could make the play situation and reality coincide. One day two sisters, aged five and seven, said to each other: "Let's play sisters." Here Sully was describing a case in which two sisters were playing at being sisters, i.e., playing at reality. The above-mentioned experiment based its method on children's play, suggested by the experimenter, that dealt with real relationships. In certain cases I have found it very easy to evoke such play in children. It is very easy, for example, to make a child play with its mother at being a child while the mother is the mother, i.e., at what is, in fact, true. The vital difference in play, as Sully describes it, is that the child in playing tries to be a sister. In life the child behaves without thinking that she is her sister's sister. She never behaves with respect to the other Just because she is her sister–except perhaps in those cases when her mother says, "Give in to her." In the game of sisters playing at "sisters," however, they are both concerned with displaying their sisterhood; the fact that two sisters decided to play sisters makes them both acquire rules of behaviour.

(I must always be a sister in relation to the other sister in the whole play situation.) Only actions that fit these rules are acceptable in the play situation.

In the game a situation is chosen that stresses the fact that these girls are sisters: they are dressed alike, they walk about holding hands–in short, they enact whatever emphasizes their relationship as sisters vis-à-vis adults and strangers. The elder, holding the younger by the hand, keeps telling her about other people: "That is theirs, not ours." This means: "My sister and I act the same, we are treated the same, but others are treated differently." Here the emphasis is on the sameness of everything that is concentrated in the child's concept of a sister, and this means that my sister stands in a different relationship to me than other people. What passes unnoticed by the child in real life becomes a rule of behaviour in play. If play, then, were structured in such a way that there were no imaginary situation, what would remain? The rules would remain. The child would begin to behave in this situation as the situation dictates.

Let us leave this remarkable experiment for a moment and turn to play in general. I think that whenever there is an imaginary situation in play, there are rules–not rules that are formulated in advance and change during the course of the game, but rules stemming from the imaginary situation.

Therefore, to imagine that a child can behave in an imaginary situation without rules, i.e., as he behaves in a real situation, is simply impossible. If the child is playing the role of a mother, then she has rules of maternal behaviour. The role the child plays, and her relationship to the object if the object has changed its meaning, will always stem from the rules, i.e., the imaginary situation will always contain rules. In play the child is free. But this is an illusory freedom.

Although initially the investigator's task was to disclose the hidden rules in all play with an imaginary situation, we have received proof comparatively recently that the so-called pure games with rules (played by school children and late preschoolers) are essentially games with imaginary situations; for just as the imaginary situation has to contain rules of behaviour, so every game with rules contains an imaginary situation. For example, what does it mean to play chess? To create an imaginary situation. Why? Because the knight, the king, the queen, and so forth, can move only in specified ways; because covering and taking pieces are purely chess concepts; and so on. Although it does not directly substitute for real-life relationships, nevertheless we do have a kind of imaginary situation here. Take the simplest children's game with rules. It immediately turns into an imaginary situation in the sense that as soon as the game is regulated by certain rules, a number of actual possibilities for action are ruled out.

Just as we were able to show at the beginning that every imaginary situation contains rules in a concealed form, we have also succeeded in demonstrating the reverse–that every game with rules contains an imaginary situation in a concealed form. The development from an overt imaginary situation and covert rules to games with overt rules and a covert imaginary situation outlines the evolution of children's play from one pole to the other.

All games with imaginary situations are simultaneously games with rules, and vice versa. I think this thesis is clear.

However, there is one misunderstanding that may arise, and must be cleared up from the start. A child learns to behave according to certain rules from the first few months of life. For a very young child such rules–for example, that he has to sit quietly at the table, not touch other people's things, obey his mother–are rules that make up his life. What is specific to rules followed in games or play? It seems to me that several new publications can be of great aid in solving this problem. In particular, a new work by Piaget has been extremely helpful to me. This work is concerned with the development in the child of moral rules. One part is specially devoted to the study of rules of a game, in which, I think, Piaget resolves these difficulties very convincingly.

Piaget distinguishes what he calls two moralities in the child–two distinct sources for the development of rules of behaviour.

This emerges particularly sharply in games. As Piaget shows, some rules come to the child from the one-sided influence upon him of an adult. Not to touch other people's things is a rule taught by the mother, or to sit quietly at the table is an external law for the child advanced by adults. This is one of the child's moralities. Other rules arise, according to Piaget, from mutual collaboration between adult and child, or among children themselves. These are rules the child himself participates in establishing.

The rules of games, of course, differ radically from rules of not touching and of sitting quietly. In the first place, they are made by the child himself; they are his own rules, as Piaget says, rules of self-restraint and self-determination. The child tells himself: I must behave in such and such a way in this game. This is quite different from the child's saying that one thing is allowed and another thing is not. Piaget has pointed out a very interesting phenomenon in moral development–something he calls moral realism. He indicates that the first line of development of external rules (what is and is not allowed) produces moral realism, i.e., a confusion in the child between moral rules and physical rules. The child confuses the fact that it is impossible to light a match a second time and the rule that it is forbidden to light matches at all, or to touch a glass because it might break: all "don'ts" are the same to a very young child, but he has an entirely different attitude toward rules he makes up himself.

Outline two basic ideas. play with an imaginary situation is something essentially new, impossible for a child under three; it is a novel form of behaviour in which the child is liberated from situational constraints through his activity in an imaginary situation.

To a considerable extent the behaviour of a very young child–and, to an absolute extent, that of an infant–is determined by the conditions in which the activity takes place, as the experiments of Lewin and others have shown. Lewin's experiment with the stone is a famous example. This is a real illustration of the extent to which a very young child is bound in every action by situational constraints. Here we find a highly characteristic feature of a very young child's behaviour in the sense of his attitude toward the circumstance at hand and the real conditions of his activity. It is hard to imagine a greater contrast to Lewin's experiments showing the situational constraints on activity than what we observe in play. In the latter, the child acts in a mental, not a visible, situation. I think this conveys accurately what occurs in play. It is here that the child learns to act in a cognitive, rather than an externally visible, realm, relying on internal tendencies and motives, not on incentives supplied by external things. I recall a study by Lewin on the motivating nature of things for a very young child; in it Lewin concludes that things dictate to the child what he must do: a door demands to be opened and closed, a staircase to be run up, a bell to be rung. In short, things have an inherent motivating force in respect to a very young child's actions and determine the child's behaviour to such an extent that Lewin arrived at the notion of creating a psychological topology, i.e., of expressing mathematically the trajectory of the child's movement in a field according to the distribution of things with varying attracting or repelling forces.

What is the root of situational constraints on a child? The answer lies in a central fact of consciousness that is characteristic of early childhood: the union of affect and perception. At this age perception is generally not an independent feature, but an initial feature of a motor-affective reaction, i.e., every perception is in this way a stimulus to activity. Since a situation is always communicated, psychologically through perception, and perception is not separated from affective and motor activity, it is understandable that with his consciousness so structured, the child cannot act otherwise than as constrained by the situation–or the field–in which he finds himself.

In play, things lose their motivating force. The child sees one thing but acts differently in relation to what he sees. Thus, a situation is reached in which the child begins to act independently of what he sees. Certain brain-damaged patients lose the ability to act independently of what they see; in considering such patients one can begin to appreciate that the freedom of action we adults and more mature children enjoy is not acquired in a flash, but has to go through a long process of development.

Action in a situation that is not seen, but only conceived on an imagined level and in an imaginary situation, teaches the child to guide his behaviour not only by immediate perception of objects or by the situation immediately affecting him but also by the meaning of this situation.

Experiments and day-to-day observation clearly show that it is impossible for very young children to separate the field of meaning from the visible field. This is a very important fact. Even a child of two, when asked to repeat the sentence "Tanya is standing up" when Tanya is actually sitting in front of him, will change it to "Tanya is sitting down." In certain diseases we are faced with exactly the same situation. Goldstein and Geib have described a number of patients who were unable to state something that was not true. Gelb has data on one patient who was left-handed and incapable of writing the sentence "I can write well with my right hand." When looking out of the window on a fine day he was unable to repeat "The weather is nasty today," but would say, "The weather is fine today." Often we find that a patient with a speech disturbance is incapable of repeating senseless phrases–for example, "Snow is black"–whereas other phrases equally difficult in their grammatical and semantic construction can be repeated.

In a very young child there is such an intimate fusion between word and object, and between meaning and what is seen, that a divergence between the meaning field and the visible field is impossible.

This can be seen in the process of children's speech development. You say to the child, "clock." He starts looking and finds the clock, i.e., the first function of the word is to orient spatially, to isolate particular areas in space; the word originally signifies a particular location in a situation.

It is at preschool age that we first find a divergence between the fields of meaning and vision. It seems to me that we would do well to restate the notion of the investigator who said that in play activity thought is separated from objects, and action arises from ideas rather than from things.

Thought is separated from objects because a piece of wood begins to be a doll and a stick becomes a horse. Action according to rules begins to be determined by ideas, not by objects. This is such a reversal of the child's relationship to the real, immediate, concrete situation that it is hard to evaluate its full significance. The child does not do this all at once. It is terribly difficult for a child to sever thought (the meaning of a word) from object. Play is a transitional stage in this direction. At that critical moment when a stick–i.e., an object–becomes a pivot for severing the meaning of horse from a real horse, one of the basic psychological structures determining the child's relationship to reality is radically altered.

The child cannot yet sever thought from object; he must have something to act as a pivot. This expresses the child's weakness; in order to imagine a horse, he needs to define his actions by means of using the horse in the stick as the pivot. But nevertheless, the basic structure determining the child's relationship to reality is radically changed at this crucial point, for his perceptual structure changes. The special feature of human perception–which arises at a very early age–is so-called reality perception. This is something for which there is no analogy in animal perception. Essentially it lies in the fact that I do not see the world simply in color and shape, but also as a world with sense and meaning. I do not see merely something round and black with two hands, I see a clock; and I can distinguish one thing from another. There are patients who say, when they see a clock, that they are seeing something round and white with two thin steel strips, but they do not know that this is a clock; they have lost real relationship to objects. Thus, the structure of human perception could be figuratively expressed as a fraction in which the object is the numerator and the meaning is the denominator; this expresses the particular relationship of object and meaning that arises on the basis of speech. This means that all human perception is not made up of isolated perceptions, but of generalized perceptions. Goldstein says that this objectively formed perception and generalization are the same thing. Thus, for the child, in the fraction object-meaning, the object dominates, and meaning is directly connected to it. At the crucial moment for the child, when the stick becomes a horse, i.e., when the thing, the stick, becomes the pivot for severing the meaning of horse from a real horse, this fraction is inverted and meaning predominates, giving meaning/object.

Nevertheless, properties of things as such do have some meaning: any stick can be a horse, but, for example, a postcard can never be a horse for a child. Goethe's contention that in play any thing can be anything for a child is incorrect. Of course, for adults who can make conscious use of symbols, a postcard can be a horse. If I want to show the location of something, I can put down a match and say, "This is a horse." And that would be enough. For a child it cannot be a horse: one must use a stick. Therefore, this is play, not symbolism. A symbol is a sign, but the stick is not the sign of a horse. Properties of things are retained, but their meaning is inverted, i.e., the idea becomes the central point. It can be said that in this structure things are moved from a dominating to a subordinate position.

Thus, in play the child creates the structure meaning/object, in which the semantic aspect–the meaning of the word, the meaning of the thing–dominates and determines his behaviour. To a certain extent meaning is freed from the object with which it was directly fused before. I would say that in play a child concentrates on meaning severed from objects, but that it is not severed in real action with real objects.

A highly interesting contradiction therefore arises in which the child operates with meanings severed from objects and actions, but in real action with real objects operates with them in fusion. This is the transitional nature of play, which makes it an intermediary between the purely situational constraints of early childhood and thought that is totally free of real situations.

In play a child deals with things as having meaning. Word meanings replace objects, and thus an emancipation of word from object occurs. (A behaviourist would describe play and its characteristic properties in the following terms: the child gives ordinary objects unusual names and ordinary actions unusual designations, despite the fact that he knows the real ones.) Separating words from things requires a pivot in the form of other things. But the moment the stick–i.e., the thing–becomes the pivot for severing the meaning of "horse" from a real horse, the child makes one thing influence another in the semantic sphere. (He cannot sever meaning from an object or a word from an object except by finding a pivot in something else, i.e., by the power of one object to steal another's name.) Transfer of meanings is facilitated by the fact that the child accepts a word as the property of a thing; he does not see the word, but the thing it designates. For a child the word "horse" applied to the stick means, "There is a horse," i.e., mentally he sees the object standing behind the word.

Play is converted to internal processes at school age, going over to internal speech, logical memory, and abstract thought. In play a child operates with meanings severed from objects, but not in real action with real things. To sever the meaning of horse from a real horse and transfer it to a stick (the necessary material pivot to keep the meaning from evaporating) and really acting with the stick as if it were a horse is a vital transitional stage to operating with meanings. A child first acts with meanings as with objects and later realizes them consciously and begins to think, just as a child, before he has acquired grammatical and written speech, knows how to do things but does not know that he knows, i.e., he does not realize or master them voluntarily. In play a child unconsciously and spontaneously makes use of the fact that he can separate meaning from an object without knowing he is doing it; he does not know that he is speaking in prose just as he talks without paying attention to the words.

Hence we come to a functional definition of concepts, i.e., objects, and hence to a word as part of a thing. And so I should like to say that the creation of an imaginary situation is not a fortuitous fact in a child's life; it is the first effect of the child's emancipation from situational constraints. The first paradox of play is that the child operates with an alienated meaning in a real situation. The second is that in play h adopts the line of least resistance, i.e., he does what he feels like most because play is connected with pleasure. At the same time, he learns to follow the line of greatest resistance; for by subordinating themselves to rules, children renounce what they want, since subjection to rule and renunciation of spontaneous impulsive action constitute the path to maximum pleasure in play.

The same thing can be observed in children in athletic games. Racing is difficult because the runners are ready to start off when one says, "Get ready, get set. . ." without waiting for the "go." It is evident that the point of internal rules is that the child does not act on immediate impulse.

Play continually creates demands on the child to act against immediate impulse, i.e., to act according to the line of greatest resistance. I want to run off at once–this is perfectly clear–but the rules of the game order me to wait. Why does the child not do what he wants, spontaneously and at once? Because to observe the rules of the play structure promises much greater pleasure from the game than the gratification of an immediate impulse. In other words, as one investigator puts it, recalling the words of Spinoza: "An affect can be overcome only by a stronger affect." Thus, in play a situation is created in which, as Nohl puts it, a dual affective plan occurs. For example, the child weeps in play as a patient, but revels as a player. In play the child renounces his immediate impulse, coordinating every act of his behaviour with the rules of the game. Groos describes this brilliantly. He thinks that a child's will originates in, and develops from, play with rules. Indeed, in the simple game of sorcerer as described by Groos, the child must run away from the sorcerer in order not to be caught, but at the same time he must help his companion and get him disenchanted. When the sorcerer has touched him, he must stop. At every step the child is faced with a conflict between the rule of the game and what he would do if he could suddenly act spontaneously. In the game he acts counter to what he wants. Nohi showed that a child's greatest self-control occurs in play. He achieves the maximum display of willpower in the sense of renunciation of an immediate attraction in the game in the form of candy, which by the rules of the game the children are not allowed to eat because it represents something inedible. Ordinarily a child experiences subordination to a rule in the renunciation of something he wants, but here subordination to a rule and renunciation of acting on immediate impulse are the means to maximum pleasure.

Thus, the essential attribute of play is a rule that has become an affect. "An idea that has become an affect, a concept that has turned into a passion"–this ideal of Spinoza's finds its prototype in play, which is the realm of spontaneity and freedom. To carry out the rule is a source of pleasure. The rule wins because it is the strongest impulse. (Cf. Spinoza's adage that an affect can be overcome by a stronger affect.) Hence it follows that such a rule is an internal rule, i.e., a rule of inner self-restraint and self-determination, as Piaget says, and not a rule the child obeys as a physical law. In short, play gives the child a new form of desires, i.e., teaches him to desire by relating his desires to a fictitious "I"–to his role in the game and its rules. Therefore, a child's greatest achievements are possible in play–achievements that tomorrow will become his average level of real action and his morality.

Now we can say the same thing about the child's activity that we said about things. Just as we have the fraction object/meaning, we also have the fraction action/meaning.

Whereas action dominated before, this structure is inverted, meaning becoming the numerator, and action taking the place of the denominator. It is important to realize how the child is liberated from actions in play. An action, for example, is realized as finger movements instead of real eating–that is, the action is completed not for the action itself, but for the meaning it carries. At first, in a child of preschool age, action dominates over meaning and is incompletely understood; a child is able to do more than he can understand. It is at preschool age that there first arises an action structure in which meaning is the determinant; but the action itself is not a sideline or subordinated feature: it is a structural feature. Nohl showed that children, in playing at eating from a plate, performed actions with their hands reminiscent of real eating, but all actions that did not designate eating were impossible. Throwing one's hands back instead of stretching them toward the plate turned out to be impossible, that is, such action would have a destructive effect on the game. A child does not symbolize in play, but he wishes and realizes his wishes by letting the basic categories of reality pass through his experience, which is precisely why in play a day can take half an hour, and a hundred miles be covered in five steps. The child, in wishing, carries out his wishes; and in thinking, he acts. Internal and external action are inseparable: imagination, interpretation, and will are internal processes in external action.

The meaning of action is basic, but even by itself action is not neutral. At an earlier age the position was the reverse: action was the structural determinant, and meaning was a secondary, collateral, subordinated feature. What we said about severing meaning from object applies equally well to the child's own actions. A child who stamps on the ground and imagines himself riding a horse has thus accomplished the inversion of the fraction action/meaning to meaning/action.

Once again, in order to sever the meaning of the action from the real action (riding a horse, without having the opportunity to do so), the child requires a pivot in the form of an action to replace the real one. But once again, whereas before action was the determinant in the structure "action-meaning," now the structure is inverted and meaning becomes the determinant. Action retreats to second place and becomes the pivot; meaning is again severed from action by means of another action. This is a repetition of the point leading to operations based solely on the meanings of actions, i.e., to volitional choice, a decision, a conflict of motives, and to other processes sharply separated from fulfillment: in short, to the development of the will. Just as operating with the meanings of things leads to abstract thought, in volitional decision the determining factor is not the fulfillment of the action, but its meaning. In play an action replaces another action just as an object replaces another object. How does the child "float" from one object to another, from one action to another? This is accomplished by movement in the field of meaning–not connected with the visible field or with real objects–which subordinates all real objects and actions to itself. This movement in the field of meaning predominates in play: on the one hand, it is movement in an abstract field (a field that thus appears before voluntary operation with meanings), but the method of movement is situational and concrete (i.e., it is not logical, but affective, movement). In other words, the field of meaning appears, but action within it occurs just as in reality; herein lies the main genetic contradiction of play.

Thus we find in play–if you will–the negative of a child's general, everyday behaviour. Therefore, to consider play the prototype of his everyday activity and its predominant form is completely without foundation. This is the main flaw in Koffka's theory. He regards play as the child's other world. According to Koffka, everything that concerns a child is play reality, whereas everything that concerns an adult is serious reality. A given object has one meaning in play, and another outside it. In a child's world the logic of wishes and of satisfying urges dominates, not real logic. The illusory nature of play is transferred to life. This would be true if play were indeed the predominant form of a child's activity. But it is hard to envisage the insane picture that a child would bring to mind if the form of activity we have been speaking of were to become the predominant form of his everyday activity–even if only partially transferred to real life.

Koffka gives a number of examples to show how a child transfers a situation from play into life. But the real transference of play behaviour to real life can be regarded only as an unhealthy symptom. To behave in a real situation as in an illusory one is the first sign of delirium.

As research has shown, play behaviour in real life is normally seen only in the type of game in which sisters play at "sisters," i.e., when children sitting at dinner can play at having dinner, or (as in Katz's example) when children who do not want to go to bed say, "Let's play that it's night time and we have to go to sleep." They begin to play at what they are in fact doing, evidently creating associations that facilitate the execution of an unpleasant action.

Thus, it seems that play is not the predominant type of activity at preschool age. Only theories maintaining that a child does not have to satisfy the basic requirements of life, but can live in search of pleasure, could possibly suggest that a child's world is a play world.

Is it possible to suppose that a child's behaviour is always guided by meaning, that a preschooler's behaviour is so arid that he never behaves with candy as he wants to simply because he thinks he should behave otherwise? This kind of subordination to rules is quite impossible in life, but in play it does become possible; thus, play also creates the zone of proximal development of the child. In play a child is always above his average age, above his daily behaviour; in play it is as though he were a head taller than himself. As in the focus of a magnifying glass, play contains all developmental tendencies in a condensed form; in play it is as though the child were trying to jump above the level of his normal behaviour.

The play-development relationship can be compared with the instruction-development relationship, but play provides a background for changes in needs and in consciousness of a much wider nature. Play is the source of development and creates the zone of proximal development. Action in the imaginative sphere, in an imaginary situation, the creation of voluntary intentions and the formation of real-life plans and volitional motives–all appear in play and make it the highest level of preschool development.

The child moves forward essentially through play activity. Only in this sense can play be termed a leading activity that determines the child's development.

The second question is: How does play develop? It is a remarkable fact that the child starts with an imaginary situation when initially this imaginary situation is so very close to the real one. A reproduction of the real situation takes place. For example, a child playing with a doll repeats almost exactly what her mother does with her; the doctor looks at the child's throat, hurts her, and she cries; but as soon as the doctor has gone, the child immediately thrusts a spoon into the doll's mouth. This means that in the original situation, rules operate in a condensed and compressed form. There is very little of the imaginary in the situation. It is an imaginary situation, but it is comprehensible only in the light of a real situation that has just occurred, i.e., it is a recollection of something that has actually happened. Play is more nearly recollection than imagination–that is, it is more memory in action than a novel imaginary situation. As play develops, we see a movement toward the conscious realization of its purpose.

It is incorrect to conceive of play as activity without purpose; play is purposeful activity for a child. In athletic games one can win or lose; in a race one can come first, second, or last. In short, the purpose decides the game; it justifies all the rest. Purpose as the ultimate goal determines the child's affective attitude toward play. When running a race, a child can be highly agitated or distressed; and little may remain of pleasure, because he finds it physically painful to run, and if he is overtaken, he will experience little functional pleasure.

In sports the purpose of the game is one of its dominant features without which there would be no point–it would be like examining a piece of candy, putting it in one's mouth, chewing it, and then spitting it out.

In play the object, to win, is recognized in advance.

At the end of play development, rules emerge; and the more rigid they are, the greater the demands on the child's application, the greater the regulation of the child's activity, the more tense and acute play becomes. Simply running around without purpose or rules of play is a dull game that does not appeal to children.

Nohl simplified the rules of croquet for children and showed how this demagnetized the game, for the child lost the sense of the game in proportion to the simplification of the rules. Consequently, toward the end of development in play, what was originally embryonic has a distinct form, finally emerging as purpose and rules. This was true before, but in an undeveloped form. One further feature has yet to come, essential to sporting games; this is some sort of record, which is also closely connected with purpose.

Take chess, for example. For a real chess player it is pleasant to win and unpleasant to lose a game. Nohl says that it is as pleasing to a child to come first in a race as it is for a handsome person to look at himself in a mirror; there is a certain feeling of satisfaction.

Consequently, a complex of originally undeveloped features comes to the fore at the end of play development–features that were secondary or incidental in the beginning occupy a central position at the end, and vice versa.

Finally, the third question: What sort of changes in a child's behaviour can be attributed to play? In play a child is free, i.e., he determines his own actions, starting from his own "I." But this is an illusory freedom. His actions are in fact subordinated to a definite meaning, and he acts according to the meanings of things.

A child learns to consciously recognize his own actions and becomes aware that every object has a meaning.

From the point of view of development, the fact of creating an imaginary situation can be regarded as a means of developing abstract thought. I think that the corresponding development of rules leads to actions on the basis of which the division between work and play becomes possible, a division encountered as a fundamental fact at school age.

I should like to mention just one other aspect: play is really a particular feature of preschool age.

As figuratively expressed by one investigator, play for a child under three is a serious game, just as it is for an adolescent, although, of course, in a different sense of the word; serious play for a very young child means that he plays without separating the imaginary situation from the real one.

For the schoolchild, play begins to be a limited form of activity, predominantly of the athletic type, which fills a specific role in the schoolchild's development, but lacks the significance of play for the preschooler.

Superficially, play bears little resemblance to what it leads to, and only a profound internal analysis makes it possible to determine its course of movement and its role in the preschooler's development.

At school age play does not die away, but permeates the attitude toward reality. It has its own inner continuation in school instruction and work (compulsory activity based on rules). All examinations of the essence of play have shown that in play a new relationship is created between the semantic and the visible–that is, between situations in thought and real situations.

A Healthy Start to a Lifetime of Learning on Play

Academic training is increasingly replacing imaginative play and experiential hands-on learning in the early years of our children's lives. Education is now seen as a race, and the earlier you start, the sooner and the better you finish.

Yet there is no evidence that this push for early academics, such as the effort to have children start reading by age five, produces any lasting advantage for children. If anything, research and experience point in the opposite direction.

The current emphasis on teaching reading through formal instruction to five-year-olds is not working, leading many concerned parents and policy makers to assume that reading instruction must start sooner—at three or four. But that assumption is based on a narrow and thus flawed approach to child development, early education, and the development of literacy.

The key to developing literacy—and all other skills—is to pace the learning so that it is consistent with the child's development, enabling him or her to succeed at the early stages. Ensure this initial success and the child's natural love of learning blooms. Doom him to failure in the beginning by making inappropriate demands and he may well be unable to overcome the resulting sense of inadequacy. This is especially true of children whose families are already under social and economic stress.

Recent research confirms that early cognitive development is inextricably linked with physical, emotional, and social development. All grow out of early relationships with family and care-givers. Relationships with parents are of primary importance.

Essential capacities of childhood that must be fostered and developed during the first five years are listed below. These can be used as indicators of kindergarten readiness, but only when combined with appropriate expectations of a five-year-old development so that children are not handicapped by unrealistic demands. Five-year-olds entering kindergarten generally can:

- Use ideas and words meaningfully and creatively to make themselves understood and to understand others. This requires an environment that is rich in face-to-face verbal exchanges, including conversation, nursery rhymes, storytelling, and the sharing of books aloud. Morality is a precursor to literacy.

- Form close relationships with adults and other children. From these come the beginnings of empathy and human understanding.
- Read and respond appropriately to emotional and social cues and be able to work in groups.
- Engage in imaginative play, alone and with others.
- Express creativity through a range of activities, including visual arts, music, dance, etc.
- Feel at home exploring and caring about the world of nature.
- Interact with the world through hands-on experiences, handcrafts, and other physically engaging activities.
- Quiet themselves for short times in order to digest experiences or engage in focused activity.
- Perceive patterns, follow simple directions, and solve simple problems.
- Learn to attend to, focus on, and process experiences in an integrated way through motor, sensory, and affective pathways.

Guidelines for Policymaking

How should the recognition of these capacities be translated into policy? As the Institute of Medicine's report, From Neurons to Neighbourhoods, states, "The policy issue is therefore not one of getting children ready to learn, but rather one of appreciating that they are born to learn and crafting policies and programs that actively build on their considerable capabilities" (p. 148). Children love to learn. This love needs to be fostered at home and in early care and education programs. Policy can support this in a number of ways:

- Provide funding opportunities for parents to educate themselves about the needs of young children and their own capacities for parenting. Possible options include courses for adolescents on child development and the care of children; and for parents, pre-birth and parenting classes, parent-child programmes, home visits, etc.
- Create a renewed focus on early-childhood teacher training and better compensation to help teachers and child care staff. In training programmes, place a new emphasis on understanding the broad range of capacities children need to develop, especially the capacity to play, and help develop the creativity and insight of the teachers themselves.
- Focus assessments of early care programs on whether children's prime needs for close relationships with caring, responsible adults and for developmentally appropriate care are being met. Developmentally appropriate care includes: a daily rhythm of healthy meals, rest, and activities; daily periods of play, both outdoors and indoors, in a safe environment; music and the other arts; hands-on and other physically engaging activities, which literally embody the most effective first lessons for young children in the sciences and mathematics; and a rich variety of face-to-face verbal interactions, including conversation, nursery rhymes, storytelling, and books read aloud with attentive adults.
- Recognize that when families are under great stress for reasons of poverty or illness this has a profound impact on children and their emotional readiness to learn. The social and economic stresses on the family need to be addressed as well as the specific needs of the child in the classroom.

Fund long-term research to identify: when children are developmentally ready to read and to acquire other academic skills; factors that may interfere with their ability to learn, such as overexposure to electronic media; and the best approaches in early education that will lead to a lifelong love of reading and learning.

Types of Play

Throwing balls, reading books, dressing up, painting pictures—children can learn and play in so many ways! Often times, customers are stumped when it comes to choosing the perfect toy for a child's interests or needs. To help find appropriate toys for children, Growing Tree Toys provides information on 6 types of play, which outline the various play behaviors associated with our toys. Through our child development research and toy knowledge, Growing Tree Toys separated play into the following six types: quiet, creative, active, cooperative, dramatic, and manipulative. These types of play provide further information on what to expect from a particular toy and how a child will interact with the toy.

Why are the Types of Play Important?

Knowing the types of play for a toy is essential to mother as they assess the environment in which the child is learning, the specific interests of the child, or the areas in which the child needs development.

1. *Active Play:* Play that involves movement and physical activity. Active play is the perfect type of play to tucker any youngster out! Whether running around in the yard, or building sand castles at a local playground, active play is an essential part of a child's development. Some examples of active play are: Riding Bikes Swinging at the playground Kickball.
2. *Cooperative Play:* Play for your child and a group of friends. Cooperative play can take place almost anywhere—outside on the playground or downstairs in the basement. In any environment, children learn from watching other children play and interacting with them socially. Some fun

cooperative play activities are: Interactive pretend play Basketball Board games Game time, make believe time—it's all fun time when other children are around to take part in play!

3. *Creative Play:* Play that explores your child's imagination and makes something out of nothing! A box of crayons, construction paper, pipe cleaners, scissors and glue. They are all staples in the home, but when they come together in the hands of a child, they become magical works of art. But, creativity extends beyond art, entering a world of music, dance, building—even dirt! Creative play includes such things as: Painting Sculpting play dough Building or creating crafts Providing a child a creative outlet will lead to many amazing things, and as you may know already, some not so amazing things if it involves drawing on furniture or a wall!
4. *Dramatic Play:* Play that involves pretend and make believe, or whatever the imagination dreams. Have you ever found a child in your clothes? Carrying your briefcase? Wearing your old uniform? What seems commonplace to you opens a whole new world of possibilities to a child. Dramatic play can include: Simple role playing. Using props to create a "new" environment. Creating scenes or situations with dolls and puppets. Children love role-playing and exploring worlds outside of their everyday, creating new and fun situations with every costume and prop. Imagine what they think you do at work!
5. *Manipulative Play:* Play that involves hand-eye coordination and motor skills. Children need the opportunity to work on finer skills that involve a little more control and direction. Manipulative play develops the sense of coordination, challenging their little fingers to follow the lines or use their tools properly. Some examples of manipulative play are: Colouring, especially in a defined area Paper crafts

and art involving moving parts that need to be "put together". Using a safe and simple tool kit to help with tasks around the house. Cutting out a sunshine for the window or painting within the lines—all these activities are the perfect exercise for this type of play.

6. *Quiet Play:* Play that keeps children's mouths shut but their minds open. Playtime for children should have the opportunity to be quiet—the playtime for which adults are sometimes grateful! Children need quiet time to intently digest the items in their learning environment, like books and puzzles. Quiet play provides children an opportunity to think and reason and can include such activities as: Beading a necklace working on puzzles reading or looking at pictures By providing a silent environment, children can focus on their toys and playthings and really get down to the work of being a child. After all, play is the work of children!
7. *Motor/Physical Play:* Motor play provides critical opportunities for children to develop both individual gross and fine muscle strength and an overall integration of muscles, nerves, and brain functions. Recent research has confirmed the critical link between stimulating activity and brain development. Young children must have ample opportunities to develop physically, and motor play instills this disposition toward physical activity in young children.
8. *Social Play:* A variety of opportunities for children to engage in social play are the best mechanisms for progressing through the different social stages. By interacting with others in play settings, children learn social rules such as, give and take, reciprocity, cooperation, and sharing. Through a range of interactions with children at different social stages children also learn to use moral reasoning to devel

a mature sense of values. To be prepared to function effectively in the adult world, children need to participate in lots of social

9. *Constructive Play:* Constructive play is when children manipulate their environment to create things. This type of play occurs when children build towers and cities with blocks, play in the sand, construct contraptions on the woodworking bench, and draw murals with chalk on the sidewalk. Constructive play allows children to experiment with objects; find out combinations that work and don't work; and learn basic knowledge about stacking, building, drawing, making music and constructing. It also gives children a sense of accomplishment and empowers them with control of their environment. Children who are comfortable manipulating objects and materials also become good at manipulating words, ideas and concepts.

10. *Fantasy Play:* Children learn to abstract, to try out new roles and possible situations, and to experiment with language and emotions with fantasy play. In addition, children develop flexible thinking; learn to create beyond the here and now; stretch their imaginations, use new words and word combinations in a risk-free environment, and use numbers and words to express ideas, concepts, dreams, and histories. In an ever—more technological society, lots of practice with all forms of abstraction-time, place, amount, symbols, words, and ideas—is essential.

5

Intelligence Development

Introduction

The terms 'intelligent', 'brilliant', 'slow' and 'dull' are used by teachers and parents to categories children according to intellect. While we all have an intuitive grasp of what intelligence is, we find it hard to define it. Intelligence is an abstract construct that eludes definition. Yet, we feel that it is something that can be measured and quantified. Furthermore, we have woven a web of biases of what an intelligent person should or shouldn't do. For example, a more intelligent child is encouraged to pursue a professional degree, while a less intelligent child is streamlined into softer options like the humanities. The history of formal intelligence testing dates back to the 1800s when Alfred Binet, a French psychologist, was commissioned by the French Ministry of Education to construct tests to determine which children were not likely to succeed in school so that they could receive special attention. This test was later adapted by Stanford psychologists Lewis Terman, who developed the Standford-Binet Test. A number of intelligence tests have sprung up since then—the Wechsler Intelligence Scale for children and adults, Kaufman's Intelligence Test and Raven's Progressive Matrices.

Most intelligence tests consist of a number of subtests that assess abilities such as verbal and mathematical reasoning, logical thinking, vocabulary and general knowledge—abilities that are generally required in a traditional scholastic environment. A significant contribution towards intelligence testing was made by Charles Spearman, who used the statistical procedure of factor analysis to show that a "general faculty" sub served all intelligence subtests. While different subtests tapped independent and separate abilities, a "general faculty" also operated upon them. Spearman based his supposition on the fact that most of the subtests of traditional psychometric tests of intelligence tend to correlate with each other to some extent.

In India, The Standford-Binet test has been adapted as the Binet-Kamath Test. Most intelligence tests are designed to provide an I.Q. (intelligence quotient) score, which is defined as: I.Q. = Mental Age/Chronological Age × 100. Thus, a ten-year old child who has a mental age of a 14 year-old, will have an I.Q. of 140. The mental age is based on a set of norms that have been devised by collecting data on a fairly large sample of children of different ages, whom the test makers believe are representative of a population at large. One of the criticisms of I.Q. tests is that most tests are not truly representative, especially regarding lower income and minority groups. Even if I.Q. tests are truly representative, they have some drawbacks. Foremost, traditional psychometric tests of intelligence are based on the proposition that human beings are endowed with a single, "general faculty" for acquiring information. Secondly, as a person is given a fixed I.Q. score, his/her intelligence is taken to be a fixed, unchanging entity. Traditional tests of intelligence do not take situational and contextual information into account. Thirdly, they penalize a child for a creative or unconventional answer.

Fortunately, I.Q. tests are used selectively in India, mainly by psychologists who assess children with learning problems. In such situations, an intelligence test may provide valuable information regarding a child's cognitive profile over and above the single I.Q. score. Even though I.Q. testing has not pervaded the Indian educational scene in a big way, our conception of intelligence in school settings is similar to those who developed psychometric assessments. Parents and educators view intelligence within a narrow framework. Thus, even though most children do not undergo formal I.Q. testing, school tests and examinations serve as proxy intelligence tests. Children who score high marks in school are deemed more intelligent than those who do not. Our marks-oriented approach, which streamlines children into future careers as early as Class IX, has a number of drawbacks.

Firstly, the term 'intelligent' quite narrowly and measure it based on performance on academic tests which, by and large, do not provide an index of a student's creative or critical reasoning skills. Performance on mathematical and linguistic tasks, which form the bulk of academic assessments, are taken as a yardstick of the student's overall intelligence. Second, overlook other abilities and do not provide sufficient opportunities for students to explore and excel in other domains. The cultivation of positive self-esteem is often neglected in schools as children are judged solely by their marks in scholastic tasks. Children who excel in sports, music, dance or drawing are often not given due recognition by the system. Third, overlook the contribution of environmental factors for the development of intelligence. As a culture we tend to view 'intelligence' as being more innate; and do not give due recognition to the external factors that are as important as, if not more, than our biological endowment.

An alternative view to the traditional conception of intelligence has been put forth by the neurophysiologist Howard Gardner. His theory of multiple intelligences looks at human potential in its broadest sense. He defines 'intelligence' as a "biopsychological potential to process information that can be activated in a cultural setting to solve problems or create products that are of value in a culture". Thus, he broadens the scope of 'intelligence' by pluralizing it. He believes that we are endowed with separate faculties for dealing with different kinds of symbol systems. Drawing evidence from eclectic sources, including neuropsychological, experimental and developmental psychology, Gardner claims that there are at least eight distinct intelligences. These are

(1) linguistic; (2) logical mathematical; (3) bodily kinesthetic; (4) spatial; (5) musical; (6) interpersonal; (7) intrapersonal; (8) naturalist. The first two intelligences are those required for scholastic tasks and have been traditionally viewed as the faculties comprising intellect. However, the theory of multiple intelligences has broadened the scope of how we conceive of intelligence—Gardner argues that people who excel in other areas such as dance or music should also be considered 'intelligent'. Gardner also stresses the importance of socio-cultural variables in the development of an intelligence. While a child may be inclined towards a particular type of intelligence, he/she is not going to excel in that field unless given an opportunity to cultivate and hone it. We need to be aware that our school system stresses the importance of linguistic and mathematical intelligences, often to the exclusion of other faculties.

What are the implications of the theory of multiple intelligences of educators and school administrators? First, the theory questions the disproportionate importance given to linguistic and mathematical skills in traditional forms of testing. Most schools also tend to evaluate students solely on these skills. Thus, educators need to be a aware of the fact that different types of intelligences exist, and that a child who does not perform well on a task that requires a certain type of intelligence may excel at a task that taps a different type of intelligence. Second, the fact that Gardner used eclectic sources of data while formulating his theory also throw light on the nature of the intelligences and their assessment. Intelligence is complex, and a number of tasks in appropriate contexts are required to assess it. Plain paper and pencil tasks simply will not do. Gardner, however, remains wary regarding assessment, and is aware of the pitfalls of any standardized test. Teachers need to be aware of the fact that traditional tests do not necessarily reveal a student's potential.

While the theory of multiple intelligences has gained popularity in many schools all over the world, Gardner remains skeptical of whether his theory is being misunderstood or misrepresented when applied in school settings. As he himself does not offer concrete application criteria and leaves it to the educators to develop for themselves, his skepticisms is fair. Even in India there are a few elite schools that claim to be applying the theory. Often, this application is at a very superficial level—a pitfall that Gardner himself has warned against. He has also cautioned educators from labeling children according to types of intelligences.

However, what the theory can offer educators at this point is a framework to shape their philosophy of how they view children and intelligence—two areas of concern for any institution dedicated to the cause of education. The theory of multiple intelligences offers a broad framework for educators to review their pedagogical. In intelligence, Piaget focuses on the mental processes that occur, rather than on the actual measure of the intellect. He uses four are as to define intelligence. These areas are: a biological approach to looking at intelligence, the succession of the stages, knowledge, and intellectual competence.

Piaget's biological approach, or biological adoption, focuses on the physical and mental aspects of our bodies. This includes our reflexes which occur when certain stimuli trigger an instinctive response. He also discusses how we adapt to certain situations using assimilation and accommodation. Assimilation occurs when new information is introduced to a person. The person begins to integrate the new information into existing files, or "schema". Accommodation occurs when the person reorganizes schema to accommodate themselves with the environment.

The succession of stages involves the movement through four stages that Piaget has set and defined. Children must move through these stages during their childhood. These include Sensory motor, Preoperational, Concrete operational, and Formal operational. Stage movement is an important factor of Piaget's definition of intelligence, because Piaget states there are a specific set of criteria that must be met and mastered at each stage. In order to move from the first stage to the next, the child must master that specific set of criteria.

To define Intellectual Competence, Piaget focuses on the highest level of functioning that can occur at a specific stage. Although Piaget has approximate ages assigned to stages, a child's competence is only measured by what stage they are in, not by age. If the child can only perform tasks that are at the preoperational stage, that is the highest level the child is at regardless of age.

Goals and priorities: As assessment is an integral component of most schools, educators will benefit from critiquing their own assessment standards and criteria.

Definition on Intelligence

Intelligence is an abstract construct that eludes definition. Yet, we feel that it is something that can be measured and quantified. Furthermore, we have woven a web of biases of what an intelligent person should or should not do.

Concept of Intelligence

"It seems that in intelligence there is a fundamental faculty, the alteration or the lack of which, is of the utmost importance for practical life. This faculty is judgment, otherwise called good sense, practical sense, initiative, the faculty of adapting one's self to circumstances. A person may be a moron or an imbecile if he is lacking in judgment; but with good judgment he can never be either. Indeed the rest of the intellectual faculties seem of little importance in comparison with judgment"

Nature of Intelligence

there are two major contribution on the nature of intelligence. The first, supported by such psychologists as Eysenck, Galton, Jensen, and Spearman, believe that all intelligence comes from one general factor, known as *g*. The proponents of the other school of thought include Gardner, Sternberg, and Thurstone. These psychologists think that there is more than one general type of intelligence, or in other words, that there are different types of intelligences. Following are the type of intelligence:

Types of Intelligence

General Intelligence

There are strong arguments to support the theory of one general type of intelligence. The most convincing evidence for a single general intelligence model is the fact that there is proof of a single general factor that governs the level of intelligence of an individual. This is also known as the positive manifold. There is a very high correlation between I.Q. and very simple cognitive tasks, which supports the theory of one general intelligence.

Positive Manifold: The first argument in support of one general intelligence is the fact that there is a high positive correlation between different tests of cognitive ability. Spearman (1904), in doing his research, administered to many people different types of tests, covering several different areas of cognitive ability. When he examined the results of these different tests, he found that there was a positive correlation between the tests for a given individual. In other words, if a certain person performed well on a test of verbal abilities, then that same person also performed well on another test of another cognitive ability, for instance, a mathematics test. Spearman named this positive correlation among tests the positive manifold. This positive manifold was also called the general intelligence factor, or *g*. This is the single factor that determines the intelligence of the individual. Jensen (1997) supported the theory of one general intelligence by stating, "the positive correlation between all cognitive test items is a given, an inexorable fact of nature. The all-positive inter item correlation matrix is not an artifact of test construction or item selection, as some test critics mistakenly believe". This positive manifold led Spearman (1904) to find a large first factor that was dubbed general intelligence, or *g*.

Reaction Time and *g*: Another strong argument in support of one general intelligence is the fact that there is a very high correlation between reaction time and I.Q. According to Eysenck (1982), "I.Q. correlates very highly (. 8

and above, without correction for attenuation) with tests which are essentially so simple, or even directly physiological that they can hardly be considered cognitive in the accepted sense". For instance, an example of the type of tests used to measure reaction time is a test in which a light is turned on. The participant is asked to press a button as soon as he or she sees the light go on. From tests such as these, the reaction time can be measured. Given that only very simple sensory and motor movements are necessary to respond, it is difficult to argue that cultural, environmental, gender, socio-economic, or educational discrepancies will affect the participants ability to respond to the testers' questions (Eysenck, 1982).

Common definitions of intelligence are "success in problem solving, ability to learn, capacity for producing no genetic solutions, understanding of complex instructions or simply all-round cognitive ability" (Eysenck, 1982). A common thread in all of these definitions of intelligence is that they all require the nervous system, especially the brain, and sensory organs to be functioning properly. Furthermore, in order for these types of tasks to be completed, they require that the information processing that goes on within the bodily systems is relatively without error.

Jensen (1993), as well as others, synthesized these facts and conjectured that "the most obvious hypothesis is that speed of information processing is the essential basis if *g*, and one possible neurological basis of speed of processing is the speed of transmission through nerve pathways" (p. 54). The speed of information transmission can be reasonably well measured or extrapolated from reaction time scores. Therefore, if an individual has faster neural processing speed, then he or she have a better reaction time. In turn, given that reaction time is highly correlated with I.Q., then those individuals with faster neural processing speeds have higher IQ's. Consequently, neural processing speed determines the level of intelligence of the individual; this intelligence is the one general intelligence, *g*.

Sternberg and Gardner (1982) summarized the theory of one general intelligence by stating "general intelligence can be understood componentially as deriving in part from the execution of general components in information processing behaviour". And Spearman (1973/1923) concluded that "cognitive events do, like those of physics, admit throughout of being reduced to a small number of definitely formula table principles in the sense of ultimate laws". These psychologists, as well as many others, believe that intelligence can be defined by a single factor. Whether that single factor be termed positive manifold, neural processing speed, or *g*, the complexities of the human mind and its processes can be reduced to a single factor, defined as intelligence.

Multiple Intelligences

The different proponents of one general intelligence all agree that there is a single factor that determines intelligence, and the proponents of multiple intelligences agree that there is more than one single type of intelligence. However, the different proponents of multiple intelligences do not agree on how many different intelligences there are, or could be. I believe that the theories put forth by Gardner and Sternberg have the most merit. Both of them have their own theory on multiple intelligences; Gardner (1983) believes there are seven forms of intelligence; Sternberg (1985) believes there are three forms of intelligences.

Gardner's Theory: Gardner's theory of multiple intelligences suggests that there are seven different forms of intelligence. They are linguistic, musical, spatial, bodily, interpersonal, intrapersonal and logic-mathematical. In developing his theory, Gardner (1983) attempted to rectify some of the errors of earlier psychologists who "all ignore[d] biology; all fail[ed] to come to grips with the higher levels of creativity; and all [were] insensitive to the range of roles highlighted in human society". So, Gardner based his own theory of intelligence on biological facts. Li (1996) summarizes Gardner's theory as follows:

Premise 1: If it can be found that certain brain parts can distinctively map with certain cognitive functioning (A), then that cognitive functioning can be isolated as one candidate of multiple intelligences (B) (If A, then B). Premise 2: Now it has been found that certain brain parts do distinctively map with certain cognitive functioning, as evidenced by certain brain damage leading to loss of certain cognitive function (Evidence of A). Conclusion: Therefore, multiple intelligences (Therefore B).

Gardner's theory has a very solid biological basis. Premise two takes into account the brain as a major physical determinant of intelligence. By studying individuals who had speech impairment, paralysis, or other disabilities, Gardner could localize the parts of the brain that were needed to perform the physical function. He studied the brains of people with disabilities postmortem and found that there was damage in specific areas, in comparison to those who did not have a disability. Gardner found seven different areas of the brain, and so his theory consists of seven different intelligences, each related to a specific portion of the human brain (Li, 1996).

Gardner looked to develop a theory with multiple intelligences also because he felt that the current psychometric tests only examined the linguistic, logical, and some aspects of spatial intelligence, whereas the other facets of intelligent behaviour such as athleticism, musical talent, and social awareness were not included.

Sternberg's Theory: The triarchic theory of intelligence developed by Sternberg is "a comprehensive theory, more encompassing. . . because it takes into account social and contextual factors apart from human abilities" (Li, 1996). Sternberg (1985) felt that the theories that preceded him were not incorrect, but, rather, incomplete. Consequently, his theory, like Gardner's, takes into account creative or musical intelligence. But as for the other six intelligences from Gardner's theory, Sternberg classifies them into two different types of intelligences: analytic (or academic) and practical. These two types of intelligences differ and are defined as follows: Analytic problems tend to have been formulated by other people, be clearly defined, come with all information needed to solve them, have only a single right answer, which can be reached by only a single method, be disembodied from ordinary experience, and have little or no intrinsic interest. Practical problems tend to require problem recognition and formulation, be poorly defined, require information seeking, have various acceptable solutions, be embedded in and require prior everyday experience, and require motivation and personal involvement (Neisser et al., 1996).

If an individual could solve one or the other of these types of problems well, then that individual would have a high analytic or practical intelligence, respectively. Also, there exist virtuosos, or individuals who are extremely talented in the fine arts, these people would have a high creative intelligence.

One reason why Sternberg's theory has received so much acclaim is that in real-life situations, is has proven itself. For example, Brazilian street children can do the math that they need to know in order to run their street businesses, but they are unable to pass a math class in school (Carraher, Carraher, and Schliemann, 1985). Evidence such as this shows that there are two different types of mathematical intelligence, an academic classroom mathematical intelligence and a street wise practical intelligence.

Other Theories: In addition to Gardner's and Sternberg's theories on multiple intelligences, there are other theories as well, including Turnstone's and Guilford's. Both were proponents of multiple intelligences. Thurstone (1924) stated that "the biological function of intelligence is to protect the organism from bodily risk and to satisfy its wants with the least possible chance of recording failure on the environment"). With this in mind, he found several primary mental abilities. As expected, these abilities are those abilities that the individual uses in order to survive and succeed in society. He found this using factor analysis, like Spearman, but Thurstone took the factor analysis a step further and rotated the factors. He arrived at 13 different factors as opposed to Spearman's one and called these primary mental abilities. These factors included spatial, perceptual, numerical, logical, verbal, memory, arithmetical reasoning, and deductive abilities (Thurstone, 1938). Guilford (1967) found that the structure of intellect was composed of 4 contents, 5 operations, and 6 processes. Each of these was mixed and matched to come up with 120 different combinations of abilities.

What is Multiple Intelligence?

There are seven main areas in which all people have special skills; he calls them intelligences. Binet's work led to the formation of an intelligence test; we are all familiar with the "intelligence quotient," or "I.Q.," the way that intelligence is measured on his test.

This type of IQ test was used as the basis of another one with which most of us are familiar: the Scholastic Aptitude Test (SAT), which is taken my most college-bound high school students.

Both of these tests look predominantly at two types of intelligences: verbal and math. If a person does well on these, s/he is considered "intelligent," and is a candidate for one of the better colleges or universities. But what about everyone else? How many of you who are reading these words have used the phrase "not good at taking tests," when talking either about yourself or your child?

The Multiple Intelligences (MI) theory proposes that there are other measures of intelligence beside these two. I offer this information to you so that you can understand that while many teachers have some knowledge of MI theory, most of our schools are not fully set up to use it to the advantage of all students.

That being the case, perhaps you can either (1) be involved in helping your child's teachers and school to provide a more balanced program that develops his intelligences that are not more included in the curriculum or (2) find activities outside of the school environment in which your child can develop his dominant areas of intelligence.

You should also know that MI theory posits that each of us has, to some degree or another, all of these intelligences. Some of them are simply more developed than others. Furthermore, we are all able to improve our ability in each of these areas.

Howard Gardner stresses that the intelligences are equal in their importance. In alphabetical order, they are:

Bodily-Kinesthetic: Using one's body to solve problems and express ideas and feelings. Actors, athletes, and dancers use their whole bodies in this way, much the same way that craftspeople, sculptors, and mechanics use their hands.

These are some questions to determine if children may be exhibiting a well-developing Bodily-Kinesthetic Intelligence. Does your child:

- excel in more than one sport?
- move various body parts when required to sit still for long periods of time?
- have the ability to mimic others' body movements?
- enjoy taking things apart and putting them back together?
- have a hard time keeping hands off objects?
- enjoy running, jumping, or other physical activities?
- show skill in activities that require fine-motor coordination, such as origami, making paper airplanes, building models, finger-painting, clay, or knitting?
- use his body well to express himself?

Interpersonal: Perceiving the moods, feelings, and needs of others. It includes salespeople, teachers, counselors, and those we have come to call the helping professions.

These are some questions to determine if children may be exhibiting a well-developing Interpersonal Intelligence. Does your child:

- enjoy socializing with friends?

- seem to be a natural leader?
- empathize easily with others, which leads to his give advice to friends who come to him with problems?
- seem to be street-smart?
- enjoy belonging to organizations?
- enjoy teaching other kids-either peers or younger ones?
- have two or more close friends?
- serve as a magnet for social activities with others?

Intrapersonal: Turning inward with a well-developed self-knowledge and using it successfully to navigate oneself through the world.

These are some questions to determine if children may be exhibiting a well-developing Intrapersonal Intelligence. Does your child:

- show a sense or independence or a strong will?
- have a realistic sense of her abilities and weaknesses?
- do well when left alone to play or study?
- "march to the beat of a different drummer" in living and learning?
- have a hobby or interest she doesn't talk about much?
- have a good sense of self-direction?
- prefer working alone to working with others?
- accurately express how he is feeling?
- learn from failures and successes?
- have good self-esteem?

Linguistic: Using words, either orally or written, in an effective manner. This intelligence is associated with storytellers, politicians, comedians, and writers.

These are some questions to determine if children may be exhibiting a well-developing Linguistic Intelligence. Does your child:

- write better than average for her age?
- enjoy telling stories and jokes?
- have a good memory for names, places, dates, and other information?
- enjoy word games, either visually or auditorally?
- enjoy reading books?
- spell better than other children the same age?
- appreciate rhymes, puns, tongue twisters?
- enjoy books on tape without needing to see the book itself?
- enjoy hearing stories without seeing the book?
- have an excellent vocabulary for his age?
- communicate thoughts, feelings, and ideas well?

Logical-Mathematical: Understanding and using numbers effectively, as well as having good powers to reason well. Exemplars are mathematicians, scientists, computer programmers, and accountants.

These are some questions to determine if children may be exhibiting a well-developing Logical-Mathematical Intelligence. Does your child:

- demonstrate curiosity about how things work?
- have fun with numbers?
- enjoy math at school?
- enjoy math and/or computer games?
- play and enjoy strategy games such as chess and checkers, brain teasers, or logic puzzles?
- easily put things into categories?
- like to do experiments, either at school when assigned or on her own?

- show an interest in visiting natural history or discovery-type museums and exhibits?

Musical: Relating in a wide range of ways to music. This can take many forms, as a performer, composer, critic, and music-lover.

These are some questions to determine if children may be exhibiting a well-developing Musical Intelligence. Does your child:

- tell you when she recognizes that music is off-key?
- easily remember song melodies and sing them?
- have a pleasant singing voice, either alone or in a chorus?
- play a musical instrument?
- speak or move in a rhythmical way?
- hum or whistle to himself?
- tap on the tabletop or desktop while working?
- show sensitivity to noises in the environment?
- respond emotionally to music she hears?

Naturalist Intelligence: Excellent at recognizing and classifying both the animal and plant kingdoms, as well as showing understanding of natural phenomena.

These are some questions to determine if children may be exhibiting a well-developing Naturalist Intelligence. Does your child:

- talk about favourite pets or preferred natural spots?
- enjoy nature preserves, the zoo, or natural history museum?
- show sensitivity to natural formations? (Note that in urban environments, this type of "formation" can include cultural icons.)
- like to play in water?
- hang around the pet in school or at home?

- enjoy studying environment, nature, plants, and animals?
- speak out about animal rights and earth preservation?
- collect bugs, flowers, leaves, or other natural things to show to others?

Spatial: Perceiving the visual-spatial world in an accurate way, so as to be able to work in it effectively. The people who do this cover a wide range of fields that, upon first glance, do not seem to have much in common. Compare, for example, hunters, sailors, engineers, inventors, and surgeons to interior decorators, architects, painters, and sculptors.

These are some questions to determine if children may be exhibiting a well-developing Spatial Intelligence. Does your child:

- recall visual details in objects?
- have an easy time learning to read and understand maps and charts in books?
- daydream a lot?
- enjoy the visual arts?
- demonstrate ability in using art materials and creating drawings, sculptures, or other three-dimensional objects?
- enjoy visual presentations such as videos, television, and movies?
- get a lot of information from illustrations in books she reads?
- scribble, doodle, or draw on all available surfaces?

Development of Intelligence Theory

Ideas and Interests

After receiving his law degree in 1878, Alfred Binet began to study science at the Sorbonne. However, he was not overly interested in his formal schooling, and started educating himself by reading psychology texts at the National Library in Paris. He soon became fascinated with the ideas of John Stuart Mill, who believed that that the operations of intelligence could be explained by the the laws of associationism. Binet eventually realized the limitations of this theory, but Mill's ideas continued to influence his work.

In 1883, Binet began to work in Jean-Martin Charcot's neurological laboratory at the Salpêtrière Hospital in Paris. At the time of Binet's tenure, Charcot was experimenting with hypnotism. Binet was strongly influenced by this great man, and published four articles about his work in this area. Unfortunately, Charcot's conclusions did not hold up under professional scrutiny, and Binet was forced to make an embarrassing public admission that he had been wrong in supporting his teacher.

When his intrigue with hypnosis waned as a result of failure to establish professional acceptance, he turned to the study of development spurred on by the birth of his two daughters, Madeleine and Alice (born in 1885 and 1887, respectively). In the 21 year period following his shift in career interests, Binet "published more than 200 books, articles, and reviews in what now would be called experimental, developmental, educational, social, and differential psychology" (Siegler, 1992). Bergin and Cizek (2001) suggest that this work may have influenced Jean Piaget, who later studied with Binet's collaborator Theodore Simon in 1920. Binet's research with his daughters helped him to further refine his developing conception of intelligence, especially the importance of attention span and suggestibility in intellectual development.

Despite Binet's extensive research interests and wide breadth of publications, today he is most widely known for his contributions to intelligence. Wolf (1973) postulates that this is the result of his not being affiliation with a major university. Because Binet did not have any formalized graduate study in psychology, he did not hold a professorship with a prestigious institution where students and funds would be sure to perpetuate his work (Siegler, 1992). Additionally, his more progressive theories did not provide the practical utility that his intelligence scale would evoke.

In 1904 a French professional group for child psychology, *La Société Libre pour l'Etude Psychologique de l'Enfant*, was called upon by the French government to appoint a commission on the education of retarded children. The commission was asked to create a mechanism for identifying students in need of alternative education. Binet, being an active member of this group, found the impetus for the development of his mental scale.

Binet and Simon, in creating what historically is known as the Binet-Simon Scale, comprised a variety of tasks they thought were representative of typical children's abilities at various ages. This task-selection process was based on their many years of observing children in natural settings. They then tested their measurement on a sample of fifty children, ten children per five age groups. The children selected for their study were identified by their school teachers as being average for their age. The purpose of this scale of normal functioning, which would later be revised twice using more stringent standards, was to compare children's mental abilities relative to those of their normal peers (Siegler, 1992).

The scale consisted of thirty tasks of increasing complexity. The easiest of these could be accomplished by all children, even those who were severely retarded. Some of the simplest test items assessed whether or not a child could follow a lighted match with his eyes or shake hands with the examiner. Slightly harder tasks required children to point to various named body parts, repeat back a series of 3 digits, repeat simple sentences, and to define words like house, fork or mama. More difficult test items required children to state the difference between pairs of things, reproduce drawings from memory or to construct sentences from three given words such as "Paris, river and fortune." The hardest test items included asking children to repeat back 7 random digits, find three rhymes for the French word *obéisance* and to answer questions. He has received in turn a doctor, a lawyer, and then a priest.

For the practical use of determining educational placement, the score on the Binet-Simon scale would reveal the child's mental age. For example, a 6 year-old child who passed all the tasks usually passed by 6 year-olds—but nothing beyond—would have a mental age that exactly matched his chronological age, 6.0. (Fancher, 1985).

Binet was upfront about the limitations of his scale. He stressed the remarkable diversity of intelligence and the subsequent need to study it using qualitative as opposed to quantitative measures. Binet also stressed that intellectual development progressed at variable rates, could be impacted by the environment and was therefore not based solely on genetics, was malleable rather than fixed, and could only be used on children with comparable backgrounds (Siegler, 1992). Given Binet's stance that intelligence testing was subject to variability and was not generalizable, it is important to look at the metamorphosis that mental testing took on as it made its way to the U.S.

While Binet was developing his mental scale, the business, civic, and educational leaders in the U.S. were facing issues of how to accommodate the needs of a diversifying population, while continuing to meet the demands of society. There arose the call to form a society based on meritocracy (Siegler, 1992) while continuing to underline the ideals of the white upper class. In 1908, H.H. Goddard, a champion of the eugenics movement, found utility in mental testing as a way to evidence the superiority of the white race. After studying abroad, Goddard brought the Binet-Simon Scale to the United States and translated it into English.

Following Goddard in the U.S. mental testing movement was Lewis Terman who took the Simon-Binet Scale and standardized it using a large American sample. The new Standford-Binet scale, was no longer used solely for advocating education for all children, as was Binet's objective. A new objective of intelligence testing was illustrated in the Stanford-Binet manual with testing ultimately resulting in "curtailing the reproduction of feeble-mindedness and in the elimination of an enormous amount of crime, pauperism, and industrial inefficiency" (White, 2000).

It follows that we should question why Binet did not speak out concerning the newfound uses of his measure. Siegler (1992) pointed out that Binet was somewhat of an isolationist in that he never traveled outside of France and he barely participated in professional organizations. Additionally, his mental scale was not adopted in his own country during his lifetime and therefore was not subjected to the same fate. Finally, when Binet did become aware of the "foreign ideas being grafted on his instrument" he condemned those who with 'brutal pessimism' and 'deplorable verdicts' were promoting the concept of intelligence as a single, unitary construct (White, 2000).

6

Intellectual Development

Introduction

A child's growth and development may be divided into four periods: infancy, the preschool years, the middle childhood years, and adolesecence. Immediately after birth, an infant normally loses approximately 5 per cent to 10 per cent of his or her birth weight. However, by about 2 weeks of age, an infant should start to have rapid weight gain and growth.

By 4 to 6 months of age, an infant's weight should be double the birth weight. During the second half of the first year of life, growth is not as rapid. Between the ages of 1 and 2, a toddler will gain only about 5 pounds. Weight gain will remain at about 5 pounds per year between the ages of 2 and 5.

Between the ages of 2 and 10 years, a child will continue to grow at a steady pace. A final growth spurt begins with the onset of puberty, sometime between the ages of 9 and 15.

Nutrient needs correspond with these changes in rates of growth, meaning an infant needs more calories in relation to size than a preschooler or school-age child needs. Nutrient needs increase again as a child approaches adolescence.

At the age of 2, most children understand the concept of time in broad terms. Many 2-and 3-year-olds believe that anything that happened in the past happened "yesterday," and anything that will happen in the future will happen "tomorrow." A child at this age has a vivid imagination but has difficulty distinguishing fantasy from reality. By age 4, most children have a more complicated understanding of time. They realize that the day is divided into morning, afternoon, and night. They can even appreciate the change in seasons.

From 18 months to 5 years of age, a child's vocabulary quickly expands from about 50 words to several thousand words. Children can begin to name and to actively ask about objects and events. By age 2, they begin to put two words together in short phrases, progressing to simple sentences by age 3. Pronunciation improves, with speech being half-understandable to a stranger by age 2 and fully understandable by age 4. A 4-year-old child can tell simple stories and can engage in conversation with adults or other children.

Even before 18 months of age, children can listen to and understand a story being read to them. By age 5, children are able to recite the alphabet and to recognize simple words in print. These skills are all fundamental to learning how to read simple words, phrases, and sentences. Depending on exposure to books and natural abilities, most children begin to read by age 7.

By age 7, a child's intellectual capabilities have become more complex. By this time, a child becomes increasingly able to focus on more than one aspect of an event or situation at the same time. For example, a school-aged child can appreciate that a tall, slender container can hold the same amount of water as a short, broad one. He can appreciate that medicine can taste bad but can make him feel better, or that his mother can be mad at him but can still love him. The child is increasingly able to understand another person's perspective and so learns the essentials of taking turns in games or conversations. In addition, a school-aged child is able to follow agreed-upon rules of games. The child is also increasingly able to reason using the powers of observation and multiple points of view.

Jean Piaget—Intellectual Development

Jean Piaget was born in Neufchatel (Switzerland) on August 9, 1896. He died in Geneva on September 16, 1980. He was the oldest child of Arthur Piaget, professor of medieval literature at the University, and of Rebecca Jackson. At age 11, while he was a pupil at Neufchatel Latin high school, he wrote a short notice on an albino sparrow. This short paper is generally considered as the start of a brilliant scientific career made of over sixty books and several hundred articles.

Piaget may be best known for his stages of intellectual development. Piaget discovered that children think and reason differently at different periods in their lives. He believed that everyone passed through an invariant sequence of four qualitatively distinct stages. Invariant means that a person cannot skip stages or reorder them. Although every normal child passes through the stages in exactly the same order, there is some variability in the ages at which children attain each stage. The four stages are: sensori motor-birth to 2 years; preoperational-2 years to 7 years; concrete operational-7 years to 11 years; and formal operational (abstract thinking) 11 years and up. Each stage has major cognitive tasks which must be accomplished. In the sensori motor stage, the mental structures are mainly concerned with the mastery of concrete objects. The mastery of symbols takes place in the preoperational stage. In the concrete stage, children learn mastery of classes, relations, and numbers and how to reason. The last stage deals with the mastery of thought.

Piaget has been labeled an interactionist as well as a constructivist. His interest in cognitive development came from his training in the natural sciences and his interest in epistemology. Piaget was very interested in knowledge and how children come to know their world. He developed his cognitive theory by actually observing children (some of whom were his own children). Using a standard question or set of questions as a starting point, he followed the child's train of thought and allowed the questioning to be flexible. Piaget believed that children's spontaneous comments provided valuable clues to understanding their thinking. He was not interested in a right or wrong answer, but rather what forms of logic and reasoning the child used (Singer, 1978). After many years of observation, Piaget concluded that intellectual development is the result of the interaction of hereditary and environmental factors. As the child develops and constantly interacts with the world around him, knowledge is invented and reinvented. His theory of intellectual development is strongly grounded in the biological sciences. He saw cognitive growth as an extension of biological growth and as being governed by the same laws and principles. He argued that intellectual development controlled every other aspect of development-emotional, social, and moral.

Intellectual Development in Children

Probably the most cited theory in the cognitive development in children is Jean Piaget (1896-1980). As with all stage theories, *Piaget's Theory of intellectual Development* maintains that children go through specific stages as their intellect and ability to see relationships matures. These stages are completed in a fixed order with all children, even those in other countries. The age range, however can vary from child to child.

Sensory Motor Stage: This stage occurs between the ages of birth and two years of age, as infants begin to understand the information entering their sense and their ability to interact with the world. During this stage, the child learns to manipulate objects although they fail to understand the permanency of these objects if they are not within their current sensory perception. In other words, once an object is removed from the child's view, he or she is unable to understand that the object still exists.

The major achievement during this stage is that of Object Permanency, or the ability to understand that these objects do in fact continue to exist. This includes his ability to understand that when mom leaves the room, she will eventually return, resulting in an increased sense of safety and security. Object Permanency occurs during the end of this stage and represents the child's ability to maintain a mental image of the object (or person) without the actual perception.

Sensory Motor Period (0-24 Months)

Developmental stage and age	*Characteristics behaviours*
Reflexive Stage (0-2 months)	Simple reflex activity such as grasping, sucking.
Primary Circular Reactions (2-4 months)	Reflexive behaviors occur in stereotyped repetition such as opening and closing fingers repetitively.
Secondary Circular Reactions (4-8 months)	Repetition of change actions to reproduce interesting consequences such as kicking one's feet to more a mobile suspended over the crib.
Coordination of Secondary Reactions (8-12 months)	Responses become coordinated into more complex sequences. Actions take on an "intentional" character such as the infant reaches behind a screen to obtain a hidden object.
Tertiary Circular Reactions (12-18 months)	Discovery of new ways to produce-the same consequence or obtain the same goal such as the infant may pull a pillow toward him in an attempt to get a toy resting on it.
Invention of New Means Through Mental Combination (18-24 months)	Evidence of an internal representational system. Symbolizing the problem-solving sequence before actually responding. Deferred imitation.

The Preoperational Period (2-7 Years)

Pre-operational Stage: The second stage begins after Object Permanency is achieved and occurs between the ages of two to seven years of age. During this stage, the development of language occurs at a rapid pace. Children learn how to interact with their environment in a more complex manner through the use of words and images. This stage is marked by Egocentrism, or the child's belief that everyone sees the world the same way that she does. The fail to understand the differences in perception and believe that inanimate objects have the same perceptions they do, such as seeing things, feeling, hearing and their sense of touch.

A second important factor in this stage is that of Conservation, which is the ability to understand that quantity does not change if the shape changes. In other words, if a short and wide glass of water is poured into a tall and thin glass. Children in this stage will perceive the taller glass as having more water due only because of it's height. This is due to the children's inability to understand reversibility and to focus on only one aspect of a stimulus, such as height, as opposed to understanding other aspects, such as glass width.

Developmental stage and age	*Characteristics behaviours*
Preoperational Phase (2-4 years)	Increased use of verbal representation but speech is egocentric. The beginnings of symbolic rather than simple motor play. Transductive reasoning. Can think about something without the object being present by use of language.
Intuitive Phase (4-7 years)	Speech becomes more social, less egocentric. The child has an intuitive grasp of logical concepts in some areas. However, there is still a tendency to focus attention on one aspect of an object while ignoring others. Concepts formed are crude and irreversible. Easy to believe in magical increase, decrease, disappearance. Reality not firm. Perceptions dominate judgment.

In moral-ethical realm, the child is not able to show principles underlying best behaviour. Rules of a game not develop, only uses simple do's and don'ts imposed by authority.

Period of Concrete Operations (7-11 Years)

Concrete Operations Stage: Occurring between ages 7 and about 12, the third stage of cognitive development is marked by a gradual decrease in centristic thought and the increased ability to focus on more than one aspect of a stimulus. They can understand the concept of grouping, knowing that a small dog and a large dog are still both dogs, or that pennies, quarters, and dollar bills are part of the bigger concept of money.

They can only apply this new understanding to concrete objects (those they have actually experienced). In other words, imagined objects or those they have not seen, heard, or touched, continue to remain somewhat mystical to these children, and abstract thinking has yet to develop.

Evidence for organized, logical thought. There is the ability to perform multiple classification tasks, order objects in a logical sequence, and comprehend the principle of conservation. thinking becomes less transductive and less egocentric. The child is capable of concrete problem-solving.

Some reversibility now possible (quantities moved can be restored such as in arithmetic: 3+4 = 7 and 7-4 = 3, etc.).

Class logic-finding bases to sort unlike objects into logical groups where previously it was on superficial perceived attribute such as color. Categorical labels such as "number or animal" now available.

Period of Formal Operations (11-15 Years)

Formal Operations Stage: In the final stage of cognitive development (from age 12 and beyond), children begin to develop a more abstract view of the world. They are able to apply reversibility and conservation to both real and imagined situations. They also develop an increased understanding of the world and the idea of cause and effect. By the teenage years, they are able to develop their own theories about the world. This stage is achieved by most children, although failure to do so has been associated with lower intelligence.

Thought becomes more abstract, incorporating the principles of formal logic. The ability to generate abstract propositions, multiple hypotheses and their possible outcomes is evident. Thinking becomes less tied to concrete reality.

Formal logical systems can be acquired. Can handle proportions, algebraic manipulation, other purely abstract processes. If a + b = x then x = a-b. If ma/ca = IQ = 1.00 then Ma = CA.

Prepositional logic, as-if and if-then steps. Can use aids such as axioms to transcend human limits on comprehension.

Activity Intellectual Development

One-year-old Children

- They are curious.
- They point to objects that they want.
- They imitate animal sounds.
- They name familiar people and objects.
- They combine two words to form a basic sentence.
- They use the pronouns me and mine.
- They use "no" frequently.
- They name body parts and familiar pictures.
- They use objects for their intended purpose.
- They begin to include a second person in pretend play.
- Their attention span is short.
- They can hold a pencil and scribble.
- They are very active.
- Because of their developing imagination, they have trouble knowing what is real and what is pretend.

Two-year-old Children

- They follow simple directions.
- They use three or more words in combination.
- They express their feelings and wishes.
- They use objects to represent other objects.
- They still have a very limited attention span.

- They can memorize short rhymes.
- They join in simple songs.
- They begin to think about doing something before doing it.
- They have trouble making choices, but they want to make choices.

Three-year-old Children

- They can communicate their needs, ideas, and questions.
- Their attention span is a little longer so they can participate in group activities.
- Preschool children learn best by doing. They need a variety of activities. They need indoor and outdoor space. They need a balance between active and quiet play.

Four-year-old Children

- They are very talkative.
- They enjoy serious discussions.
- They ask lots of questions, including "how" and "why" questions.
- Their language includes silly words and profanity.
- Their classification skills and reasoning ability are developing.
- They should understand some basic concepts such as number, size, weight, color, texture, distance, time, and position.

How Children Learn

. . . we discovered that education is not something which the teacher does, but that it is a natural process which develops spontaneously in the human being. It is not acquired by listening to words, but in virtue of experiences in which the child acts on

his environment. The teacher's task is not to talk, but to prepare and arrange a series of motives for cultural activity in a special environment made for the child. (Dr. Maria Montessori)

A central component of Piaget's developmental theory of learning and thinking is that both involve the participation of the learner. Knowledge is not merely transmitted verbally but must be constructed and reconstructed by the learner. Piaget asserted that for a child to know and construct knowledge of the world, the child must act on objects and it is this action which provides knowledge of those objects; the mind organizes reality and acts upon it. The learner must be active; he is not a vessel to be filled with facts. Piaget's approach to learning is a readiness approach. Readiness approaches in developmental psychology emphasize that children cannot learn something until maturation gives them certain prerequisites. The ability to learn any cognitive content is always related to their stage of intellectual development. Children who are at a certain stage cannot be taught the concepts of a higher stage.

Intellectual growth involves three fundamental processes: assimilation, accommodation, and equilibration. Assimilation involves the incorporation of new events into preexisting cognitive structures. Accommodation means existing structures change to accommodate to the new information. This dual process, assimilation-accommodation, enables the child to form schema. Equilibration involves the person striking a balance between himself and the environment, between assimilation and accommodation. When a child experiences a new event, disequilibrium sets in until he is able to assimilate and accommodate the new information and thus attain equilibrium. There are many types of equilibrium between assimilation and accommodation that vary with the levels of development and the problems to be solved. For Piaget, equilibration is the major factor in explaining why some children advance more quickly in the development of logical intelligence than do others.

Implications for Education

A Piagetian-inspired curricula emphasizes a learner-centered educational philosophy. The teaching methods which most American school children are familiar with-teacher lectures, demonstrations, audio-visual presentations, teaching machines, and programmed instruction-do not fit in with Piaget's ideas on the acquisition of knowledge. Piaget espoused *active* discovery learning environments in our schools. Intelligence grows through the twin processes of assimilation and accommodation; therefore, experiences should be planned to allow opportunities for assimilation and accommodation. Children need to explore, to manipulate, to experiment, to question, and to search out answers for themselves-activity is essential. However, this does not mean that children should be allowed to do whatever they want. So what is the role of the teacher? Teachers should be able to assess the child's present cognitive level; their strengths and weaknesses. Instruction should be individualized as much as possible and children should have opportunities to communicate with one another, to argue and debate issues. He saw teachers as facilitators of knowledge—they are there to guide and stimulate the students. Allow children to make mistakes and learn from them. Learning is much more meaningful if the child is allowed to experiment on his own rather than listening to the teacher lecture. The teacher should present students with materials and situations and occasions that allow them to discover new learning. In his book *To Understand is to Invent* Piaget said the basic principle of active methods can be expressed as follows: "to understand is to discover, or reconstruct by rediscovery, and such conditions must be complied with if in the future individuals are to be formed who are capable of production and creativity and not simply repetition". In active learning, the teacher must have confidence in the child's ability to learn on his own.

Intellectual Development and Diet

Malnutrition has been associated with serious problems with intellectual development. A child who is undernourished may experience early fatigue and may be unable to fully participate in learning at school. Additionally, malnutrition can increase the susceptibility to illness, possibly causing a child to miss school.

Children who are chronically undernourished have unacceptable growth patterns accompanied by scholastic underachievement. A good variety of food choices and adequate intake are essential to achieve the best possible intellectual development. Breakfast is particularly important as children may feel fatigued, sleepy, and unmotivated when breakfast is skimpy or is skipped altogether.

Nutrition is considered critical enough to intellectual development that U.S. government programs have been put in place to insure at least one healthy, balanced meal a day for children. This is usually breakfast, because the relationship between breakfast and improved learning has been clearly demonstrated. Programs are available in impoverished and underserved areas of the United States.

7

Creativity Development

Introduction

Creativity is the freest form of self-expression. There is nothing more satisfying and fulfilling for children than to be able to express themselves openly and without judgment. The ability to be creative, to create something from personal feelings and experiences, can reflect and nurture children's emotional health. The experiences children have during their first years of life can significantly enhance the development of their creativity.

Importance

All children need to be truly creative is the freedom to commit themselves completely to the effort and make whatever activity they are doing their own. What's important in any creative act is the process of self-expression. Creative experiences can help children express and cope with their feelings. A child's creative activity can help teachers to learn more about what the child may be thinking or feeling. Creativity also fosters mental growth in children by providing opportunities for trying out new ideas, and new ways of thinking and problem-solving. Creative activities help acknowledge and celebrate children's uniqueness and diversity as well as offer excellent opportunities to personalize our teaching and focus on each child.

Opportunities for Creativity

Children need plenty of opportunities for creative play and creative thinking. Start by providing activities that are based on the children's interests and ideas. This means learning how to listen intently to what children are saying. It is very helpful to tape record and transcribe children's conversations as well as take notes and review them with your co-teachers.

Be sure to offer children a wide range of creative materials and experiences. Being creative is more than drawing or painting. There's also photography, music, field trips, working with wire, clay, paper, wood, water or shadows. The possibilities are endless. It's important to provide children lots of time to explore materials and pursue their ideas. This includes time to think about how to plan, design, construct, experiment and revise project ideas. Don't forget to build in time to talk these ideas over with other people-both teachers and children.

Varieties of Experience

Look for ways to provide multi-ethnic, multi-cultural and other community experiences for children. Activities such as field trips, celebrating holidays and activities with other ethnic groups, and encouraging children to bring visitors to school enhances the creative process. The more varied experiences children have in their lives, the wider the range of creative expression. The more personal experiences children have with people and situations outside of their own environment, the more material they can draw on to incorporate in their play. Our challenge is to try not to be intimidated by the variety and diversity of artistic expression in our classroom.

Fostering the Creative Process

Encouraging children to make their own choices is important. Children should be permitted frequent opportunities—and lots of time-to experience and explore expressive materials. Put your emphasis on the process of creativity and not on the finished product. What children learn and discover about themselves is vital to their development. Show your support for the creative process by appreciating and offering support for children's efforts. Independence and control are important components in the creative process. This is especially true when working with children with disabilities.

In this stage, children:

- Are amazed at their ability to make marks.
- Spend much time practicing motor skills.
- Draw circles first, then squares and other geometric shapes.
- Begin trying to create (draw) their world.
- May want to point to and name parts of their drawings.

Pre-schematic Stage (Late Preschool to Approximately Age 7)

At this stage, children

- Make first attempts to represent people or objects. Efforts are recognizable to adults.
- Are fascinated with the wide variety of colours.
- Achieve obvious connections between different parts of a drawing.
- Value signs of approval from teachers and peers.
- Are easily discouraged and fatigued.
- Are active, hands on, eager to learn, and self-centered.
- Are highly imaginative yet tend to focus on one idea at a time.
- Search for ways to represent their ideas.

Schematic Stage (Approximately 7 to 9 Years)

Children at this stage

- Increase the use of symbols, such as a heart for love or dark colors to represent night.

- Are less self-centered.
- Still do not have a realistic understanding of their environment. For example, the sky in a child's picture may not meet the ground at the horizon.
- Show improved eye-hand coordination and fine motor skills.
- Have an increased attention span.
- Begin developing a sense of humor.
- Divide by gender in play.
- Represent special characteristics for each person or object in their drawings. For example, if Mom wears glasses and has curly hair, the child will include these characteristics in the drawing.

Realistic Stage (9 to 12 Years)

Children at this stage

- Are greatly affected by peer influence.
- Increase the amount of detail and use of symbols in drawings.
- Have expanded individual differences.
- Begin to develop a set of values.
- Want to do things "right."

Pseudo-naturalistic stage (12-14 Years)

At this stage, children

- Are highly critical of the products they make.
- Use a more adult-like mode of expression.
- Experience a period of great individual differences physically, mentally, emotionally, and socially.
- Have art class available only as an elective in school. For many children, this will be the last opportunity to have art instruction.

Experience a period of heightened self-consciousness. Children in this age group often feel a need to conform to their peers, which can stifle their creativity.

Creativity in Young Children

Creativity is more than a product-it's a process. An interesting painting, a thought provoking writing, a unique comment-these may be examples of creative work, but the decisions people make as they paint, sculpt, write, speak, play, and think are at the core of the creative process.

Art and music are common examples of creativity, but creative thought appears in almost all aspects of life-from the way a parent quiets a crying child to the methods a scientist uses to discover a cure for a disease.

Children who amaze their teachers with unusual responses to questions or display a keen sense of humor are thinking creatively. Even children who perhaps are nonconforming and unpredictable are thinking creatively.

Because creative thought often goes against the set rules of a strict classroom or home, adults may be irritated by the behaviour of a creative child. Adults often do not recognize the value creative children bring to families and classrooms. All children become adults who will make a difference in our world with their creative problem-solving skills.

Encouraging Creativity through Teacher and Parents

Teachers and parents can help children learn to think and solve problems in creative ways by giving them the freedom to make mistakes and by respecting their ideas. This happens with greater mobility and use of language through modeling and being allowed to experiment without fearing failure.

To solve a problem creatively, children need to be able to see a variety of perspectives and to generate several solutions. When working on a problem, adults should teach young children to examine their surroundings for "cues" that will help them generate a pool of possible solutions. In addition, adults can encourage creative thought simply by providing

- *Choices:* Children who are given choices show more creativity than do children who have all choices made for them.
- *Stimulation:* Physical environments designed to stimulate the senses can enhance creative problem solving. For example, when shown an object in the shape of a half-moon and asked, "What can we use this for?" children will exhaust their first mental images and begin developing ideas from what they see in their surroundings. Research has found that children who keep looking around a classroom or playroom for cues are using a creative problem-solving method. An environment that provides both novelty and variety will greatly aid creativity.
- *Time for play and fantasy:* Dramatic play just before engaging in problem-solving tasks can lead to more creative thought.

Reality Behind Creativity

The joining together of two or more irrelevant elements, called synectics, can lead to creative answers. The process of synectics can take many forms:

- *Independence (with reasonable limits):* Parents and teachers should encourage children to think and act without adult direction but within the limits of rules.
- *Exposure to a diverse community:* Give children the opportunity to see and experience other cultures and ways of living, acting, and being to teach them how to respect the choices of other people.
- *Brainstorming sessions:* Encourage children to tackle problems as a group by freely expressing their

ideas with no fear of a negative response. Brainstorming can take place between a child and an adult or between two or more children.

Activities

- Hand a child a piece of modeling clay and ask the child to imagine that he or she is the modeling clay.
- Place a child in a different time and place. For instance, ask a child to describe how he or she would cook a meal without electricity, silverware, dishes, etc.
- Ask a child to describe a problem or an event using pictures instead of words.
- Ask a child to solve a problem using the most unusual solutions he or she can come up with.
- *Encouragement:* When children show special aptitudes, such as an ability to generate many questions, a keen memory, advanced reading or pre-reading skills, artistic skills, or other above-average abilities, adults should encourage them to build on and expand their skills.
- *Honest critiques:* Evaluate students' work constructively so they can see ways to improve their work and still feel positive about themselves and what they have created.
- *An environment where there is no one right answer for every problem:* Teachers who enthusiastically encourage children to develop more than one solution to a problem see greater creativity in problem solving.

Barriers to Creativity

Often people are not able to perform at their best because of outside influences that make them feel pressured or insecure:

- *Reward:* When people do not expect a reward, they are more creative and enjoy the process more. An unexpected reward that comes after a project is completed is valuable but not necessary to the creative process.
- *Intrinsic versus extrinsic motivation:* As in the case of reward, external motivation (such as money or special privileges) undermines creativity. Artists say that when they are working for the enjoyment of the process, they are far more effective and productive than when they are commissioned to create for money.
- *Expected external evaluation:* Knowing beforehand that a piece of art is going to be graded can lead to a decrease in creativity.
- *Peer pressure:* There is some evidence that pressure to conform can lead to temporary decreases in creativity.
- *Surveillance:* Being observed by others while engaged in a creative process can undermine creativity.

Creativity Develop Through Art

- Art is only one way children can express themselves but because it develops before writing, or abstract thinking, adults can see creativity expressed in art more easily with young children.

The following is a brief overview of the developmental stages of children's art. Please keep in mind that the ages given are general guidelines and that children will enter and leave each stage at their own pace.

Role of Parent and Teacher

Children want their art to look like the object they are looking at. Failing in this attempt can be discouraging. Children need to be taught that art is not limited to copying what they see. Adults can show children other styles of art (such as impressionistic or cubist art) to help them see that the free expression of ideas and emotions is more important than creating a mirror image.

Never compare one child's work to another's or select one piece to be the "model" or "ideal." Children will go through these developmental stages in the same order, but the pace at which they enter and leave them will vary.

Tips for Parents and Teachers How to Develop Creativity

- Avoid projects that can be completed in only one way(paint-by-numbers, kits to be assembled, for example).
- Do not use art as indoor recess or as a reward for behaving well. Art activities should be well thought out and planned.
- Make a wide variety of materials available to children.
- Suggest options, but let children make the final decisions for art projects.
- Ask children about their art while they are creating it, not just at the end.
- Ask children to tell you about the work (as opposed to guessing, possibly incorrectly, from an adult's point of view).
- Praise the effort, use of colour, and uniqueness rather than just the final product-the trip is more important than the destination.
- Display art at a child's eye level.
- Encourage individual expression.

Avoid the regimented use of materials and adult-directed projects. A classroom full of samples of individual creativeness (as opposed to 23 identical pieces hanging in a row) indicates that the teacher has given children choices and has focused on the process rather than the product.

Characteristics of Creative Children

The creativity children are more sociable, more warm-hearted and anxious. Three characteristics of personality shows the difference between the highly creative children from less creative but equally intelligent children.

- The highly creative have a reputation for having wild and silly ideas.
- Their work is characterized by production of ideas, "outside this world".

"Humour, playfulness, lack of rigidity and realization" characterize their work.

The common characteristics of creative individual is his high level of effective intelligence, his openness to experience, his freedom from incapacitate restraints and impoverishing inhibition, his independence in thoughts and action, his high level of creative energy, his unquestioning commitment to creative endeavor and his continuous striving for solution to the ever more difficult problems that be constantly sets for himself.

Developing Creativity Among Children

The child should be encouraged and facilitate openness in thought and action and provide for discovering new ideas. An important condition for the development of creativity in child is to encourage them to socially interact with the people and children around.

Researchers have shown that for the development of creative thinking non-authorization ways of learning should be encouraged.

Suggestions for Creative in Thinking and Writing

- Curiosity and wide interest in intellectual matters should be developed at an early age.
- Some children prefer to learn by discovering rather than by set rules therefore variety of learning tasks should be included in day-to-day activities.

- Learning experiences should be stimulated more often.
- You should indulge your child in questioning such questions to which he/she gives unique or original answers.
- You should accept and appreciate the unique responses given by children.
- Indulge your children in more creative activities, progressing slowly from simple to complex.
- You should avoid helping your child when seeking creative efforts.
- If possible break the set-rules of learning to develop new ideas in child.
- Full time should be provided for the development of an idea as some children are slow starters and need more time to think independently and act accordingly.

Methods of Teaching Creativity

- Ask open-ended questions to involve your child in general discussions. For example: what would happen, if there were no rivers? Such questions will stimulate free-thinking and provide scope for many possible answers, but none of them is wrong.
- Involve your child to challenge the assumptions underlying the ideas presented by you.
- Involve your child in the activities, which stimulate creativity and fantasy. For example: Present some meaningless similarities, 'I am a horse', and let the child find out how it is possible.
- Involve your child in exploring activity, like make a list of as many problems as possible related to environment, or list of things around you.

- Present some statements of observation to explore the possibility of its reversal, for example 'The rose is red' 'Red is the rose'.
- Provide your child with as many activities and opportunities as possible, for the expression of ideas, which should be continuous, and in the area of children's interest.
- Whenever possible provide your child with supplementary materials, books and other experiences, you should avoid emphasizing the textual information.
- Provide your children with activities and projects which interest them and give them openness to think originally and express their ideas in their own way.
- Encourage your child to pursue their hobbies.
- Appreciate openly when ever a child expresses creative behaviors like asking usual questions, giving unusual ideas and taking self initiated action etc.
- Appreciate the child when he/she makes ambiguous statements.
- Encourage the child to make as many as guesses as possible about the solution while solving the problems.
- Do not always insist on correct answers. Allow the child to think and rethink the correctness of the answer. Do not evaluate the goodness of the answer but insist on the number of ideas. Quality of the answer is automatically taken care of when the child examine all the possible answer of each question.
- Take care that child is not taunted by his friends or brother/sister for his answers to the questions posed by you.

- Do not make sarcastic and insulting remarks in front of the child or on the child.
- You should discourage self-criticism.
- Allow your child to think and express freely and find the facts for themselves. Do not tell them every thing.
- Let children do their best in finding the solution to the problem without giving any hint.
- Do not encourage rote learning or memorizing the facts. Allow them to pursue as much as they want without bothering themselves about giving the expected solution or answer.

Enhance Creativity

- Try to explain your child the same think in different ways.
- Give various type of challenging activities to your child.
- Evaluate the answers given by your child in different

Creative Play

One of the most important types of creative activity for young children is creative play. Creative play is expressed when children use familiar materials in a new or unusual way, and when children engage in role-playing and imaginative play. Nothing reinforces the creative spirit and nourishes a child's soul more than providing large blocks of time to engage in spontaneous, self-directed play throughout the day. Play is the serious business of young children and the opportunity to play freely is vital to their healthy development.

Even as early as infancy, play fosters physical development by promoting the development of sensory exploration and motor skills. Through play and the repetition of basic physical skills, children perfect their abilities and become competent at increasingly difficult physical tasks. Play fosters mental development and new ways of thinking and problem solving. Through block play, children are confronted with many mental challenges having to do with measurement, equality, balance, shape, spatial relationships and physical properties.

One of the strongest benefits of play is the way it enhances social development. Playful social interactions begin from the moment of birth. Dramatic play helps children experiment with and understand social roles. It can also give them countless opportunities for acquiring social skills as they play with others. Through dramatic play, children gradually learn to take each other's needs into account, and appreciate different values and perspectives.

Through play, children are able to express and cope with their feelings. Play also helps relieve stress and pressure for children. They can just be themselves. There's no need to live up to adult standards during play. Play offers children an opportunity to achieve mastery of their environment. They control the experience through their imaginations, and they exercise their powers of choice and decision-making as the play progresses.

Play helps develop each child's unique perspective and individual style of creative expression. Play expresses the child's personal, unique responses to the environment. Play is a self-expressive activity that draws on the child's powers of imagination. Play is open-ended, free-form and children have the freedom to try out new ideas as well as build on and experiment with the old.

Play provides an excellent opportunity for integrating and including children with disabilities in your program. The opportunities play provides for control and independence are important issues for any child but are especially important for these youngsters.

What are some of the ways we can encourage play in our classrooms? As caregivers, we must be careful to avoid dominating the play ourselves. Play should be the result of the children's ideas and not directed by the adult. Through play, we should try to foster children's abilities to express themselves. We should also try to help children base play on their own inspirations—not ours. Our goal is to stimulate play-not control it—and to encourage children's satisfaction in playing with each other.

Pay attention to play, plan for it, encourage it. Learn how to extend children's play through comments and questions. Stimulate creative ideas by encouraging children to come up with new and unusual uses of equipment. Try to remain open to new and original ideas, and encourage children to come up with more than one solution or answer. Be careful about over-restricting equipment and make sure to have play materials quickly available when children want them. Buy and use equipment in ways that encourage the use of imagination. Avoid toys and activities that spell everything out for the child and leave nothing to the imagination. Provide children with a good range and balance of equipment, and keep equipment exciting by changing it frequently or changing its location.

8

Language Development

Introduction

Language is a communication form. It is a media by which distinguishes baby from animal. child feel more secure when he gets command over language. It is a communication skill which display the behaviour. Language is a form of speech by which one can understand feeling of others. Speech is a media between two person which convey the meaning. Speech means utteration or pronunciation of words which is known as language. Speech is one type of behaviour that helps the child to move from world of socialized relationship. Child with good language able establish better social relationship. Child expresses his feeling, thought and attitudes more freely. Speech is a complex process. Language is closely associated with corresponding developments in speech organs, mouth development and ability of the child to associate sounds with meaningful events, objects and persons.

Language has two different aspects:

1. language production.
2. language comprehension.

Stages of Language Development

This presents information on the development of language in children. The chart below presents typical language development. There is a wide range of normal development. Most children will not follow the chart to the letter. It is presented so you will know what to expect for your child.

Language Development Chart

Age of Child	*Typical Language Development*
6 Months	Vocalization with intonation Responds to his name Responds to human voices without visual cues by turning his head and eyes Responds appropriately to friendly and angry tones
12 Months	Uses one or more words with meaning (this may be a fragment of a word) Understands simple instructions, especially if vocal or physical cues are given Practices inflection Is aware of the social value of speech
18 Months	Has vocabulary of approximately 5-20 words Vocabulary made up chiefly of nouns Some echolalia (repeating a word or phrase over and over) Much jargon with emotional content Is able to follow simple commands
24 Months	Can name a number of objects common to his surroundings Is able to use at least two prepositions, usually chosen from the following: in, on, under Combines words into a short sentence-largely noun-verb combinations (mean) length of sentences is given as 1. 2 words Approximately 2/3 of what child says should be intelligible Vocabulary of approximately 150-300 words Rhythm and fluency often poor Volume and pitch of voice not yet well-controlled Can use two pronouns correctly: I, me, you, although me and I are often confused My and mine are beginning to emerge Responds to such commands as "show me your eyes (nose, mouth, hair)"
36 Months	Use pronouns I, you, me correctly Is using some plurals and past tenses Knows at least three prepositions, usually in, on, under Knows chief parts of body and should be able to indicate these if not name Handles three word sentences easily Has in the neighborhood of 900-1000 words About 90% of what child says should be intelligible Verbs begin to predominate Understands most simple questions dealing with his

(Contd.)

Age of Child	*Typical Language Development*
	environment and activities Relates his experiences so that they can be followed with reason Able to reason out such questions as "what must you do when you are sleepy, hungry, cool, or thirsty?" Should be able to give his sex, name, age Should not be expected to answer all questions even though he understands what is expected
48 Months	Knows names of familiar animals Can use at least four prepositions or can demonstrate his understanding of their meaning when given commands Names common objects in picture books or magazines Knows one or more colors Can repeat 4 digits when they are given slowly Can usually repeat words of four syllables Demonstrates understanding of over and under Has most vowels and diphthongs and the consonants p, b, m, w, n well established Often indulges in make-believe Extensive verbali-zation as he carries out activities Understands such concepts as longer, larger, when a contrast is presented Readily follows simple commands even thought the stimulus objects are not in sight Much repetition of words, phrases, syllables, and even sounds
60 Months	Can use many descriptive words spontaneously-both adjectives and adverbs Knows common opposites: big-little, hard-soft, heave-light, etc. Has number concepts of 4 or more Can count to ten Speech should be completely intelligible, in spite of articulation problems Should have all vowels and the consonants, m, p, b, h, w, k, g, t, d, n, ng, y (yellow) Should be able to repeat sentences as long as nine words Should be able to define common objects in terms of use (hat, shoe, chair) Should be able to follow three commands given without interruptions Should know his age Should have simple time concepts: morning, afternoon, night, day, later, after, while Tomorrow, yesterday, today Should be using fairly long sentences and should use some compound and some complex sentences Speech on the whole should be grammatically correct
6 Years	In addition to the above consonants these should be mastered: f, v, sh, zh, th, 1 He should have concepts of

(Contd.)

Age of Child	*Typical Language Development*
	7 Speech should be completely intelligible and socially useful Should be able to tell one a rather connected story about a picture, seeing relationships Between objects and happenings
7 Years	Should have mastered the consonants s-z, r, voiceless th, ch, wh, and the soft g as in George Should handle opposite analogies easily: girl-boy, man-woman, flies-swims, blunt-sharp short-long, sweet-sour, etc Understands such terms as: alike, different, beginning, end, etc. Should be able to tell time to quarter hour Should be able to do simple reading and to write or print many words
8 Years	Can relate rather involved accounts of events, many of which occurred at some time in the past Complex and compound sentences should be used easily Should be few lapses in grammatical constrictions-tense, pronouns, plurals All speech sounds, including consonant blends should be established Should be reading with considerable ease and now writing simple compositions Social amenities should be present in his speech in appropriate situations Control of rate, pitch, and volume are generally well and appropriately established Can carry on conversation at rather adult level Follows fairly complex directions with little repetition Has well developed time and number concepts

Infants Age between 0-6 Months

Right from the start, babies are interested in language. Baby will stare at anyone speaking to him. He will turn in the direction of a voice. He will make cries and snorts and whimpers of his own.

From about two months old, he will begin to make cooing sounds. From three months old, your baby will make sounds back when you speak to him. He is trying to communicate with you. He also begins to have different cries for hunger, tiredness, wet diaper, and a need for attention. Between four and six months of age, your baby will begin to add consonant sounds like d, p and m.

Activities

1. Stand on one side of your infant and speak to him. Watch for his head to turn toward you.
2. Whisper into child's ear.
3. Talk to baby while facing him at eight to twelve inches so you will be in focus.
4. Let him touch your lips with his hands.
5. Sing songs to him. Pick songs with various tempos and pitches. Don't worry about whether you have a beautiful voice. Your singing will be beautiful to him!
6. Chant nursery rhymes to him. Nursery rhymes have a singsong quality which helps children become used to the rhythm of our language.
7. Talk to him about all of his daily routines as you carry them out.
8. Read to him several times a day. Choose board books or cloth books or vinyl books and don't be surprised when he seems more interested in sucking and chewing books than being read to. He is learning through his senses. He'll soon pass through the chewing books stage to become an interested listener.

Infants Age between 6-12 Months

During this stage, baby will babble more and more. He'll even start to talk in "sentences." He'll string long groups of sounds together in sentence-like structures. He may even end the talk with a rising question-like sound. The amount of babbling a baby does is directly related to the amount of social stimulation he receives. Babies this age prefer to be with people rather than alone. They love to laugh and smile and babble. They begin making syllables like "pa-pa" and "uh-oh" and "ma-ma."

Baby understands many things you say to him now even though he can't say them. If you ask, "Where's your shoe?"

he will crawl to find it. During this period you will begin using the word "no" with your child for his safety. He can definitely get around and will try to explore everything, including many things he must leave alone. Be patient with your baby, and explore with him. Remember, babies seldom stop just because they hear "no." They can't believe you would deny them anything. Next year, you will actually hear child say "no" to himself, and then keep doing the forbidden thing. This is a step on the road to self regulation and impulse control.

Activities

1. Talk to him as often as possible.
2. Name things for him as hold or point to them.
3. Read to him often and with emotion in your voice. You will still need to choose board books.
4. Begin to describe objects to him as you hold them. For example, hold a ball and talk about its color, size, hardness or softness, and bounce it.
5. When he talks to you, answer him. If he vocalizes again, answer him again. You and your child are having a conversation.
6. Begin naming body parts and encourage him to point to them when you name them.
7. Take him for a stroll and name things you see.
8. Play pat-a-cake with him and encourage him to pat his hands together.
9. This is the age when he will start waving when he hears someone say "hi" or "bye-bye." He will probably begin to say "bye-bye" himself soon.
10. Ask your baby to "look" at things and name them as he looks.

Toddlers Age between 1-2 Years

Toddler is full of himself and full of fun! He is walking now and his environment is open for his exploration. As he learns to walk, that becomes the dominant goa' in his life. Language may take a back burner for a month or two. But don't worry if he's trying to walk more than talk! As soon as he is walking, his desire to learn to talk will be back stronger that ever. He will begin to copy words, and his words will sound something like what you said. He will also use gestures to communicate. He will point and he may shrug his shoulders when you ask him something he doesn't know. He can now follow simple directions even those with two parts. He may start having some temper tantrums. If you ignore them, they will usually fade away.

By 18 months, he will use at least three words meaningfully, and by age two, he may have a 50-100 word vocabulary. He will refer to himself by name and he will know the words "my" and "mine." He will love to play peek-a-boo and will laugh every time. He is convinced you cannot see him through those little wide spread fingers when he is covering his eyes. Children this age enjoy books with familiar animals and little children in them. By the age of two, he will begin to put two words together in conversation.

Activities

1. Hide a favourite toy or article of clothing and ask your child to find it.
2. Point to familiar things and ask him to name them.
3. Act out some action words like "sit" and "run" for him.
4. Call grandmother on the phone and let him talk to her.
5. Sing songs, say nursery rhymes, do finger plays and counting rhymes.
6. Play imitative games like "This is the Way We Wash Our Face."
7. Read predictable books.
8. Listen to some favourite children's recordings together.

9. Buy a book of nursery rhymes to read to your child.
10. Play simple matching games together. Say the names of the objects as you match them.

Toddlers Age between 2-3 Years

Two-year-old is becoming more involved with the world around him. Show him pictures of common objects, like a cat or dog, and he will point to them when you name them. He knows his first and last name. He can ask "what" and "where" questions, and may ask them all day long. He can identify many objects. He understands the word "no." He can make his own negative statements. He likes to chant syllables and sing silly songs. He will begin to speak in short sentences such as, "Me go!" He will also have some favourite phrases that he attaches to other words in order to make sentences ("Daddy go home" or "Doggy go home" or "Bird go home"). He is learning concepts like in, on, under, behind.

Activities

1. Play copy cat games where you copy every utterance your child makes and encourage him to copy you.
2. Show him a picture of a chair in a magazine and ask him to find one in the room.
3. Say nursery rhymes to him and say them with him if he knows them.
4. Play silly games where you read a book with the wrong words or name objects in your home with the wrong words. Let your child correct you.
5. Begin using descriptive words with your child. Find common items and describe them. For example, an easy chair might be soft, brown, and fuzzy.
6. Work simple puzzles together and talk about what to look for as you work a puzzle.
7. Make or buy a simple lotto or matching game to play together.

8. When child asks for something using one word, encourage him to add to his description. If he wants a book, ask "Which one?".
9. Read to him often. Hold him on your lap so you are seeing the book together. Let him pick out a favourite story and you pick out one, too. Talk about why you both like the one you chose.
10. When you are at the grocery, have your child point to and name items he knows. Ask him what he likes to eat.

How to Learn Child

Help your child recognize the shapes and sounds of letters by pronouncing them and using them in words.

According to child development experts, preschoolers' language develops in four important ways:

1. Preschoolers' speech becomes clearer, and pronunciation, fluency, and articulation all improve. They can be expected to have difficulty with speech sounds throughout much of this period because a number of various parts must be synchronized to produce many of our words.
2. Preschoolers acquire many more words, and they also come to understand word meanings more fully. It is estimated that five-year-olds understand over 8,000 words. They also have a working vocabulary of about 2,300 words.
3. Preschoolers' sentences grow in length and complexity. The typical two-year-old speaks an average of two words per sentence, while four-year-olds average over four words per sentence.
4. Finally, preschoolers become quite adept at using language socially. Young children learn how to phrase requests to achieve a desired outcome. They convince a parent to give them an extra cookie. Also, they use intonation in play to persuade peers to let them play. Preschoolers also learn the social rules

of language such as politeness, body language, speaking so the listener understands, and turn taking.

Children's Literacy Development

Reading and Writing

Early writing attempts by young children look like scribbling, however, these marks on paper represent ideas or even whole stories. The next step after the early scribble marks is the appearance of letters. The first letters are often letters found in the children's names. At this point, children are not associating the letters with their sounds. By the end of the preschool period, some children do begin to use letters that are associated with the sounds in the message or story they are writing.

Children seem to go through a series of early reading stages. In the initial stage they believe that words of a story come from the pictures. You may have noticed this when your child demands that you, "read!" even on a page that only has pictures and no words. In the second stage, children begin to notice print and know that the story comes from the text. An example of this stage is when child points to a letter and declares, "That letter's in my name." During the third stage, children tell their favourite story word for word by heart. In fact, if your child is in this stage, he may correct you if you make a mistake in reading to him. In the fourth stage, children attempt to find the place in the text where the memorized story is written. Your child will make matches but may also make errors. As he tries to match up the memorized story with the text, your child learns more about reading. In the last stage, the child finds the exact place in the text where the memorized story is written.

As a parent, you play an important role in your child's language and literacy development. You are an important language model for your child by introducing new vocabulary, asking and answering questions, and using appropriate grammatical forms. In addition, you show the importance of literacy when your child sees you reading and writing. You can assist your child's development in this area by reading stories, books, and poetry with them each day.

Activities

1. Be positive about your child's speech. Remember it is common for preschoolers to make what adults consider to be pronunciation errors. These "errors" mean your child is thinking and trying out new forms.
2. Sing with your child.
3. Encourage imaginative play; it motivates and promotes language growth in young children.
4. Take outings with your child and converse with them about all the objects, people, and animals you see along the way. It doesn't have to be a costly outing. A walk around the block or a trip to the grocery store provide opportunities for conversation.
5. Spend time talking at mealtimes. Talk naturally about anything that interests you or your child.
6. Read many stories and tell many stories to your preschooler. Discuss your child's favourite stories. Ask him what he likes best or which character he would like to be.
7. If you have a tape recorder available, encourage your child to record her favourite story or song.
8. Read rhymes to your child. Make up some of your own rhymes.
9. Provide your child with a variety of writing materials including pens, pencils, markers, colored pencils, and chalk and chalkboard.
10. Purchase developmentally appropriate software

Activities for Three and Four-Year-Olds

Story Starters

Have a younger child dictate a story to you or write one together. Reread the story the next day. You are helping him learn that each word says something and that each word remains the same from day to day.

He might want to "write" on a copy of the story sheet himself and then tell you his story. If your child is already writing words, just give him a copy and let him write his own story. Ask him to share it with you after he finishes. You can write a story, too, and share it with your child. Besides being a fun family activity, you are helping to stretch child's imagination and develop his creativity

Principles of Language Teaching

1. teach listening and speaking first, reading and writing next. Writing does not represent intonation, thythm, stress, and structures etc. and transfer from audio to visual learning is greater. Good models of speech should be available for language teaching.
2. Have the students memorize basic conventional sentences accurately. This principle has psychological and linguistic justification.
3. Encourage the students to use the patterns learnt in practice so that it becomes a habit.
4. Teach sound system structurally by demonstration, imitation, contrast and encourage children to produce speech than simply comprehending it. Practice will increase fluency and flexibility.
5. Keep the vocabulary load to a minimum while students are mastering sound system and grammatical patterns, because it is not the vocabulary that constitute language but the pattern, sound contrast and the sequence.
6. Teach the patterns gradually in cumulative grades and steps. Language acquisition is a complex habit and it has to be acquired slowly.

7. Avoid teaching language through translation. Psychologically the process of translation is more complex and unnecessary because it presupposes conceptual understanding of both languages.
8. Teach the language as it is true of the educated native speakers of the language not in terms of what it ought to be. If communicate the intention of the speaker.
9. Quantity and permanence of learning are dependent on practice. Hence it encourages child for practicing language, linguistics have also emphasized practice through memorization and pattern practice. Experiments show 85 per cent should be for practice.
10. Shaping and prompting are necessary for helping child to respond. hence give articulator or other hints to help the students to articulate response.
11. Give immediate reward or appreciation when language learning is up to the mark.
12. Teach the meaning of language as it exists in a particular culture where the language is spoken natively.

Language Disorders

Speech and language are both tools of communication. They are separate from each other, though. Speech deals with how children say words. It refers to the way a child can pronounce or use the different speech sounds in words. Language, on the other hand, refers to how well a child can express ideas and understand others. It deals with understanding and being understood through communication.

So a child with a language problem might be able to say words well but may not be able to put words together to share ideas very well. A child with a speech problem, on the other hand, may put lots of words together but is hard to understand. Some children may have both speech and language problems.

A child's communication is considered delayed when she is behind other children her age in speech and language skills. "Delayed" means the child is doing things in the right way and in the right order, but is slower than other children in learning them. On the other hand, a child might have a disorder if his speech or language is very different from that of other children who are like him in other ways. There also might be a disorder if a child's speech and/or language is difficult to understand. Another sign of a disorder is when a child seems to be very worried about how she talks or avoids communicating with other people.

Causes Language Disorder

Speech and language disorders may be caused by:

- Hearing loss
- Ear infections
- Neurological (brain or nerve) disorders
- Brain or head injury
- Mental retardation (developmental delay)
- Stroke
- Viral infections
- Physical problems such as cleft lip or cleft palate

Language disorders may also be connected with other disabilities such as:

- Autism
- Cerebral palsy
- Learning disabilities

Defective Speech

Speech defects arise either due to malformation of the speech organ or due to emotional disturbances. Following are the some common defective speech:

1. Lisping

It is structured of letter sound substitution, children while pronounce " simple simon" pronounce "thimple thimon" or "red rose" called as "wed wose". This happens due to defective teeth, jaw, tongue or fascination for using baby speech. Children due one or other reason substitute the for "s" "Z" "w" for "r" and so on. After their permanent teeth appear, their lisping decreases. In rare cases due to organic defects or space between teeth lisping may be occur.

2. Stammering

Stammering is a type of stuttering means prolongation of the sound of the opening letter of a word i. e.b......... bath. stammering occurs when a child cannot get a word out. Some children have problems with consonants and not in another.

3. Stuttering

It is a kind a kind of speech defect and also repetitive speech, it occurs due to failure of speech muscle to co-ordinate. It appears that the person dose not know suddenly what to say, often accompanied by stammering. There is check of speech followed by sudden speech which then is followed by no speech and so on. It appears due to poor vocabulary, overprotective parents, dominant and over anxious parents. These factors are responsible for stuttering. It is a form of speech impediment which is common in pre school children. The most complicated task the child faces during preschool year is the process of learning to talk. Stuttering disappears if the parents do not make an issues of it and if they let the child finish his utterance without correcting him, or calling attention to his difficulties interrupting. It can be treated with build sense of security and self confidence.

4. Slurring

Not clear speech in child called slurring. It occurs due to inactivity of the lips, paralysis of vocal organs, timidity, excitement or fear for the strangers. It mostly appears during post school years. Slurring is corrected if the child opens his mouth while speaking so that sound s can come outside. They speak so fast that no body can understand what they say.

5. Cluttering

It is a jumping speech defects. IT a rapid, confused and jumbled type of speech. It is just like stuttering. But the more one tries to control it, the more of it you shall have. Children whose speech development has been delayed give evidence of cluttering.

Factors Affecting Language Development

Following are some factors which influenced the speech and language development.

Health

The child suffers from severe and prolonged illness during the first two years of life, language development is impaired. Illness not only delays the development of speech organs but isolation and seclusions confines communication with adults concurrently.

Intelligence

Intelligence play a vital role in language development. Babbling at an early age are better predictor of child's intelligence. Children of high intelligence show better linguistic competence both in vocabulary, length of sentences uttered and correctness of sentence structure.

Socio-economic Condition of Family

Those children from high socio-economic status talk faster, talk better than the poor children. lower group of children suffer from listening elaborative language, suffer from under and over stimulation, and commit more articulation errors. The relationship between socio-economic condition and language ability is well established and the gap in language competence and production becomes more between high and low socio-economic groups as age advances.

Sex

Boys are faster then the girls in learning to talk. Compared to girls the mea length of sentence uttered by boys is less. The comprehension vocabulary is also small in case of boys. Boys commit more grammatical errors and their pronunciation is less accurate. Sex difference in favor of girls remain and become quite pounced with every increase in age.

Family Relationship

A healthy stimulating environment facilitates language development, particularly the relationship between mother and child. Children reared in institutions are slow in learning to talk, and remain retarded in language development throughout their lives. This happens primarily because of lack of adequate adult contact and personal relationship in the institution.

Twins

Twins and triplets are slower to learn the language than the single child. Their vocabulary skill is so faster than the twins.

Bilingual Homes

In bilingual homes the child face several problems to the language because the learn more than two languages at a time so it is very difficult to child remember the two or three languages at a time.

Common Techniques to Improve the Language Development of Child

- according to Brown in1958—the best index of language development is "mean length of utterance".
- According to Schlanger in 1967—
  1. Story telling to children, exposing the child to different play things, naming the object, describing the object.

2. Acquinting the children with different concrete objects and teaching words.
3. Encouraging the children to play and communicate with playmates verbally etc. have been effective in accelerating the rate of language acquisition in children.

- According to Stearns in 1966—language lessons are useful to develop the skill.
- According to Smith in 1965—Montessori technique of playing with materials or sensory training enables the child to speak and increase his working vocabulary.

Communication

From the moment of birth, baby began to communicate. At first, newborn's cries may seem like a foreign language to you. But before you know it, you will learn baby's "language" and be able to provide him with what he needs.

Right after birth, introduced baby to own ways of communicating: touching, soothing, holding and making facial gestures. Your baby will learn your "language," just as you will learn his.

How does Baby Communicate?

Baby is born with the ability to cry, which is how he will do most of his communicating for a while. Your baby's cries generally tell you that something is wrong in his world: his belly is empty, his bottom is wet, his feet are cold, he's tired, he needs to be held and cuddled. Soon you will be able to recognize which need your baby is expressing and respond accordingly. In fact, sometimes what a baby needs can be identified by his cry-for example, the "I'm hungry" cry may be short and low-pitched, while "I'm upset" may sound choppy.

Baby may also cry when he is overwhelmed by all of the sights and sounds of the world. Sometimes he may cry for no apparent reason at all. Don't be too upset when your baby cries and you aren't able to console him immediately: crying is one of his ways of shutting out stimuli when he's overloaded.

Crying is your baby's main method of communication, but he is also capable of other, more subtle forms. Learning to recognize them is exciting and rewarding and can strengthen your bond with your baby.

A newborn can differentiate between the sound of a human voice and other sounds. Try to pay attention to how he responds to your voice. He already associates your voice with care: food, warmth, touch. If he's crying in his bassinet, see how quickly your approaching voice quiets him. See how closely he listens when you are talking to him in loving tones. He may not yet coordinate looking and listening, but even if he stares into the distance, he'll be paying close attention to your voice as you speak. He may subtly adjust his body position or facial expression, or even move his arms and legs in time with your speech.

Sometime during your newborn's first month, you may get a glimpse of his first smile and perhaps hear his first laugh or giggle. What welcome additions these are to his communication repertoire!

What should Mother Do?

As soon as you hold your baby after birth, mother will begin to communicate with each other by exchanging your first glances, sounds, and touches. newborn is already learning about the world through his senses.

As the days after birth pass newborn will become accustomed to seeing and will begin to focus on face. His senses of touch and hearing are especially important, though. Your infant will be curious about noises he hears, but none more so than the spoken voice. Talk to baby whenever the chance. Communicating with a newborn is really a matter of meeting his needs. Always respond to your newborn's cries-he cannot be spoiled with too much attention. Your prompt response when your baby communicates will let him know that he's important and worthy of attention.

There will probably be times when mother have met all of your baby's needs, yet he continues to cry. Don't despair-baby may be overly stimulated, have gastric distress, or may have too much energy and need a good cry. It is common for babies to have a fussy period at the same time every night, generally between early evening and midnight. This can be very upsetting, but the good news is that it's short-lived; most babies outgrow it around three months. There are some things you can try to soothe your baby. Some babies are comforted by motion, such as rocking or being walked back and forth across the room, while others respond to sounds, like soft music or the hum of a vacuum cleaner. It may take some time to find out what best comforts your baby during these stressful periods.

Should Mother be Concerned?

Mother may want to talk to doctor if baby seems to cry for an unusual length of time, if the cries sound odd to you, or if the crying is associated with decreased activity, poor feeding, or unusual breathing or movements. doctor will be able to reassure mother or look for a medical reason for baby's distress. Chances are there is nothing wrong, and knowing this can help relax and stay calm when baby is upset.

Here are some other reasons for prolonged crying:

- The baby is ill. A baby who cries more when being held or rocked may be sick. Call your doctor.
- The baby has an eye irritation. A scratched cornea or "foreign body" in a baby's eye can cause redness and tearing. Call your doctor.
- The baby is in pain. An open diaper pin or other object could be hurting the baby's skin. Take a close look everywhere.

Communication(Infant 1-2 Years Old)

Language development really takes off during this time, especially as baby approaches his second birthday. He is better able to comprehend what mother say and express what the child wants. He will take joy in his ability to understand more complex directions-and he won't hesitate to give directions.

How does Baby Communicate?

Most babies say their first words toward the beginning of this period, though some start even sooner and others don't start talking until they are nearly 2 years old. If baby is preoccupied with learning to walk, he may push talking to the back burner; this is not unusual and nothing to be alarmed about.

Baby may have learned fragments of dozens of words that probably won't be recognizable yet. When he gets around to talking, though, he'll probably progress quickly. He'll soon be able to point at something familiar and say its name, and recognize names of familiar people, objects and body parts. By two years, he may use phrases and even two-to four-word sentences.

No matter when child says his first words, it's a sure bet he'll be understanding much of what you say to him well before that. He should be able to respond to commands ("Roll the ball to Mommy") and should be fully aware of the names of familiar objects and family members.

Mother will undoubtedly find yourself struggling with toddler to do, only to have him ignore or scream in protest. He's merely testing your limits and his degree of control. By 18 months, he will probably have mastered saying "no" with authority, and by age 2 he may throw a tantrum when he's unwilling to do something ask. He'll also show signs of possessiveness, and mother will frequently hear "mine" or see tears if something is taken away or show attention toward someone else.

What should Mother Do?

Baby is listening to everything you say, and he's storing it away at an incredible rate. Instead of using "baby" words, teach him the correct names for people, places and things. Speak slowly and clearly, and keep it simple.

Baby may still be communicating with gestures such as pointing to something he wants. Gestures are OK, but you should use a running commentary such as, "Do you want a drink?" (when he points to the refrigerator), then wait for a response. Then say, "What do you want? Apple juice? OK, let's get some apple juice." Such behaviour encourages your baby to respond and participate in conversations. But don't frustrate your baby by withholding food or drink waiting for a response.

Between 15 months and 18 months, baby will probably begin to enjoy language games that ask him to identify things, such as: "Where's your ear?" and "Where is Mommy?" His vocabulary will grow quickly, but his pronunciation isn't likely to keep pace. Resist the temptation to correct your baby's pronunciation; most babies mispronounce their words. Instead, emphasize the correct pronunciation in your response.

Should Mother be Concerned?

Some babies don't talk until their second birthday and choose instead to get by with the use of gestures and sounds. Vocabulary varies widely at this age, too; some babies say dozens of words, others only a few.

Most babies this age have these communication milestones in common:

- Speak about 15 words by 18 months
- Put two words together to form a sentence by age 2
- Follow simple directions by age 2

Hearing problems may become more apparent during this stage because of the emergence of speech. Don't hesitate to report any concerns you have to your doctor immediately, especially if you feel your child is not babbling or responding to your speech patterns. Sometimes chronic ear infections can leave children with excessive fluid buildup that can interfere with normal hearing. Special tests can check for hearing loss.

Communication (Toddlers 2-3 Years)

Communicating with child, from infancy onward, is one of the most pleasurable and rewarding experiences for both parent and child. Children are avid learners at all ages, absorbing information through daily interactions and experiences with other children, adults, and the world.

Parents Communicate with a Child

The more interactive conversation and play a child is involved in, the more a child learns. Reading books, singing, playing word games, and simply talking to your child will increase her vocabulary while providing increased listening opportunities. Here are a few suggestions to help improve your child's communication skills:

- Talk to your toddler about what she did during the day or what she plans to do tomorrow. "I think it's going to rain this afternoon. What shall we do?" Or discuss the day's events at bedtime.
- Play make-believe games.
- Read your child's favourite books over and over and encourage her to join in with words she knows. Encourage "pretend" reading (let your child pretend she is reading the book to you).

Typical Communication Patterns

Between the ages of 2 and 3, children experience a tremendous "growth spurt" in language skills. Although each child develops at her own individual pace, when it comes to language skills, by the age of 2, most children can follow simple directions and can speak about 50 to 200 words. By age 2, children may also begin to echo what they hear and begin to combine words in short phrases.

By about 2½ years of age, a child should have at least 200 words in her vocabulary and use fragmented phrases and small phrases. She will also be able to follow additional instructions, such as "Come to Daddy." A 3-year-old child's vocabulary will be between 200 and 300 words, and, by this time, many children will begin to string words together in short sentences.

Kids at this stage of language development will understand more and speak more clearly, and they are usually able to use language to engage in a simple question-and-answer format. By age 3, children should be using language freely, experimenting with verbal sounds, and beginning to use language to solve problems and learn concepts.

Role of Parents when Problem in Communication

Parents who suspect that their child is having trouble with hearing, language acquisition, or speech clarity should not hesitate to talk with their child's doctor. A hearing test can be one of the first referral/diagnostic measures to determine if there might be a hearing problem. If you suspect that your child has a hearing problem at any age, she should undergo an evaluation. Two years of age is not too young for a referral for a speech/language evaluation, particularly if a child is not following directions or answering "yes" or "no" to simple questions.

After an evaluation, the speech-language pathologist (an expert who evaluates and treats speech and language disorders) may recommend direct therapy, referral to a developmental pediatrician if there is suspicion of a global developmental delay (delay in more than one area of development, including gross motor, fine motor, problem solving, language, and social skills), early intervention services, or simply a follow-up assessment to see if a child will catch up.

Communication Problem

Communication problems for 2-to 3-year-olds include:

- Hearing difficulties
- Problems following directions
- Poor vocabulary acquisition

- Speech disfluencies (difficulty initiating or sustaining sounds)
- Delayed acquisition of phrasing skills
- Unclear speech

Problems-such as stuttering-may be a developmental process that some children will outgrow. For others, more intensive therapy may be needed. These communication problems can be helped by medical professionals, such as speech pathologists, therapists, or your child's doctor.

Communication (Child 4-5 Years)

Parents to Communicate with a Child

Communicating with your child, from infancy onward, is one of the most pleasurable and rewarding experiences for both parent and child. Children are avid learners at all ages, absorbing information through daily interactions and experiences with other children, adults and the world.

Between the ages of 4 and 5, many children begin to enter preschool or kindergarten programs, making language competency necessary for better learning in the classroom.

The more interactive conversation and play a child is involved in, the more a child learns. Reading books, singing, playing word games, and simply talking to your child will increase his vocabulary while providing increased listening opportunities. Here are a few suggestions to help improve your child's communication skills:

- Help your child relate to books by selecting stories that mirror families like yours or people from your cultural or ethnic group.
- Make a special spot for books, magazines and other reading material where your child is able to reach books without help.
- Help your child create his own "This Is Me" or "This Is Our Family" album; then enjoy looking and talking about the photographs or special memorabilia.

- Talk to your child about books or TV programs and videos you watch together.

Typical Communication Pattern

As children gain more mastery over their language skills, they become more sophisticated in their conversational abilities. A 4- to 5-year-old child follows complex directions and enthusiastically talks about things that happen to him. He can make up stories, listen attentively to stories and retell stories himself.

Children ages 4 to 5 are also able to understand that letters and numbers are symbols of real things and ideas, "write" as a way to tell stories and offer information, and "read" on their own.

Sentence structures now incorporate up to eight words, while vocabulary is between 1,000 and 2,000 words. Ninety per cent of the time, speech should be clearly intelligible; although there may be some developmental sound errors and stuttering, particularly among boys.

Young preschoolers make comments and requests and tell others what to do. By 4 or 5, they should know the names and gender of family members and other personal information. They often play with words and make up silly words and stories.

Role of Parents when Problem Arise in Communication

Parents worried about a child's hearing, language acquisition, or speech clarity should not hesitate to consult with their child's doctor. A hearing test may be one of the first referral/diagnostic measures to determine if there has been a hearing problem. If the doctor suspects a specific communication deficit or delay, a referral for a speech-language evaluation may be recommended. If a child appears to be delayed in all areas of development, it may be more appropriate to refer him to a developmental pediatrician and/or psychologist.

After an evaluation, the speech-language pathologist (an expert who evaluates and treats speech and language disorders) may recommend direct therapy, preschool special education services, or possible referrals to an audiologist (a hearing specialist), developmental pediatrician, and/or psychologist.

Communication Problems

Communication problems among children in this age group include:

- Hearing difficulties
- Problems following complex/compound directions
- Difficulty with conversational interaction
- Poor vocabulary acquisition
- Difficulty learning preschool concepts, such as colors and counting
- Stuttering
- Difficulties with grammar and syntax
- Unclear speech

Common problems, such as stuttering, often may be a developmental process that some children will outgrow. For others, more intensive therapy may be needed. These communication problems can be helped by medical professionals, such as speech pathologists, therapists, or your child's doctor

Communication (Child 6 to 12 Years)

Communicating with your child, from infancy onward, is one of the most pleasurable and rewarding experiences for both parent and child. Children are avid learners at all ages, absorbing information through daily interactions and experiences with other children, adults, and the world.

Parents Communicate with Children

As children enter their grade-school years they become increasingly independent, spending much of their days outside the home in school and with peers. Talking with your child is essential to bond with her and share ideas, opinions, and information. Here are a few suggestions to aid communication with your child:

- Make time during the day or evening to hear about your child's activities; be sure she sees that you are actively interested and listening carefully.
- Remember to talk with your child, not at her.
- Ask questions that go beyond "yes" or "no" answers to prompt more developed conversation.
- Take advantage of "stolen" moments, during car trips or standing in line at the supermarket, to talk with your child.
- Provide activities that offer opportunities to improve communication skills, such as attending or engaging in sporting and school events, talking about current events, and reading stories to younger children that are slightly above their competency level.

Typical Communication Pattern

As children progress in school, both their comprehension and usage of language will become more sophisticated. Usually, they will understand more vocabulary and concepts than they may express. Children should be able to engage in narrative discourse and share ideas and opinions in clear speech.

Role of Parents when Problem in Communication

Parents need to have ongoing communication with their child's teacher about overall language skills and progress. Children with language comprehension and usage problems are at risk for increased academic difficulties.

If a child has a specific communication difficulty, such as persistent stuttering or a lisp, he should be referred to the school speech-language pathologist (an expert who evaluates and treats speech and language disorders). If this is the case, the parents should routinely communicate with the therapist regarding the therapy goals, language activities that are to be practiced at home, and progress.

If a school suspects a language-based learning disability, comprehensive testing will be necessary. This can include a hearing test, psycho educational assessment (standardized testing to assess a child's learning style as well as cognitive processes as measured by normative values, such as IQ), and speech-language evaluation.

Communication Problems

Problems in communication skills for children ages 6 to 12 years may include:

- Hearing difficulties
- Difficulty with attention, following complex/ compound directions in the classroom
- Difficulty retaining information
- Poor vocabulary acquisition
- Difficulties with grammar and syntax
- Difficulties with organization of expressive language or with narrative discourse
- Difficulties with academic achievement, reading, and writing
- Unclear speech
- Persistent stuttering or a lisp
- Voice-quality abnormalities, such as a strained, hoarse quality (may require a medical examination by an otolaryngologist [an ear, nose and throat specialist])

These communication problems can be helped by medical professionals, such as speech pathologists, therapists or your child's doctor.

What is Language? What is Speech?

Language is different from speech. Language is a code made up of a group of rules that include:

- What words mean
- How to make new words

- How to combine words together
- What word combinations are best in what situations

When a person cannot understand the language code, then there is a receptive problem. If a person does not know enough language rules to share thoughts, ideas, and feelings completely, then there is an expressive problem. One problem can exist without the other, but often they occur together in both children and adults.

The language code can be correct, but if the right body parts are not moved at the right time, then the message will not sound right. Children who stutter, and people whose voices sound rough, hoarse or nasal all have speech problems.

Language and speech problems can exist together. The problem can be mild or severe. In any case, a comprehensive evaluation by a speech-language pathologist certified by the American Speech-Language-Hearing Association is the first step to improving language and speech problems.

Definition of Speech and Language Disorders

Speech and language disorders refer to problems in communication and related areas such as oral motor function. These delays and disorders range from simple sound substitutions to the inability to understand or use language or use the oral-motor mechanism for functional speech and feeding. Some causes of speech and language disorders include hearing loss, neurological disorders, brain injury, mental retardation, drug abuse, physical impairments such as cleft lip or palate, and vocal abuse or misuse. Frequently, however, the cause is unknown.

Incidence

More than one million of the students served in the public schools' special education programs in the 1997-98 school year were categorized as having a speech or language impairment. This estimate does not include children who have speech/language problems secondary to other conditions such as deafness. Language disorders may be related to other disabilities such as mental retardation, autism, or cerebral palsy. It is estimated that communication disorders (including speech, language, and hearing disorders) affect one of every 10 people in the United States.

Characteristics of Language Development

A child's communication is considered delayed when the child is noticeably behind his or her peers in the acquisition of speech and/or language skills. Sometimes a child will have greater receptive (understanding) than expressive (speaking) language skills, but this is not always the case.

Speech disorders refer to difficulties producing speech sounds or problems with voice quality. They might be characterized by an interruption in the flow or rhythm of speech, such as stuttering, which is called dysfluency. Speech disorders may be problems with the way sounds are formed, called articulation or phonological disorders, or they may be difficulties with the pitch, volume or quality of the voice. There may be a combination of several problems. People with speech disorders have trouble using some speech sounds, which can also be a symptom of a delay. They may say "see" when they mean "ski" or they may have trouble using other sounds like "l" or "r". Listeners may have trouble understanding what someone with a speech disorder is trying to say. People with voice disorders may have trouble with the way their voices sound.

A language disorder is an impairment in the ability to understand and/or use words in context, both verbally and nonverbally. Some characteristics of language disorders include improper use of words and their meanings, inability to express ideas, inappropriate grammatical patterns, reduced vocabulary and inability to follow directions. One or a combination of these characteristics may occur in children who are affected by language learning disabilities or developmental language delay. Children may hear or see a word but not be able to understand its meaning. They may have trouble getting others to understand what they are trying to communicate.

Educational Implications

Because all communication disorders carry the potential to isolate individuals from their social and educational surroundings, it is essential to find appropriate timely intervention. While many speech and language patterns can be called "baby talk" and are part of a young child's normal development, they can become problems if they are not outgrown as expected. In this way an initial delay in speech and language or an initial speech pattern can become a disorder which can cause difficulties in learning. Because of the way the brain develops, it is easier to learn language and communication skills before the age of 5. When children have muscular disorders, hearing problems or developmental delays, their acquisition of speech, language and related skills is often affected.

Speech-language pathologists assist children who have communication disorders in various ways. They provide individual therapy for the child; consult with the child's teacher about the most effective ways to facilitate the child's communication in the class setting; and work closely with the family to develop goals and techniques for effective therapy in class and at home. Technology can help children whose physical conditions make communication difficult. The use of electronic communication systems allow nonspeaking people and people with severe physical disabilities to engage in the give and take of shared thought.

Vocabulary and concept growth continues during the years children are in school. Reading and writing are taught and, as students get older, the understanding and use of language becomes more complex. Communication skills are at the heart of the education experience. Speech and/or language therapy may continue throughout a student's school year either in the form of direct therapy or on a consultant basis. The speech-language pathologist may assist vocational teachers and counselors in establishing communication goals related to the work experiences of students and suggest strategies that are effective for the important transition from school to employment and adult life.

Communication has many components. All serve to increase the way people learn about the world around them, utilize knowledge and skills, and interact with colleagues, family and friends

Articulation

- Articulation is the process by which sounds, syllables, and words are formed when your tongue, jaw, teeth, lips, and palate alter the air stream coming from the vocal folds.

Articulation Problem

- A person has an articulation problem when he or she produces sounds, syllables. or words incorrectly so that listeners do not understand what is being said or pay more attention to the way the words sound than to what they mean.

Articulation problem just same as "baby talk"

- An articulation problem sometimes sounds like baby talk because many very young children do mispronounce sounds, syllables, and words. But words that sound cute when mispronounced by young children interfere with the communication of older children or adults. Older children and adults have so many severe errors that their articulation problems are very different from "baby talk."

Causes of Articulation Problem

- Articulation problems may result from physical handicaps, such as cerebral palsy, cleft palate. or hearing loss, or may be related to other problems in the mouth, such as dental problems. However, most articulation problems occur in the absence of any obvious physical disability. The cause of these so-called functional articulation problems may be faulty learning of speech sounds

Accent an Articulation Problem

It can be for some persons. We all have accents-Southern, Eastern, Northern, Western, Chicago, Pittsburgh, Brooklyn, or Boston. An accent may be a problem if it interferes with a person's goals in life.

Types of Sound Errors

Most errors fall into one of three categories: omissions, substitutions, or distortions.

1. An example of an omission is "at" for "hat" or "oo" for "shoe."
2. An example of a substitution is the use of "w" for "r." which makes "rabbit" sound like "wabbit, ".
3. An example of the distortions of "th" for "s" so that "sun" is pronounced "thun." When the sound is said inaccurately, but sounds something like the intended sound, it is called a distortion.

Ear problems during infancy have any effect on late sound development

- Children learn their speech sounds by listening to the speech around them. This learning begins very early in life. If children have frequent ear problems during this important listening period. they may fail to learn some speech sounds.

Child Outgrow a Functional Articulation Problem

- A child's overall speech pattern will usually become more understandable as he or she matures. but some children will need direct training to eliminate all articulation errors. The exact speech pattern of the individual child will determine the answer to this question.

Children Learn all Sounds at once

- Sounds are learned in an orderly sequence. Some sounds, such as "p," "m," and "b," are learned as early as 3 years of age. Other sounds, like "s," "r,' and "l," often are not completely mastered until the early school years.

- At what age should a child be producing all sounds correctly? Children should make all the sounds of English by 8 years of age. Many children learn these sounds much earlier.

To Help a Child Pronounce Words Correctly

- By setting a good example. Don't interrupt or constantly correct the child. Don't let anyone tease or mock (including friends or relatives). Instead, present a good model. Use the misarticulated word correctly with emphasis. If the child says, "That's a big wabbit," you say "Yes, that is a big rabbit. A big white rabbit. Would you like to have a rabbit?"

To Help Adult with an Articulation Problem

- As most articulation problems can be helped regardless of a person's age, but the longer the problem persists, the harder it is to change. Some problems. such as those relating to nerve impulses to the muscles of articulation (dysarthria), are particularly difficult and generally will require a longer period of help than a functional disorder. Other conditions that may influence progress in a child or adult include hearing ability, condition of the oral structures such as the teeth, frequency of help obtained, motivation, intelligence, and cooperation.

Remedies of Articulation Problems

Contact a speech-language pathologist if you are concerned about speech. A speech-language pathologist is a professional trained at the master's or doctoral level to evaluate and help the child or adult with an articulation problem as well as other speech and/or language disorders. The speech-language pathologist should be certified by the American Speech-Language-Hearing Association and/or licensed by your state. The speech-language pathologist can advise whether professional help is indicated and how to arrange for assistance. The speech-language pathologist can also give you guidance or provide services to help prevent or eliminate a problem. Early help is especially important for more severe problems.

To Correct an Articulation Problem

When you consider the possible impact an articulation problem may have on one's social, emotional, educational, and/or vocational status, the answer becomes obvious. Our speech is an important part of us. The quality of our lives is affected by the adequacy of our speech.

Language-based Learning Disabilities

Reading, spelling, and/or writing. This disorder does not impair intelligence; in fact, most people diagnosed with learning disabilities possess average to superior intelligence. Learning disabilities are caused by a difference in brain structure that is present at birth, is often hereditary, and often related to specific language problems.

The term dyslexia has been used to refer to the specific learning problem of reading. Because of the increased recognition of the relationship between spoken and written language, and the frequent presence of spoken language problems in children with reading problems, the term language-based learning disabilities, or just learning disabilities, is more accurate.

Children at Risk

Children at risk for dyslexia and other learning disabilities may have several of the following characteristics:

- A family history of delayed speech-language development or literacy problems
- Difficulty processing sounds in words
- Difficulty finding the words needed to express basic thoughts/ideas and more complex explanations/ descriptions

- Difficulty with the comprehension of spoken and/ or written language, including, for older children, classroom handouts and textbooks
- Delayed vocabulary development
- Problems with the understanding and use of grammar in sentences
- Difficulty remembering numbers and letters in sequence, questions, and directions
- Difficulty with organization and planning, including, for older students, the drafting of school papers and longer-term school projects.

Language Problems

The child with dyslexia has trouble almost exclusively with the written (or printed) word. The child who has dyslexia as part of a larger language learning disability has trouble with both the spoken and the written word. These problems may include:

- Expressing ideas coherently, as if the words needed are on the tip of the tongue but won't come out Consequently, utterances can be vague and difficult to understand (e.g., using unspecific vocabulary, such as "thing" or "stuff" to replace words that cannot be remembered). Filler words like "um" may be used to take up time while a word is being retrieved from memory
- Learning new vocabulary that the child hears (e.g., taught in lectures/lessons) and/or sees (e.g., in books)
- Understanding questions and following directions that are heard and/or read
- Recalling numbers in sequence, e.g., telephone numbers and addresses
- Understanding and retaining the details of a story's plot or a classroom lecture

- Slow reading and reduced comprehension of the material
- Learning words to songs and rhymes
- Telling left from right, making it hard to read and write since both skills require this directionality
- Letters and numbers
- Learning the alphabet
- Identifying the sounds that correspond to letters, making learning to read a formidable task
- While writing, mixing up the order of letters in words
- Mixing up the order of numbers that are a part of math calculations
- Poor spelling
- Memorizing the times tables
- Telling time

Other Possible Problem

- *Inattention and distractibility:* Irrelevant thoughts, ambient noise, and/or excessive visual stimulation "get in the way" of paying attention to incoming information.
- *Organizational skills:* These children lose track of possessions, and have trouble completing tasks efficiently and thoroughly. Planning and organizing for writing letters and papers is also affected, resulting in a lack a focus or an unorganized sequence of ideas/thoughts.
- *Motor coordination:* Some children are delayed in learning how to tie their shoes or may appear clumsy on the playground.

Role of Speech-Language Pathologist

As part of a collaborative team consisting of the parents and educational professionals (i.e., teacher(s), special educators, psychologist), the speech-language pathologist has several responsibilities. He or she:

- informs teachers and other school professionals as to how to identify children who are at risk for developing problems before they experience failure in the classroom.
- works with professionals to help prevent problems before they occur by promoting opportunities for success with spoken and written language at home and school.
- performs assessments of spoken (speaking and listening) and written (reading and writing) language for children who have been identified by their teachers and parents as having difficulty.
- provides treatment for those children who have language problems contributing to difficulties with reading and writing.

Prevention

The speech-language pathologist consults with both educators and parents to teach and model language activities that promote success. He or she may:

- explain the importance of joint book reading and provides demonstration lessons. For example, the speech-language pathologist may illustrate how to improve students vocabulary skills by having children name items in story pictures and describe the action in these pictures.
- model how to sharpen comprehension skills by asking questions related to a story plot and having the child predict what may happen next in the story.
- have the child retell a story in their own words or act out the story.
- teach how to increase the child's awareness of print in their environment and the conventions of print.
- demonstrate strategies to teach letters and their corresponding sounds

- show ways that teachers and parents can model literacy activities (e.g., by reading newspapers and magazines, by writing notes and letters, by making writing materials available for everybody's use).

Assessment

- The clinician begins by interviewing the parents and teacher regarding academic concerns and the child's performance in the classroom.
- For preschool students, the speech-language pathologist gathers information about literacy experiences in the home. For example, are there books and other types of reading material around the home? How frequently does the child see family members writing letters, notes, lists, etc.? How often do family members read stories to the child?
- The speech-language pathologist observes the child during classroom activities. He or she evaluates the child's ability to understand verbal and written directions and to attend to written information on the blackboard, daily plans, etc.
- The speech-language pathologist assesses the student's phonological awareness skills (ability to hear and "play with" the sounds in words.
- spelling, writing, and reading are assessed with older students. In some settings, the speech-language pathologist completes these assessments as part of a team while in other settings he or she helps the educational team interpret the results of reading and writing assessments completed by other evaluators. The reading evaluation focuses on the student's ability to *decode* (sound out) words, read irregular spelling patterns, read fluently, comprehend texts that differ in length and complexity, and comprehend different types of material (e.g., stories versus non-fiction texts).

- The speech-language pathologist completes a formal evaluation of speech and language skills. Speech *articulation* (pronunciation and clarity of speech) is assessed. Understanding and use of grammar (*syntax*), understanding and use of vocabulary (*semantics*), and the client's ability to provide an extended narrative (*language sample*) are evaluated. Can the child explain something or retell a story, centering on a topic and chaining a sequence of events together? Does the narrative make sense or is it difficult to follow? Can the child describe the "plot" in an action picture?
- Executive functioning is evaluated. The speech-language pathologist assesses the child's ability to plan, organize, and attend to details (e.g., does he or she plan/organize his or her writing? is he or she able to keep track of assignments and school materials). The speech-language pathologist may read an incomplete story and ask the child to provide a logical beginning, middle, or conclusion. The child is also asked to provide solutions to problems (*reasoning and problem solving*). For example, what would you do if you locked your keys in your car? How can this problem be avoided in the future?).

Treatment

The goals of speech and language treatment for the child with a reading problem target the specific aspects of reading and writing that the student is missing. For example, if the student is able to decode text but is unable to understand the details of what has been read, comprehension is addressed. If a younger student has difficulty distinguishing the different sounds that make up words, treatment will focus on activities that support growth in this skill area (rhyming, tapping out syllables, etc.).

- Individualized programs always relate to the curriculum. Therefore, materials for treatment are taken from or are directly related to curricular content (e.g., textbooks for reading activities, assigned papers for writing activities, practice of oral reports for English class). The student is taught to apply newly learned language strategies to classroom activities and assignments. To assist the child best, the speech-language pathologist may work side-by-side with the child in his or her classroom(s).

- Intervention with spoken language (speaking and listening) can also be designed to support the development of written language. For example, after listening to a story, the student may be asked to state and write answers to questions. He or she may be asked to give a verbal and then a written summary of the story.
- Articulation (pronunciation) needs are also treated in a way that supports written language. For example, if the child is practicing saying words to improve pronunciation of a certain sound, he or she may be asked to read these words from a printed list.
- The speech-language pathologist consults and collaborates with teachers to develop the use of strategies and techniques in the classroom. For example, he or she may help the teacher modify how new material is presented in lessons to accommodate the child's comprehension needs. He or she may also demonstrate what planning strategies the student uses to organize and focus written assignments.

Learning problems should be addressed as early as possible. Many children with learning disabilities that are treated later, when language demands are greater, experience lowered self-esteem due to their previous academic frustrations and failures. Learning problems that go untreated can lead to a significant decrease in confidence, school phobia (e.g., not wanting to go to school, not wanting to do homework), and depression.

9

Personality Development

Introduction

Personality is determined by the interaction of temperament traits with the environment. Each person (including your child) comes with a factory installed wiring. How your child is wired can determine whether they will be easy or difficult to raise. How well their temperament fits with the environment and how well they are received by the people in the environment will determine how a child sees himself and others.

Concept

An individual's personality is the complex of mental characteristics that makes them unique from other people. It includes all of the patterns of thought and emotions that cause us to do and say things in particular ways. At a basic level, personality is expressed through our temperament or emotional tone. However, personality also colors our values, beliefs, and expectations. There are many potential factors that are involved in shaping a personality. These factors are usually seen as coming from heredity and the environment. Research by psychologists over the last several decades has increasingly pointed to hereditary factors being more important, especially for basic personality traits such as emotional tone. However, the acquisition of values, beliefs, and expectations seem to be due more to socialization and unique experiences, especially during childhood.

Some hereditary factors that contribute to personality development do so as a result of interactions with the particular social environment in which people live. For instance, your genetically inherited physical and mental capabilities have an impact on how others see you and, subsequently, how you see yourself. If you have poor motor skills that prevent you from throwing a ball straight and if you regularly get bad grades in school, you will very likely be labeled by your teachers, friends, and relatives as someone who is inadequate or a failure to some degree. This can become a self-fulfilling prophesy as you increasingly perceive yourself in this way and become more pessimistic about your capabilities and your future. Likewise, your health and physical appearance are likely to be very important in your personality development. You may be frail or robust. You may have a learning disability. You may be slender in a culture that considers obesity attractive or vice versa. These largely hereditary factors are likely to cause you to feel that you are nice-looking, ugly, or just adequate. Likewise, skin color, gender, and sexual orientation are likely to have a major impact on how you perceive yourself. Whether you are accepted by others as being normal or abnormal can lead you to think and act in a socially acceptable or marginal and even deviant way.

There are many potential environmental influences that help to shape personality. Child rearing practices are especially critical. In North America, children are usually raised in ways that encourage them to become self-reliant and independent. Children are often allowed to act somewhat like equals to their parents. For instance, they are included in making decisions about what type of food and entertainment the family will have on a night out. Children are given allowances and small jobs around the house to teach them how to be responsible for themselves. In contrast, children in China are usually encouraged to think and act as a member of their family and to suppress their own wishes when they are in conflict with the needs of the family. Independence and self-reliance are viewed as an indication of family failure and are discouraged. It is not surprising that Chinese children traditionally have not been allowed to act as equals to their parents.

Despite significant differences in child rearing practices around the world, there are some similarities. Boys and girls are socialized differently to some extent in all societies. They receive different messages from their parents and other adults as to what is appropriate for them to do in life. They are encouraged to prepare for their future in jobs fitting their gender. Boys are more often allowed freedom to experiment and to participate in physically risky activities. Girls are encouraged to learn how to do domestic chores and to participate in child rearing by baby-sitting. If children do not follow these traditional paths, they are often labeled as marginal or even deviant—girls may be called "tomboys" and boys may be ridiculed for being "effeminate."

There are always unique situations and interpersonal events that help to shape our personalities. Such things as having alcoholic parents, being seriously injured in a car accident, or being raped can leave mental scars that make us fearful and less trusting. If you are an only child, you don't have to learn how to compromise as much as children who have several siblings. Chance meetings and actions may have a major impact on the rest of our lives and affect our personalities. For instance, being accepted for admission to a prestigious university or being in the right place at the right time to meet the person who will become your spouse or life partner can significantly alter the course of the rest of your life. Similarly, being drafted into the military during wartime, learning that you were adopted, or personally witnessing a tragic event, such as the destruction of the World Trade Center towers in New York, can change your basic perspective.

Types of Personality

We often share personality traits with others, especially members of our own family and community. This is probably due largely to being socialized in much the same way. It is normal for us to acquire personality traits as a result of enculturation. Most people adopt the traditions, rules, manners, and biases of their culture. Given this fact, it is not surprising that some researchers have claimed that there are common national personality types, especially in the more culturally homogenous societies. During the 1940's, some leading anthropologists and psychologists argued that there are distinct Japanese and German personalities that led these two nations to view other countries as trying to destroy them.

The concept of national personality types primarily had its origins in anthropology with the research of Ruth Benedict beginning in the 1920's. She believed that personality was almost entirely learned. She said that normal people acquire a distinct *ethos*, or culturally specific personality pattern, during the process of being enculturated as children. Benedict went on to say that our cultural personality patterns are assumed to be "natural" by us and other personality patterns are viewed as being "unnatural" and deviant. She said that such feelings are characteristic of all people in all cultures because we are ethnocentric. Benedict compared the typical personalities of the 19th century North American Plains Indians with those of the farming Pueblo Indians of the American Southwest. She said that the bison hunting Plains Indians had personalities that could be typified as being aggressive, prone to violence, and seeking extreme emotional states. In contrast, she said that the typical Pueblo Indian was just the opposite—peaceful, non-aggressive, and sober in personality.

Benedict's views were especially popular in the 1930's among early feminists such as her student Margaret Mead. This was because if personality is entirely learned, it means that feminine and masculine personality traits are not biologically hard-wired in. In other words, culture rather than genes, makes women nurturing towards children and passive in response to men. Likewise, culture makes men aggressive and domineering. If this is true, these stereotypical behaviors can be altered and even reversed. Mead carried out ethnographic field work among the Polynesian peoples of the South Pacific to find examples of societies in which femininity and masculinity have very different and even opposite characteristics from those found in the Western World. She also found in Samoa, a relaxed adolescence in which sex is talked about freely by boys and girls rather than hidden or suppressed.

Most anthropologists today believe that Benedict and her students went too far in their assertions about the influence of culture on personality formation and in discounting heredity. They also tended to over simplify by defining people who did not share all of the traits of the "national personality type" as being deviants. It is more accurate to see the members of a society as having a range of personality types.

Modal Personality : This is the most common personality type within a society. In reality, there is usually a range of normal personality types within each society.

In the early 1950's, David Riesman proposed that there are three common types of modal personality that occur around the world. He called them tradition oriented, inner-directed, and other directed personalities.

1. *Tradition-oriented personality* is one that places a strong emphasis on doing things the same way that they have always been done. Individuals with this sort of personality are less likely to try new things and to seek new experiences.
2. *Inner-directed personalities* are guilt oriented. That is to say, their behaviour is strongly controlled by their conscience. As a result, there is little need for police to make sure that they obey the law. These individuals monitor themselves. If they break the law, they are likely to turn themselves in for punishment.
3. *Other-directed personalities* have ambiguous feelings about right and wrong. When they deviate from a societal norm, they usually don't feel guilty. However, if they are caught in the act or exposed publicly, they are likely to feel shame.

Advocates of Riesman's concept of three modal personalities suggest that the tradition-oriented personality is most common in small-scale societies and in some subcultures of large-scale ones. Inner-directed personalities are said to be more common in some large-scale societies, especially ones that are culturally homogenous. In contrast, the other-directed personality is likely to be found in culturally diverse large-scale societies in which there is not a uniformity in socialization processes and there is considerable anonymity for city dwellers.

Temperament

Temperament is a set of in-born traits that organize the child's approach to the world. They are instrumental in the development of the child's distinct personality. These traits also determine how the child goes about learning about the world around him.

These traits appear to be relatively stable from birth. They are enduring characteristics that are actually never "good" or "bad." How they are received determines whether they are perceived by the child as being a bad or good thing. When parents understand the temperament of their children, they can avoid blaming themselves for issues that are normal for their child's temperament. Some children are noisier than other. Some are more cuddly than others. Some have more regular sleep patterns that others.

When parents understand how their child responds to certain situations, they an learn to anticipate issues that might present difficulties for their child. They can prepare the child for the situation or in other cases they may avoid a potentially difficult situation all together.

Parents can tailor their parenting strategies to the particular temperamental characteristics of the child. They can also avoid thinking that a behaviour that reflects a temperament trait represents a pathological condition that requires treatment.

Parents feel more effective as they more fully understand and appreciate their child's unique personality.

When the demands and expectations of people and the environment are compatible with the child's temperament there is said to be a "goodness-of-fit." When incompatibility exists, you have what is known as a "personality conflict." Early on parents can work with the child's temperamental traits rather than in opposition to them. Later as the child matures the parents can help the child to adapt to their world by accommodating to their temperamental traits.

Temperament Traits-9 Phases

Classic child development research conducted by Doctors Chess and Thomas has identified 9 temperamental traits:

1. *Activity Level:* This is the child's "idle speed or how active the child is generally. Does the infant always wiggle, more squirm? Is the infant difficult to diaper because of this? Is the infant content to sit and quietly watch? Does the child have difficulty sitting still? Is the child always on the go? Or, does the child prefer sedentary quiet activities? Highly active children may channel such extra energy into success in sports; may perform well in high-energy careers and may be able to keep up with many different responsibilities.
2. *Distractibility:* The degree of concentration and paying attention displayed when a child is not particularly interested in an activity. This trait refers to the ease with which external stimuli interfere with ongoing behaviour. Is the infant easily distracted by sounds or sights while drinking a bottle? Is the infant easily soothed when upset by being offered alternate activity? Does the child become sidetracked easily when attempting to follow routine or working on some activity? High distractibility is seen as positive when it is easy to divert a child from an undesirable behaviour but seen as negative when it prevents the child from finishing school work.

3. *Intensity:* The energy level of a response whether positive or negative. Does the infant react strongly and loudly to everything, even relatively minor events? Does the child show pleasure or upset strongly and dramatically? Or does the child just get quiet when upset? Intense children are more likely to have their needs met and may have depth and delight of emotion rarely experienced by others. These children may be gifted in dramatic arts. Intense children tend to be exhausting to live with.
4. *Regularity:* The trait refers to the predictability of biological functions like appetite and sleep. Does the child get hungry or tired at predictable times? Or, is the child unpredictable in terms of hunger and tiredness? As grown-ups irregular individuals may do better than others with traveling as well as be likely to adapt to careers with unusual working hours.
5. *Sensory Threshold:* Related to how sensitive this child is to physical stimuli. It is the amount of stimulation (sounds, tastes, touch, temperature changes) needed to produce a response in the child. Does the child react positively or negatively to particular sounds? Does the child startle easily to sounds? Is the child a picky eater or will he eat almost anything? Does the child respond positively or negatively to the feel of clothing? Highly sensitive individuals are more likely to be artistic and creative.
6. *Approach/Withdrawal:* Refers to the child's characteristic response to a new situation or strangers. Does the child eagerly approach new situations or people? Or does the child seem hesitant and resistant when faced with new situations, people or things? Slow-to-warm up children tend to think before they act. They are less likely to act impulsively during adolescence.

7. *Adaptability:* Related to how easily the child adapts to transitions and changes, like switching to a new activity. Does the child have difficulty with changes in routines, or with transitions from one activity to another? Does the child take a long time to become comfortable to new situations? A slow-to-adapt child is less likely to rush into dangerous situations, and may be less influenced by peer pressure.
8. *Persistence:* This is the length of time a child continues in activities in the face of obstacles. Does the child continue to work on a puzzle when he has difficulty with it or does he just move on to another activity? Is the child able to wait to have his needs met? Does the child react strongly when interrupted in an activity? When a child persists in an activity he is asked to stop, he is labeled as stubborn. When a child stays with a tough puzzle he is seen a being patient. The highly persistent child is more likely to succeed in reaching goals. A child with low persistence may develop strong social skills because he realizes other people can help.
9. *Mood:* This is the tendency to react to the world primarily in a positive or negative way. Does the child see the glass as half full? Does he focus on the positive aspects of life? Is the child generally in a happy mood? Or, does the child see the gall as half empty and tend to focus on the negative aspects of life? Is the child generally serious? Serious children tend to be analytical and evaluate situations carefully.

Difficult or Easy to Raise Your Child

Temperament is the innate behaviour style of an individual that seems to be biologically determined. Although some experts feel that labeling a child too quickly as "difficult" may create a self-fulfilling prophecy of problematic parent-child interaction, knowing what kind of temperament your child has may make the difference between a happy and a troubled child—and between an accepting and frustrated parent. You can use the table below to get a rough idea on how easy or difficult your child is to raise.

Table of Temperamental Traits

Temperamental Traits	*Easy*	*Difficult*
Activity Level (how active the child is generally)	Low	High
Distractibility (degree of concentration and paying attention when child is not particularly interested)	Low	High
Intensity (how loud the child is)	Low	High
Regularity (the predictability of biological functions like appetite and sleep)	Regular	Irregular
Sensory Threshold (how sensitive the child is to physical stimuli: touch, taste, smell, sound, light)	High	Low
Approach/Withdrawal (characteristic responses of a child to a new situation or to strangers)	Approach	Withdrawal
Adaptability (how easily the child adapts to transitions and changes like switching to a new activity)	Good	Poor
Persistence (stubbornness, inability to give up)	Low	High
Mood (tendency to react to the world primarily in a positive or negative way)	Positive	Negative

If your child weighs more heavily on one side of the spectrum than the other, he may be a classic example of the easy or difficult child. However, if your child is in-between and his behaviour presents you with problems, you may be in nee of some new management techniques.

Adjust with Your Child's Personality

The experts tell us that there's probably not a lot you can go about changing the way a child tends to reach if that tendency is inborn but there are ways you can help him manage his impulses better and spare yourself lots of grief along the way.

Realize that your child's immature behavioural style is not your "fault" because temperament is biological not something he learned from you. Still it is within your power to help your child cope with his temperament and eventually to understand himself better instead of feeling sorry for yourself for having a noisy, distractible or shy child. Learn to accept this as his nature and then develop a strategy to help him adapt in a socially acceptable way. Replace a victimized mind set with an adult resolve to help your child ameliorate his difficulties. Above all, remember that all temperamental qualities can be shaped to work to a child's advantage if they are sensibly managed.

To become a "manager of your child's temperament, make sure that you step back from his objectionable behaviour for a minute and remind yourself that his shrill shriek of excitement or his irregular sleeping habits are not deliberate reactions but one he can yet control. The key is to switch on the objective part of your mind rather than to become emotionally embroiled in his temperamental difficulties. Through this emotionally "neutral" stance, you'll be better able to help him modify his reactions because you'll be thinking rationally.

Develop specific plans ahead of time to cope with troublesome behaviour and then enforce them in a sympathetic but consistently firm ways. If your child tend to get wild on family occasions or when he's with friends, be sensitive to this tendency and take steps to quiet it before it escalates (Decide ahead if this activity is one he can handle. With younger children avoiding potential problem situations may be the best solution). With a baby you may want to tell your host that you will want to leave the party early. You can also take your child into a quiet room and sit with him until he falls asleep. Follow similar procedure with an older child, either by removing him from the activity, distracting him with something quieter such as a story hour or a snack or calling a "time out" period.

An infant with irregular biological rhythms will need special structuring from you so that he eventually learns to sleep through the night, to eat at the usual meal times and to control his bladder and bowel function. In this case, a doctor or child-behaviour expert may be able to help to develop a schedule for your baby.

For an older child who resists going to sleep, you may have to make special distinctions between bedtime and "sleep-time." To help him settle down, you can insist that the youngster get into bed at a certain time but permit him to read or play quietly until he feels sleepy. In this way, you are regulating his schedule but still allowing him to relax at his own pace.

Learn to distinguish between behaviour that is temperamentally induced and that which is learned. If a child knocks over your best vase by mistake because he is a high-energy child and was running gleefully through the living room, your response should be different than if he broke your vase deliberately.

In some instances you will probably be upset and may express your displeasure. But the action you pursue should be different. In the first case you may have to give some thought on how to prevent your child from running through the living room and remembering other ways he can work off his energy while in the house. In the second scenario, you will probably want to punish the child for his deliberate destruction of your personal property to impress upon him that this behaviour is socially unacceptable. With temperament, the goal is always to manage rather than to systematically punish.

By the same token learn to distinguish between a tantrum that is temperamentally determined and one that is deliberately manipulative. Both may look the same because in both instances the child is crying or screaming loudly but the reasons for them are different. A strong-willed and intense child may react to a disappointment with a tantrum but the parent should understand that in a sense the child really can't help it—that this is his innate behavioral reaction. This is in marked contrast to the less intense child who screams and cries in the same way when you say no because he has learned that such behaviour will weaken your resolve and make your give into him. Becoming an expert on your child's temperament will help you distinguish between the two types of tantrums-and then you can react to the tantrum appropriately.

Finally remember that one of the most important jobs a parent can do is help his child develop self-esteem. That doesn't mean over-inflating his ego but rather helping him develop a positive sense of himself with a fair sense of his strengths and weaknesses. Understanding a child temperament is the first step toward enhancing his self-esteem because you will be able to deliver praise sensitively in accordance with his innate tendencies and help him build upon those traits in a positive way.

Role of Parents for Very Intense Children

- Provide activities that are soothing such as warm bath, massage, water play, stories.
- Recognize cues that signal that intensity is rising.
- Help child learn to recognize cues that signal that intensity is rising.
- Use humor to diffuse intensity.
- Teach child to use time-out as a time to calm self-down.
- Avoid escalating intensity of child be reacting intensely to his/her behaviour. Give calm, clear, brief feedback.

Role of Parents for Slow-to-Adapt Children

- Establish clear routines.

- Prepare child by discussing plans for the day when routine changes.
- Prepare child for transitions.
- Give warnings a few minutes before transition from one activity to next occurs.

Allow time for closure of one activity before going on to next

Freud's Stages of Psychosexual Development

Sigmund Freud (1856-1939) is probably the most well known theorist when it comes to the development of personality. *Freud's Stages of Psychosexual Development* are, like other stage theories, completed in a predetermined sequence and can result in either successful completion or a healthy personality or can result in failure, leading to an unhealthy personality. This theory is probably the most well known as well as the most controversial, as Freud believed that we develop through stages based upon a particular erogenous zone. During each stage, an unsuccessful completion means that a child becomes fixated on that particular erogenous zone and either over–or under-indulges once he or she becomes an adult.

1. *Oral Stage (Birth to 18 months):* During the oral stage, the child if focused on oral pleasures (sucking). Too much or too little gratification can result in an Oral Fixation or Oral Personality which is evidenced by a preoccupation with oral activities. This type of personality may have a stronger tendency to smoke, drink alcohol, over eat, or bite his or her nails. Personality wise, these individuals may become overly dependent upon others, gullible, and perpetual followers. On the other hand, they may also fight these urges and develop pessimism and aggression toward others.

2. *Anal Stage (18 months to three years):* The child's focus of pleasure in this stage is on eliminating and retaining feces. Through society's pressure, mainly via parents, the child has to learn to control anal stimulation. In terms of

personality, after effects of an anal fixation during this stage can result in an obsession with cleanliness, perfection, and control (anal retentive). On the opposite end of the spectrum, they may become messy and disorganized (anal expulsive).

3. *Phallic Stage (ages three to six):* The pleasure zone switches to the genitals. Freud believed that during this stage boy develop unconscious sexual desires for their mother. Because of this, he becomes rivals with his father and sees him as competition for the mother's affection. During this time, boys also develop a fear that their father will punish them for these feelings, such as by castrating them. This group of feelings is known as Oedipus Complex (after the Greek Mythology figure who accidentally killed his father and married his mother).

Later it was added that girls go through a similar situation, developing unconscious sexual attraction to their father. Although Freud Strongly disagreed with this, it has been termed the Electra Complex by more recent psychoanalysts.

According to Freud, out of fear of castration and due to the strong competition of his father, boys eventually decide to identify with him rather than fight him. By identifying with his father, the boy develops masculine characteristics and identifies himself as a male, and represses his sexual feelings toward his mother. A fixation at this stage could result in sexual deviancies (both overindulging and avoidance) and weak or confused sexual identity according to psychoanalysts.

4. *Latency Stage (age six to puberty):* It's during this stage that sexual urges remain repressed and children interact and play mostly with same sex peers.

5. *Genital Stage (puberty on):* The final stage of psychosexual development begins at the start of puberty when sexual urges are once again awakened. Through the lessons learned during the previous stages, adolescents direct their sexual urges onto opposite sex peers, with the primary focus of pleasure is the genitals.

Sigmund Freud's Theory is quite complex and although his writings on psychosexual development set the groundwork for how our personalities developed, it was only one of five parts to his overall theory of personality. He also believed that different driving forces develop during these stages which play an important role in how we interact with the world.

Freud's Structural and Topographical Models of Personality

Structural Model (Id, Ego, Superego)

According to Freud, we are born with our Id. The id is an important part of our personality because as newborns, it allows us to get our basic needs met. Freud believed that the id is based on our pleasure principle. In other words, the id wants whatever feels good at the time, with no consideration for the reality of the situation. When a child is hungry, the id wants food, and therefore the child cries. When the child needs to be changed, the id cries. When the child is uncomfortable, in pain, too hot, too cold, or just wants attention, the id speaks up until his or her needs are met.

The id doesn't care about reality, about the needs of anyone else, only its own satisfaction. If you think about it, babies are not real considerate of their parents' wishes. They have no care for time, whether their parents are sleeping, relaxing, eating dinner, or bathing. When the id wants something, nothing else is important.

Within the next three years, as the child interacts more and more with the world, the second part of the personality begins to develop. Freud called this part the Ego. The ego is based on the reality principle. The ego understands that other people have needs and desires and that sometimes being impulsive or selfish can hurt us in the long run. Its the ego's job to meet the needs of the id, while taking into consideration the reality of the situation.

By the age of five, or the end of the phallic stage of development, the Superego develops. The Superego is the moral part of us and develops due to the moral and ethical restraints placed on us by our caregivers. Many equate the superego with the conscience as it dictates our belief of right and wrong.

In a healthy person, according to Freud, the ego is the strongest so that it can satisfy the needs of the id, not upset the superego, and still take into consideration the reality of every situation. Not an easy job by any means, but if the id gets too strong, impulses and self gratification take over the person's life. If the superego becomes to strong, the person would be driven by rigid morals, would be judgmental and unbending in his or her interactions with the world. You'll learn how the ego maintains control as you continue to read.

Topographical Model

Freud believed that the majority of what we experience in our lives, the underlying emotions, beliefs, feelings, and impulses are not available to us at a conscious level. He believed that most of what drives us is buried in our unconscious. If you remember the Oedipus and Electra Complex, they were both pushed down into the unconscious, out of our awareness due to the extreme anxiety they caused. While buried there, however, they continue to impact us dramatically according to Freud.

The role of the unconscious is only one part of the model. Freud also believed that everything we are aware of is stored in our conscious. Our conscious makes up a very small part of who we are. In other words, at any given time, we are only aware of a very small part of what makes up our personality; most of what we are is buried and inaccessible.

The final part is the preconscious or subconscious. This is the part of us that we can access if prompted, but is not in our active conscious. Its right below the surface, but still buried somewhat unless we search for it. Information such as our telephone number, some childhood memories, or the name of your best childhood friend is stored in the preconscious.

Because the unconscious is so large, and because we are only aware of the very small conscious at any given time, this theory has been likened to an iceberg, where the vast majority is buried beneath the water's surface. The water, by the way, would represent everything that we are not aware of, have not experienced, and that has not been integrated into our personalities, referred to as the unconscious.

Ego Defence Mechanisms

It stated earlier that the ego's job was to satisfy the id's impulses, not offend the moralistic character of the superego, while still taking into consideration the reality of the situation. We also stated that this was not an easy job. Think of the id as the 'devil on your shoulder' and the superego as the 'angel of your shoulder.' We don't want either one to get too strong so we talk to both of them, hear their perspective and then make a decision. This decision is the ego talking, the one looking for that healthy balance.

Before we can talk more about this, we need to understand what drives the id, ego, and superego. According to Freud, we only have two drives; sex and aggression. In other words, everything we do is motivated by one of these two drives.

Sex, also called Eros or the Life force, represents our drive to live, prosper, and produce offspring. Aggression, also called Thanatos or our Death force, represents our need to stay alive and stave off threats to our existence, our power, and our prosperity.

Now the ego has a difficult time satisfying both the id and the superego, but it doesn't have to do so without help. The ego has some tools it can use in its job as the mediator, tools that help defend the ego. These are called Ego Defence Mechanisms or Defenses. When the ego has a difficult time making both the id and the superego happy, it will employ one or more of these defenses:

Table: Ego Defense Mechanism

Defense	*Description*	*Example*
Denial	Arguing against an anxiety provoking stimuli by stating it doesn't exist	Denying that your physician's diagnosis of cancer is correct and seeking a second opinion
Displacement	Taking out impulses on a less threatening target	Slamming a door instead of hitting as person, yelling at your spouse after an argument with your boss
Intellectualization	Avoiding unacceptable emotions by focusing on the intellectual aspects	Focusing on the details of a funeral as opposed to the sadness and grief
Projection	Placing unacceptable impulses in yourself onto someone else	When losing an argument, you state "You're just Stupid;" homophobia
Rationalization	Supplying a logical or rational reason as opposed to the real reason	Stating that you were fired because you didn't fired because you didn't kiss up the the boss, when the real reason was your poor performance
Reaction formation	Taking the opposite belief because the true belief causes anxiety	Having a bias against a particular race or culture and then embracing that race or culture to the extreme
Regression	Returning to a previous stage of development	Sitting in a corner and crying after hearing bad news; throwing a temper tantrum when you don't get your way
Repression	Pulling into the unconscious	Forgetting sexual abuse from your childhood due to the trauma and anxiety

(Contd.)

(Contd. Table)

Defense	*Description*	*Example*
Sublimation	Acting out unacceptable impulses in a socially acceptable way	Sublimating your aggressive impulses toward a career as a boxer; becoming a surgeon because of your desire to cut; lifting weights to release 'pent up' energy
Suppression	Pushing into the unconscious	Trying to forget something that causes you anxiety

Ego defenses are not necessarily unhealthy as you can see by the examples above. In face, the lack of these defenses, or the inability to use them effectively can often lead to problems in life. However, we sometimes employ the defenses at the wrong time or overuse them, which can be equally destructive.

Psychosocial Theory: Erikson

Erikson believed that childhood is very important in personality development. He accepted many of Freud's theories, including the id, ego, and superego, and Freud's theory of infantile sexuality. But Erikson rejected Freud's attempt to describe personality solely on the basis of sexuality, and, unlike Freud, felt that personality continued to develop beyond five years of age.

All of the stages in Erikson's epigenetic theory are implicitly present at birth (at least in latent form), but unfold according to both an innate scheme and one's up-bringing in a family that expresses the values of a culture. Each stage builds on the preceding stages, and paves the way for subsequent stages. Each stage is characterized by a psychosocial crisis, which is based on physiological development, but also on demands put on the individual by parents and/or society. Ideally, the crisis in each stage should be resolved by the ego in that stage, in order for development to proceed correctly. The outcome of one stage is not permanent, but can be altered by later experiences. Everyone has a mixture of the traits attained at each stage, but personality development is considered successful if the individual has more of the "good" traits than the "bad" traits.

Ego Psychology

Erikson's theory of ego psychology holds certain tenets that differentiate his theory from Freud's. Some of these include:

- The ego is of utmost importance.
- Part of the ego is able to operate independently of the id and the superego.
- The ego is a powerful agent that can adapt to situations, thereby promoting
- mental health.
- Social and sexual factors both play a role in personality development.

Erikson's theory was more comprehensive than Freud's, and included information about "normal" personality as well as neurotics. He also broadened the scope of personality to incorporate society and culture, not just sexuality. Criticisms of his theories, in addition to the factors discussed in class, have noted that he did no statistical research to generate his theories, and it is very hard to test his theories in order to validate them.

Zones, Modes, and Modalities

"a", "b" and "c" identify the oral, anal, and gential zones, respectively; and numbers "1" through "5" pertain to the passive and active incorporative, the retentive and eliminative, and the intrusive modes, respectively.

Erikson's illustration of "the interplay of one zone with all the modes" (1950) by means of circles and arrows is among the most confusing moments in his book. Here are the diagrams (Erikson, 1950), at the point male and female development are said to diverge in loco motor/intrusive/ "phallic"/Oedipal Stage 3:

Erikson's Stages of Psychosocial Development

Like Piaget, Erik Erikson (1902-1994) maintained that children develop in a predetermined order. Instead of focusing on cognitive development, however, he was interested in how children socialize and how this affects their sense of self. *Erikson's Theory of Psychosocial Development* has eight distinct stage, each with two possible outcomes. According to the theory, successful completion of each stage results in a healthy personality and successful interactions with others. Failure to successfully complete a stage can result in a reduced ability to complete further stages and therefore a more unhealthy personality and sense of self. These stages, however, can be resolved successfully at a later time.

Trust vs. Mistrust: From ages birth to one year, children begin to learn the ability to trust others based upon the consistency of their caregiver(s). If trust develops successfully, the child gains confidence and security in the world around him and is able to feel secure even when threatened. Unsuccessful completion of this stage can result in an inability to trust, and therefore an sense of fear about the inconsistent world. It may result in anxiety, heightened insecurities, and an over feeling of mistrust in the world around them.

Autonomy vs. Shame and Doubt. Between the ages of one and three, children begin to assert their independence, by walking away from their mother, picking which toy to play with, and making choices about what they like to wear, to eat, etc. If children in this stage are encouraged and supported in their increased independence, they become more confident and secure in their own ability to survive in the world. If children are criticized, overly controlled, or not given the opportunity to assert themselves, they begin to feel inadequate in their ability to survive, and may then become overly dependent upon others, lack self-esteem, and feel a sense of shame or doubt in their own abilities.

Initiative vs. Guilt. Around age three and continuing to age six, children assert themselves more frequently. They begin to plan activities, make up games, and initiate activities with others. If given this opportunity, children develop a sense of initiative, and feel secure in their ability to lead others and make decisions. Conversely, if this tendency is squelched, either through criticism or control, children develop a sense of guilt. They may feel like a nuisance to others and will therefore remain followers, lacking in self-initiative.

Industry vs. Inferiority. From age six years to puberty, children begin to develop a sense of pride in their accomplishments. They initiate projects, see them through to completion, and feel good about what they have achieved. During this time, teachers play an increased role in the child's development. If children are encouraged and reinforced for their initiative, they begin to feel industrious and feel confident in their ability to achieve goals. If this initiative is not encouraged, if it is restricted by parents or teacher, then the child begins to feel inferior, doubting his own abilities and therefore may not reach his potential.

Identity vs. Role Confusion. During adolescence, the transition from childhood to adulthood is most important. Children are becoming more independent, and begin to look at the future in terms of career, relationships, families, housing, etc. During this period, they explore possibilities and begin to form their own identity based upon the outcome of their explorations. This sense of who they are can be hindered, which results in a sense of confusion ("I don't know what I want to be when I grow up") about themselves and their role in the world.

Intimacy vs. Isolation. Occurring in Young adulthood, we begin to share ourselves more intimately with others. We explore relationships leading toward longer term commitments with someone other than a family member. Successful completion can lead to comfortable relationships and a sense of commitment, safety, and care within a relationship. Avoiding intimacy, fearing commitment and relationships can lead to isolation, loneliness, and sometimes depression.

Generativity vs. Stagnation. During middle adulthood, we establish our careers, settle down within a relationship, begin our own families and develop a sense of being a part of the bigger picture. We give back to society through raising our children, being productive at work, and becoming involved in community activities and organizations. By failing to achieve these objectives, we become stagnant and feel unproductive.

Ego Integrity vs. Despair. As we grow older and become senior citizens, we tend to slow down our productivity, and explore life as a retired person. It is during this time that we contemplate our accomplishments and are able to develop integrity if we see ourselves as leading a successful life. If we see our lives as unproductive, feel guilt about our pasts, or feel that we did not accomplish our life goals, we become dissatisfied with life and develop despair, often leading to depression and hopelessness.

10

Moral Development

Introduction

When people talk about moral development, they are referring to their conduct and attitude towards other people in society. They look to see if you and I follow societal norms, rules, and laws. In terms of children, we are describing their ability to distinguish right from wrong.

Two noteworthy individuals, Jean Piaget and Lawrence Kohlberg, studied the moral development of children. Piaget looked at how children develop moral reasoning. He found that young children have a much more primitive understanding of right and wrong behaviour than do older children.

Moral Behaviour

Piaget determined that younger children judge bad behaviour by the amount of damage caused by a person's behaviour. He would tell children a story with a moral dilemma. He would ask them to tell him "who is naughtier:" a boy who accidentally broke fifteen cups or a boy who breaks one cup trying to reach a jam jar when his mother is not around. Younger children attributed the "naughty" behaviour to the boy who broke the most cups regardless of the other child's intent. This type of moral reasoning was called Objective Morality or Moral Realism.

Older children attributed bad behaviour to the boy who broke only one cup because his motives where bad. This, more advanced form of moral reasoning was called Subjective Morality or Autonomous Morality. Piaget did not feel that children fully achieved this stage of moral development before the ages of twelve or thirteen.

Kohlberg and Piaget Theory

Kohlberg carried Piaget's work into adolescence and adulthood. He also told children moral dilemma stories, but he would ask them to tell him what they thought would be the right thing to do. Their answers led him to the discovery of three levels of moral development with two stages each:

The first level is called Preconventional. During this level children are concerned with avoiding punishment (Stage 1: Punishment-Obedience) and getting one's own needs met (Stage 2: Individualism). This level and its stages fit into the framework of young children, up to the age of ten years.

The second level is called Conventional. During this level children are more concerned with living up to the expectations of others (Stage 3: Interpersonal Conformity) and want to do the right thing because it is good for the group, family, or institution (Stage 4: Social System and Conscience). This level and its stages fit children over the age of ten years and on to adulthood.

The third level is called Post-conventional. During this level individuals govern their behaviour by the relative values and opinions of the groups they live and interact with. Right behaviour is based on a "social contract" (Stage 5: Social Contract and Individual Rights) with others and in the validity of universal moral principles (Stage 6: Universal/ Ethical Principles) which may or may not agree with societies laws. Laws that agree with universal moral principles are obeyed but when those laws violate these principles, the individual follows the principles instead.

Although many people have criticized Piaget and Kohlberg about their stages of moral development as being culturally biased, the parenting questions remain: How do we teach children moral behaviour? Is it already hard wired into the child's development and must parents shape and direct it?

Interaction between Nature and Nurture

Robert Coles, the author, "The Moral Intelligence of Children," states that character or moral development is an interaction between nature and nurture. It develops as a result of parental interaction, balanced discipline styles, and a child's own choices. Children learn about right from wrong from their earliest experiences. When they need nurturing or feeding and parents fulfill that need without excessive indulgence, then children develop characters that accept rules and tolerate frustrations, later in life.

In book, "Love and Limits: Achieving a Balance in Parenting" discuss the two sides of discipline and the need that children have for balance between them. Too much love and a child becomes spoiled, expecting their every want and need to be met regardless of other people's wants and needs. This causes children to be stuck in those early stages of moral development based on selfish individualism. That's fine for a two-year-old, tolerable in a six-year-old, and obnoxious in a twelve-year-old or older. Too many limits and the child develop a low sense of worth and a lack of self-control. This usually results in an overly rebellious child or an unhealthy submissive one.

Achieving this balance is difficult. But it is easier to do if discipline is viewed from the vantagepoint of moral development. We are not merely punishing wrong behaviour. We are shaping character. We are not simply setting limits. We are teaching how to distinguish right from wrong. It is easier to say "no" when I know that I am guiding my child's moral development and ultimately, his or her social success.

As the later stages of moral development reveal, children can make a choice not to follow society's rules or laws. Parents must accept that reality. That's part of parents' on-going moral development. It also makes what parents do now, with children, all the more important. Understanding moral development allows parents to assess their children and have a better target for their individual development. It redefines our roles as teachers and guides over the unpleasant tasks of police and judges. Hopefully, the end result is that our child will be the one who will stop and wait for someone in need, regardless of what the crowd says he or she should do.

Moral Development Theory

Kohlberg's Theory

Kohlberg, who was born in 1927, grew up in Bronxville, New York, and attended the Andover Academy in Massachusetts, a private high school for bright and usually wealthy students. He did not go immediately to college, but instead went to help the Israeli cause, in which he was made the Second Engineer on an old freighter carrying refugees from parts of Europe to Israel. After this, in 1948, he enrolled at the University of Chicago, where he scored so high on admission tests that he had to take only a few courses to earn his bachelor's degree. This he did in one year. He stayed on at Chicago for graduate work in psychology, at first thinking he would become a clinical psychologist. However, he soon became interested in Piaget and began interviewing children and adolescents on oral issues. The result was his doctoral dissertation (1958a), the first rendition of his new stage theory.

Kohlberg is an informal, unassuming man who also is a true scholar; he has thought long and deeply about a wide range of issues in both psychology and philosophy and has done much to help others appreciate the wisdom of many of the "old psychologists," such as Rousseau, John Dewey, and James Mark Baldwin. Kohlberg has taught at the University of Chicago (1962-1968) and, since 1968, has been at Harvard University.

Traditionally, psychology has avoided studying anything that is loaded with value judgments. There is a degree of difficulty involved in trying to be unbiased about things that involve terms like "good" and "bad!" So, one of the most significant aspects of human life—morality—has had to wait quite a while before anyone in psychology dared to touch it! But Lawrence Kohlberg wanted to study morality, and did so using some of the most interesting (if controversial) techniques. Basically, he would ask children and adults to try to solve moral dilemmas contained in little stories, and to do so out loud so he could follow their reasoning. It wasn't the specific answers to the dilemmas that interested him, but rather how the person got to his or her answer.

One of the most famous of these stories concerned a man named Heinz. His wife was dying of a disease that could be cured if he could get a certain medicine. When he asked the pharmacist, he was told that he could get the medicine, but only at a very high price—one that Heinz could not possibly afford. So the next evening, Heinz broke into the pharmacy and stole the drug to save his wife's life. There are simple reasons why Heinz should or should not have stolen the drug, and there are very sophisticated reasons, and reasons in between. After looking at hundreds of interviews concerning this and several other stories, Kohlberg outlined three broad levels and six more specific stages of moral development.

Level I: **Pre-conventional morality.** While infants are essentially amoral, very young children are moral in a rather primitive way described by the two preconventional stages.

Stage 1. the reward and punishment stage. Good or bad depends on the physical consequences: This stage is based simply on one's own pain and pleasure, and doesn't take others into account.

Stage 2. the exchange stage. In this stage, there is increased recognition that others have their own interests and should be taken into account. Those interests are still understood in a very concrete fashion, and the child deals with others in terms of simple exchange or reciprocity. Children in this stage are very concerned with what's fair, but are not concerned with real justice.

Level II: **Conventional morality**. By the time children enter elementary school, they are usually capable of conventional morality, although they may often slip back into preconventional morality on occasion. But this level is called conventional for a very good reason: It is also the level that most adults find themselves in most of the time!

Stage 3. This stage is often called the good boy/good girl stage. The child tries to live up to the expectations of others, and to seek their approval. Now the concern includes motives or intentions, and concepts such as loyalty, trust, and gratitude are understood. Children in this stage often adhere to a concrete version of the Golden Rule, although it is limited to the people they actually deal with on a day-to-day basis.

Stage 4. This is called the law-and-order stage. Children now take the point of view that includes the social system as a whole. The rules of the society are the bases for right and wrong, and doing one's duty and showing respect for authority are important.

Level III: **Post-conventional morality**. Some adolescents and adults go a step further and rise above moralities based on authority to ones based on reason.

Stage 5. The social contract stage means being aware of the degree to which much of so-called morality is relative to the individual and to the social group they belong to, and that only a very few fundamental values are universal. The person at this level sees morality as a matter of entering into a rational contract with one's fellow human beings to be kind to each other, respect authority, and follow laws to the extent that they respect and promote those universal values. Social contract morality often involves a utilitarian approach, where the relative value of an act is determined by "the greatest good for the greatest number."

Stage 6. This stage is referred to as the stage of universal principles. At this point, the person makes a personal commitment to universal principles of equal rights and respect, and social contract takes a clear back-seat: If there is a conflict between a social law or custom and universal principles, the universal principles take precedence.

Bronfenbrenner's Theory

Another psychologist unafraid to tackle morality was Urie Bronfenbrenner. He is famous for his studies of children and schools in different cultures. He outlines five moral orientations:

1. *Self-oriented morality.* This is analogous to Kohlberg's pre-conventional morality. Basically, the child is only interested in self-gratification and only considers others to the extent that they can help him get what he wants, or hinder him.
2. *Authority-oriented morality.* Here, the child, or adult, basically accepts the decrees of authority figures, from parents up to heads of state and religion, as defining of good and bad.
3. *Peer-oriented morality.* This is basically a morality of conformity, where right and wrong is determined not by authority but by one's peers. In western society, this kind of morality is frequently found among adolescents, as well as many adults.
4. *Collective-oriented morality.* In this orientation, the standing goals of the group to which the child or

adult belongs over-ride individual interests. Duty to one's group or society is paramount.

5. *Objectively oriented morality.* By objectively, Bronfenbrenner means universal principles that are objective in the sense that they do not depend on the whims of individuals or social groups, but have a reality all their own.

Bronfenbrenner noted that while 1 is found among children (and some adults) in all cultures, 6 is found in relatively few people in any culture. The differences between 2, 3 and 4 are more a matter of culture than of development. Many cultures promote strict obedience to authority figures. One can see this in some middle eastern cultures, where the word of the religious authorities is law. In many western cultures, conformity to one's peers is a powerful force. And in others still, such as some Asian cultures, the welfare of the group is considered far more important than that of the individual.

Bronfenbrenner also talks about how we get movement from one orientation to another. The movement from 1 to 2, 3, or 4 involves participation in the family and other social structures, where concern for others begins to take precedent over concern for oneself.

Movement from 2, 3 or 4 to 5 occurs when a person is exposed to a number of different moral systems which at least partially conflict with each other, a situation he calls moral pluralism. This forces the person to begin to think about what might lie beneath all the variation, and lead him or her to consider ultimate moral principles.

On the other hand, sometimes people slide back down to the lowest orientation when they suffer from the disintegration of social structures, as in war and other social disasters. This can force a person's attentions back onto their own needs, and cause them to begin ignoring the welfare of larger social groupings.

Stages of Moral Development

I. Pre-conventional Level

At this level, the child is responsive to cultural rules and labels of good and bad, right or wrong, but he interprets the labels in terms of either the physical or hedonistic of action (punishment, reward, exchange of favours) or the physical power of those who enunciate the rules and labels. The level is divided into the following three stages:

Stage 0: Egocentric judgment

The child makes judgments of good on the basis of what he likes and wants or what helps him, and bad on the basis of what he does not like or what hurts him. He has no concept of rules or of obligations to obey or conform independent of his wish.

Stage 1: The Punishment and Obedience Orientation

The physical consequences of action determine its goodness or badness regardless of the human meaning or value of these consequences. Avoidance of punishment and unquestioning deference to power are values in their own right, not in terms of respect for an underlying moral order supported by punishment and authority

Stage 2: The Instrumental Orientation

Right action consists of what instrumentally satisfies one's own needs and occasionally the needs of others. Human relations are viewed in terms such as those of the market place. Elements of fairness, reciprocity, and equal sharing are present, but they are always interpreted in a physical, pragmatic way. Reciprocity is a matter of "you scratch my back and I'll scratch your", not loyalty, gratitude, or justice.

II. Conventional Level

At this level, the individual perceives the maintenance of the expectations of his family, group, or nation as valuable in its own right, regardless of immediate and obvious consequences. The attitude is not only one of *conformity* to personal expectations and social order, but of loyalty to it, of actively maintaining, supporting, and justifying the order and identifying with the persons or group involved in it. The level consists of the following two stages:

Stage 3: The Interpersonal Concordance or "Good Boy-Nice Girl" Orientation

Good behaviour is what pleases or helps others and is approved by them. There is much conformity to stereotypical images of what is majority or "natural" behaviour. Behaviour is frequently judged by intention—"he means well" becomes important for the first time. One earns approval by being "nice".

Stage 4: The "Law and Order" Orientation

The individual is oriented toward authority, fixed rules, and the maintenance of the social order. Right behaviour consists in doing one's duty, showing respect for authority, and maintaining the given social order for its own sake.

III. Post-Conventional, Autonomous or Principled Level

The individual makes a clear effort to define moral values and principles that have validity and application apart from the authority of the groups of persons holding them and apart from the individual's own identification with the group. The level has the two following stages:

Stage 5: The Legalistic Orientation (Generally with Utilitarian Overtones)

Right action tends to be defined in terms of general individual rights and standards that have been critically examined and agreed upon by the whole society. There is a clear awareness of the relativism of personal values and opinions and a corresponding emphasis upon procedural rules for reaching consensus. Aside from what is constitutionally and democratically agreed upon, right action is a matter of personal values and opinions. The result is an emphasis upon the "legal point of view", but with an additional emphasis upon the possibility of changing the law in terms of rational considerations of social utility (rather than freezing it in terms of stage 4 "law and order"). Outside the legal realm, free agreement, and contract, is the binding element of obligation. The "official" morality of the American government and Constitution is at this stage.

Stage 6: The Universal Ethical-Principle Orientation

Right is defined by the decision of conscience in accord with self-chosen ethical principles that appeal to logical comprehensiveness, universality, and consistency. These principles are abstract and ethical; they are not concrete moral rules like the Ten Commandments. At heart, these are universal principles of justice, of the reciprocity and equality of the human rights, and of respect for the dignity of human beings as individual persons.

Piaget's Stages of Moral Development

Piaget studied many aspects of moral judgment, but most of his findings fit into a two-stage theory. Children younger than 10 or 11 years think about moral dilemmas one way; older children consider them differently. As we have seen, younger children regard rules as fixed and absolute. They believe that rules are handed down by adults or by God and that one cannot change them. The older child's view is more relativistic. He or she understands that it is permissible to change rules if everyone agrees. Rules are not sacred and absolute but are devices which humans use to get along cooperatively.

At approximately the same time—10 or 11 years—children's moral thinking undergoes other shifts. In particular, younger children base their moral judgments more on consequences, whereas older children base their judgments on intentions. When, for example, the young child hears about one boy who broke 15 cups trying to help his mother and another boy who broke only one cup trying to steal cookies, the young child thinks that the first boy did worse. The child primarily considers the amount of damage—the consequences—whereas the older child is more likely to judge wrongness in terms of the motives

There are many more details to Piaget's work on moral judgment, but he essentially found a series of changes that occur between the ages of 10 and 12, just when the child begins to enter the general stage of formal operations.

Intellectual development, however, does not stop at this point. This is just the beginning of formal operations, which continue to develop at least until age 16. Accordingly, one might expect thinking about moral issues to continue to develop throughout adolescence. Kohlberg therefore interviewed both children and adolescents about moral dilemmas, and he did find stages that go well beyond Piaget's. He uncovered six stages, only the first three of which share many features with Piaget's stages.

Kohlberg's Six Stages of Moral Development

Level 1. Preconventional Morality

Stage 1. Obedience and Punishment Orientation. Kohlberg's stage 1 is similar to Piaget's first stage of moral thought. The child assumes that powerful authorities hand down a fixed set of rules which he or she must unquestioningly obey. To the Heinz dilemma, the child typically says that Heinz was wrong to steal the drug because "It's against the law," or "It's bad to steal," as if this were all there were to it. When asked to elaborate, the child usually responds in terms of the consequences involved, explaining that stealing is bad "because you'll get punished".

Although the vast majority of children at stage 1 oppose Heinz's theft, it is still possible for a child to support the action and still employ stage 1 reasoning. For example, a child might say, "Heinz can steal it because he asked first and it's not like he stole something big; he won't get punished". Even though the child agrees with Heinz's action, the reasoning is still stage 1; the concern is with what authorities permit and punish.

Kohlberg calls stage 1 thinking "preconventional" because children do not yet speak as members of society. Instead, they see morality as something external to themselves, as that which the big people say they must do.

Stage 2. Individualism and Exchange. At this stage children recognize that there is not just one right view that is handed down by the authorities. Different individuals have different viewpoints. "Heinz," they might point out, "might think it's right to take the drug, the druggist would not." Since everything is *relative,* each person is free to pursue his or her *individual* interests.

You might have noticed that children at both stages 1 and 2 talk about punishment. However, they perceive it differently. At stage 1 punishment is tied up in the child's mind with wrongness; punishment "proves" that disobedience is wrong. At stage 2, in contrast, punishment is simply a risk that one naturally wants to avoid.

Although stage 2 respondents sometimes sound a moral, they do have some sense of right action. This is a notion of *fair exchange* or fair deals. The philosophy is one of returning favors—"If you scratch my back, I'll scratch yours."

Respondents at stage 2 are still said to reason at the preconventional level because they speak as isolated individuals rather than as members of society. They see individuals exchanging favors, but there is still no identification with the values of the family or community.

Level II. Conventional Morality

Stage 3. Good Interpersonal Relationships. At this stage children—who are by now usually entering their teens—see morality as more than simple deals. They believe that people should live up to the expectations of the family and community and behave in "good" ways. Good behaviour means having good motives and interpersonal feelings such as love, empathy, trust, and concern for others.

As mentioned earlier, there are similarities between Kohlberg's first three stages and Piaget's two stages. In both sequences there is a shift from unquestioning obedience to a relativistic outlook and to a concern for good motives. For Kohlberg, however, these shifts occur in three stages rather than two.

Stage 4. Maintaining the Social Order. Stage 3 reasoning works best in two-person relationships with family members or close friends, where one can make a real effort to get to know the other's feelings and needs and try to help. At stage 4, in contrast, the respondent becomes more broadly concerned with *society as a whole.* Now the emphasis is on obeying laws, respecting authority, and performing one's duties so that the social order is maintained.

Because stage 4, subjects make moral decisions from the perspective of society as a whole, they think from a full-fledged member-of-society perspective.

You will recall that stage 1 children also generally oppose stealing because it breaks the law. Superficially, stage 1 and stage 4 subjects are giving the same response, so we see here why Kohlberg insists that we must probe into the reasoning behind the overt response. Stage 1 children say, "It's wrong to steal" and "It's against the law," but they cannot elaborate any further, except to say that stealing can get a person jailed. Stage 4 respondents, in contrast, have a conception of the function of laws for society as a whole—a conception which far exceeds the grasp of the younger child.

Level III. Post-conventional Morality

Stage 5. Social Contract and Individual Rights. At stage 4, people want to keep society functioning. However, a smoothly functioning society is not necessarily a good one. A totalitarian society might be well-organized, but it is hardly the moral ideal. At stage 5, people begin to ask, "What makes for a good society?" They begin to think about society in a very theoretical way, stepping back from their own society and considering the rights and values that a society ought to uphold. They then evaluate existing societies in terms of these prior considerations. They are said to take a "prior-to-society" perspective.

Stage 5 respondents basically believe that a good society is best conceived as a social contract into which people freely enter to work toward the benefit of all They recognize that different social groups within a society will have different values, but they believe that all rational people would agree on two points. First they would all want certain basic *rights,* such as liberty and life, to be protected Second, they would want some *democratic* procedures for changing unfair law and for improving society.

Stage 5 subjects, then, talk about "morality" and "rights" that take some priority over particular laws. Kohlberg insists, however, that we do not judge people to be at stage 5 merely from their verbal labels. We need to look at their social perspective and mode of reasoning. At stage 4, too, subjects frequently talk about the "right to life," but for them this right is legitimized by the authority of their social or religious group (e. g., by the Bible). Presumably, if their group valued property over life, they would too. At stage 5, in contrast, people are making more of an independent effort to think out what any society ought to value. They often reason, for example, that property has little meaning without life. They are trying to determine logically what a society ought to be like.

Stage 6: Universal Principles. Stage 5 respondents are working toward a conception of the good society. They suggest that we need to (a) protect certain individual rights and (b) settle disputes through democratic processes. However, democratic processes alone do not always result in outcomes that we intuitively sense are just. A majority, for example, may vote for a law that hinders a minority. Thus, Kohlberg believes that there must be a higher stage—stage 6—which defines the principles by which we achieve justice.

Kohlberg's conception of justice follows that of the philosophers Kant and Rawls, as well as great moral leaders such as Gandhi and Martin Luther King. According to these people, the principles of justice require us to treat the claims of all parties in an impartial manner, respecting the basic dignity, of all people as individuals. The principles of justice are therefore universal; they apply to all. Thus, for example, we would not vote for a law that aids some people but hurts others. The principles of justice guide us toward decisions based on an equal respect for all.

In actual practice, Kohlberg says, we can reach just decisions by looking at a situation through one another's eyes. In the Heinz dilemma, this would mean that all parties—the druggist, Heinz, and his wife—take the roles of the others. To do this in an impartial manner, people can assume a "veil of ignorance" (Rawls, 1971), acting as if they do not know which role they will eventually occupy. If the druggist did this, even he would recognize that life must take priority over property; for he wouldn't want to risk finding himself in the wife's shoes with property valued over life. Thus, they would all agree that the wife must be saved—this would be the fair solution. Such a solution, we must note, requires not only impartiality, but the principle that everyone is given full and equal respect. If the wife were considered of less value than the others, a just solution could not be reached.

Until recently, Kohlberg had been scoring some of his subjects at stage 6, but he has temporarily stopped doing so, For one thing, he and other researchers had not been finding subjects who consistently reasoned at this stage. Also, Kohlberg has concluded that his interview dilemmas are not useful for distinguishing between stage 5 and stage 6 thinking. He believes that stage 6 has a clearer and broader conception of universal principles (which include justice as well as individual rights), but feels that his interview fails to draw out this broader understanding. Consequently, he has temporarily dropped stage 6 from his scoring manual, calling it a "theoretical stage" and scoring all post conventional responses as stage 5.

Theoretically, one issue that distinguishes stage 5 from stage 6 is civil disobedience. Stage 5 would be more hesitant to endorse civil disobedience because of its commitment to the social contract and to changing laws through democratic agreements. Only when an individual right is clearly at stake does violating the law seem justified. At stage 6, in contrast, a commitment to justice makes the rationale for civil disobedience stronger and broader. Martin Luther King, for example, argued that laws are only valid insofar as they are grounded in justice, and that a commitment to justice carries with it an obligation to disobey unjust laws. King also recognized, of course, the general need for laws and democratic processes (stages 4 and 5), and he was therefore willing to accept the penalties for his actions. Nevertheless, he believed that the higher principle of justice required civil disobedience.

Summary

At stage 1 children think of what is right as that which authority says is right. Doing the right thing is obeying authority and avoiding punishment. At stage 2, children are no longer so impressed by any single authority; they see that there are different sides to any issue. Since everything is relative, one is free to pursue one's own interests, although it is often useful to make deals and exchange favors with others.

At stages 3 and 4, young people think as members of the conventional society with its values, norms, and expectations. At stage 3, they emphasize being a good person, which basically means having helpful motives toward people close to one At stage 4, the concern shifts toward obeying laws to maintain society as a whole.

At stages 5 and 6 people are less concerned with maintaining society for it own sake, and more concerned with the principles and values that make for a good society. At stage 5 they emphasize basic rights and the democratic processes that give everyone a say, and at stage 6 they define the principles by which agreement will be most just.

Concept of Moral Development

Piaget, you will recall, proposed that true mental stages meet several criteria. They (1) are qualitatively different ways of thinking, (2) are structured wholes, (3) progress in an invariant sequence, (4) can be characterized as hierarchic integrations. and (5) are cross-cultural universals. Kohlberg has taken these criteria very seriously, trying to show how his stages meet them all. Let us consider these points one at a time.

1. *Qualitative differences:* It seems fairly clear that Kohlberg's stages are qualitatively different from one another. For example, stage 1 responses, which focus on obedience to authority, sound very different from stage 2 responses, which argue that each person is free to behave as he or she wishes. The two stages do not seem to differ along any quantitative dimension, they seem qualitatively different.

2. *Structured wholes:* By "structured wholes," Kohlberg means that the stages are not just isolated responses but are *general* patterns of thought that will consistently show up across many different kinds of issues. One gets a sense that this is true by reading through his scoring manual; one finds the same kinds of thinking reappearing on diverse items.

3. *Invariant sequence.* Kohlberg believes that his stages unfold in an invariant sequence. Children always go from

stage 1 to stage 2 to stage 3 and so forth. They do not skip stages or move through them in mixed-up orders. Not all children necessarily reach the highest stages; they might lack intellectual stimulation. But to the extent they do go through the stages, they proceed in order.

Most of Kohlberg's evidence on his stage sequence comes from *cross-sectional* data. That is, he interviewed different children at various ages to see if the younger ones were at lower stages than the older ones. Stages 1 and 2 are primarily found at the youngest age, whereas the higher stages become more prevalent as age increases. Thus, the data support the stage sequence.

Cross-sectional findings, however, are inconclusive. In a cross-sectional study, different children are interviewed at each age, so there is no guarantee that any individual child actually moves through the stages in order. For example, there is no guarantee that a boy who is coded at stage 3 at age 13 actually passed through stages 1 and 2 in order when he was younger. More conclusive evidence must come from *longitudinal* studies, in which the same children are followed over time.

The first two major longitudinal studies (Kohlberg and Kramer, 1969; Holstein, 1973) began with samples of teenagers and then tested them at three-year intervals. These studies produced ambiguous results. In both, most subjects either remained at the same stage or moved up one stage, but there were also some who might have skipped a stage. Furthermore, these studies indicated that some subjects had regressed, and this finding also bothered Kohlberg, because he believes that movement through his stages should always be forward.

Kohlberg's response to these troublesome findings was to revise his scoring method. He had already become uncomfortable with his first (1958b) scoring manual, believing that it relied too heavily on the *content* of subjects' answers rather than their underlying *reasoning*. and he had made some improvements on it. So, when these longitudinal findings emerged, he decided to develop a much more precise and adequate scoring system and, to some extent, to revise his definitions of the stages.

To create the latest scoring manual, Kohlberg and his co-workers (Colby et al., 1983) worked with seven boys from his original (1958) sample who had been retested every three or four years for 20 years. It was during this work that Kohlberg decided to drop stage 6.

Kohlberg then examined the hypothesis of invariant sequence for 51 other boys from his original sample, who also had been retested at least twice (every three or four years) over the 20-year period. This time, Kohlberg and his colleagues (Colby et al., 1983) found no stage-skipping, and only about 6 per cent of the subjects showed signs of regressing. Four recent longitudinal studies have obtained similar results although, two have found somewhat more regression (up to 15 per cent) (Colby et al., 1983). In general, then, the new longitudinal studies seem to support the invariant-sequence hypothesis.

Kohlberg's new, longitudinal study has also changed the earlier picture of moral development in other ways. Stage 4 had become the dominant stage by age 16. In the new scoring system, however, it is more difficult to achieve the higher stages—the reasoning must be more clearly demonstrated—and Kohlberg finds that stage 4 does not become dominant until the boys are in their 20s and 30s. Stage 5, too, only appears in the mid-20s and never becomes very prevalent.

4. *Hierarchic integration:* When Kohlberg says that his stages are hierarchically integrated, he means that people do not lose the insights gained at earlier stages, but integrate them into new, broader frameworks. For example, people at stage 4 can still understand stage 3 arguments, but they

now subordinate them to wider considerations. They understand that Heinz had good motives for stealing, but they point out that if we all stole whenever we had a good motive, the social structure would break down. Thus stage 4 subordinates a concern for motives to a wider concern for the society as a whole.

The concept of hierarchic integration is very important for Kohlberg because it enables him to explain the direction of his stage sequence. Since he is not a maturationist, he cannot simply say that the sequence is wired into the genes. So he wants to show how each new stage provides a broader framework for dealing with moral issues. Stage 4, as mentioned, transcends the limitations of stage 3 and becomes more broadly concerned with social organization. Stage 5, in turn, sees the weakness of stage 4; a well-organized society is not necessarily a moral one. Stage 5 therefore considers the rights and orderly processes that make for a moral society. Each new stage retains the insights of the prior stage, but it recasts them into a broader framework. In this sense, each new stage is more cognitively adequate than the prior stage.

If Kohlberg is right about the hierarchic nature of his stages, we would expect that people would still be able to understand earlier stages but consider them inferior, In fact, when Rest (Rest et al., 1969; Rest, 1973) presented adolescents with arguments from different stages, this is what he found. They understood lower-stage reasoning, but they disliked it. What they preferred was the highest stage they heard, whether they fully understood it or not. This finding suggests, perhaps, that they had some intuitive sense of the greater adequacy of the higher stages.

Werner, we remember from Chapter 4, described hierarchic integration as a process that occurs alongside *differentiation,* and Kohlberg believes his stages represent increasingly differentiated structures as well. Kohlberg points out that the stage 5 value on life, for example, has become differentiated from other considerations. Stage 5 respondents say that we ought to value life for its own sake, regardless of its value to authorities (stage 1), its usefulness to oneself (stage 2), the affection it arouses in us (stage 3), or its value within a particular social order (stage 4). Stage 5 subjects have abstracted this value from other considerations and now treat it as a purely moral ideal. Their thinking, Kohlberg says, is becoming like that of the moral philosophers in the Kantian tradition (1981, p. 171).

5. *Universal sequence:* Kohlberg, like all stage theorists, maintains that his stage sequence is universal; it is the same in all cultures. At first glance, this proposal might be surprising. Don't different cultures socialize their children differently, teaching them very different moral beliefs?

Kohlberg's response is that different cultures do teach different beliefs, but that his stages refer not to specific beliefs but to underlying modes of reasoning (Kohlberg and Gilligan, 197 1). For example, one culture might discourage physical fighting, while another encourages it more. As a result, children will have different beliefs about fighting, but they will still reason about it in the same way at the same stage. At stage 1, for example, one child might say that it is wrong to fight when insulted "because you will get punished for it, "while another says that "it is all right to fight; you won't get punished." The beliefs differ, but both children reason about them in the same underlying way, in terms of the physical consequences (punishment). They do so because this is what they can cognitively grasp. Later on, the first child might argue that fighting is bad "because if everyone fought all the time there would be anarchy," while the second child argues that "people must defend their honor, because if they don't everyone will be insulting everyone, and the whole society will break down." Once again, the specific beliefs differ, reflecting different cultural teachings, but the underlying reasoning is the same—in this case it is stage 4, where people can consider something as abstract as the social order.

Children, regardless of their beliefs, will always move to stage 4 thinking some time after stage 1 thinking because it is cognitively so much more sophisticated.

Kohlberg, then, proposes that his stage sequence will be the same in all cultures, for each stage is conceptually more advanced than the next. He and other researchers have given his interview to children and adults in a variety of cultures, including Mexico, Taiwan, Turkey, Israel, the Yucatan, Kenya, the Bahamas, and India. Most of the studies have been cross sectional, but a few have been longitudinal. Thus far, the studies have supported Kohlberg's stage sequence. To the extent that children move through the stages, they appear to move in order (Edwards, 1980).

At the same time, people in different cultures seem to move through the sequence at different rates and to reach different end-points. In the United States most urban middle-class adults reach stage 4, with a small percentage using some stage 5 reasoning. In urban areas of other countries the picture is fairly similar. In the isolated villages and tribal communities of many countries, however, it is rare to find any adult beyond stage 3 (Edwards, 1980).

Kohlberg (Nisan and Kohlberg, 1982) suggests that one can understand these findings in terms of Piagetian theory. Cultural factors, in this theory, do not directly shape the child's moral thought, but they do stimulate thinking. Social experiences can challenge children's ideas, motivating them to come up with new ones. In traditional villages, however, there may be little to challenge a stage 3 morality; the norms of care and empathy work very well in governing the face-to-face interactions of the group. Thus, there is little to stimulate thinking beyond this stage.

When, in contrast, young people leave the village and go off to the city, they witness the breakdown of interpersonal ties. They see that group norms of care and empathy have little impact on the impersonal interactions of city life, and they see the need for a formal legal structure to ensure moral conduct. They begin to think in terms of stage 4 morality. Furthermore, as Keniston (1971) notes, if young people attend the universities, they may take classes in which the teachers deliberately question the unexamined assumptions of their childhoods and adolescences. Thus they are stimulated to think about moral matters in new ways.

11

Cognitive Development

While it's amazing to watch baby grow and develop, it's just as amazing to realize how her brain is "growing and developing."

Cognitive development is the development of the thinking and organizing systems of the brain. It involves language, mental imagery, thinking, reasoning, problem solving, and memory development.

Positive Role in Child's Cognitive Development

A positive role in your child's cognitive development by playing with her, having conversations with her, explaining what is happening as you go through the day together, introducing her to new activities and environments, encouraging her to explore and experiment, giving her choices, reading to her, being interested in her interests, letting her know it is okay to make mistakes, and loving and being proud of her.

Infants Age between 0-6 Months

Baby is learning to be socially aware. Shortly after birth, she will look at you and her brain will make the connection that you are an important person in her life. She will also make the connection that your voice is the voice of that special person who loves and cares for her. She will turn her head towards the sound of your voice when she hears it. She also loves to hear language and will try to converse with you almost from birth. Over the first few months of life, she will become aware of how her body moves and will begin to explore the world through her five senses.

Activities

1. Talk to your baby often. It is soothing to her and she is learning from the sounds.
2. Hold a rattle about 12 inches from her face and move it slowly from side to side. Her eyes will follow the path of the rattle for a short time. Over time she will be able to track for longer and longer periods.
3. Hold your face about 12 inches from hers and talk to her. She may try to imitate your facial expressions.
4. Hang a mobile over her crib at about 15 inches. She will enjoy watching it. At some point, she will begin to realize that her own movements make the mobile move. As infant becomes more mobile herself, you will need to raise the height of the mobile so that she will not grab it or become entangled in it.
5. Play classical music for her. This may help soothe your baby and some believe it may help with development in the music and math areas.
6. Read to baby every day. Ask your friends and relatives to read to her, too. baby is eager to hear language. It helps her learn the sounds of our language and it is very important for cognitive growth. Children who are read to often are more likely to "emerge" easily into literacy.
7. Sing to her and talk during feeding and while changing diapers.

Mobile Infants age between 6-12 months

Baby is beginning to get around under her own power! When she starts to crawl around, you'll be excited and terrified. Her horizons have expanded. She can crawl and scoot and "cruise" wherever her fancy takes her. Now she is really beginning to imitate the actions of others. She has longer periods of wakefulness and she is learning constantly.

As you perform a task, she watches you and creates mental images of how things work. She knows the difference between a familiar face and an unfamiliar one. If she has not seen a man with a mustache, she may be afraid when she sees one. She may take a little time to decide whether to trust a new person. You need to reassure her and help develop that self-confidence that will take her confidently through life. She enjoys taking things apart and putting them back together. She will now seek for an object that is hidden instead of forgetting about it. She is also learning to use simple tools like a spoon. As she begins doing simple activities, remember that she is just beginning and that she will need a lot of practice. Give her lots of praise and encouragement.

Activities

1. Invest in a set of nesting blocks or cylinders. The set has seven to nine blocks that nest inside each other. Your baby will enjoy dumping them or taking them apart and then trying to put them back together. Let her do it any way she wants. She does not care if only three blocks are nested together. Show your interest and your pleasure at her performance of this task. She will slowly get better at it as she develops.
2. Give child a kitchen cabinet that she is allowed to open. Fill it with your plastic containers. She will be happily busy in this cabinet while you are preparing dinner.
3. Play peek-a-boo with her.

4. Hide an object behind your back and let her find it.
5. Put some plastic cups in the tub while you are giving her a bath so she can fill and pour.
6. Imitate sounds she makes. She will probably imitate you right back.
7. Sing some notes of the scale to her. She will try to imitate you.
8. Read to her every day. She probably has favourite board books that she will want to hear over and over.
9. Give her safe objects to shake and discriminate sounds. She will explore them through her senses which means she will look, listen, touch, smell, and try to taste everything.
10. Place an unbreakable mirror in a spot where she can see herself.

Young Toddlers Age between 1-2 Years

12-to 24-month-old toddler is learning at an amazing rate. Sometime early in this year, if she isn't already walking, she will begin to walk. Then the world is truly open to her, and exists only for her gratification. So when she's running away from you in the grocery store to see and touch all the boxes and cans, please remember that right now, she is developmentally unable to see things.

She will begin to use words for the first time. She will also begin to imitate your actions and try to imitate your words. Her short-and long-term memory will improve dramatically during this period. She will begin to point to objects in her books when you name them.

She will respond to instructions with appropriate actions. She will be able to match two like objects and she will know the uses of many common household objects. She will learn by watching and by exploring and experimenting. Be patient with your one-year-old. This is sometimes a trying time, but it is also a fun, exciting time, watching your child progress.

Activities

1. Read to your child daily. She is picking up words quickly and she learns them by hearing you say them. Name objects in the book and let her point to them.
2. Have conversations with your child and listen when she talks.
3. Play Peek-a-Boo with her. She loves the idea of you having to search for her and she truly believes that she is invisible when she holds her hands over her eyes.
4. Ask her to find objects for you. You will be surprised at what she has noticed you doing.
5. Expand on child's words. If she says, "Block" then you say, "Did you find your block?" Do this kind of activity often to help your child begin to use sentences.
6. Put pictures of grandparents in your child's room or near the phone so she can "see" the person who is talking to her.
7. Sing simple songs with her.
8. Play "name the body parts" with her. She will love pointing to the part you name.
9. Invest in some blocks for her to stack. Do activities that show cause and effect, like hitting a block tower and watching it fall.
10. Let her experiment with paper and fat crayons with you. You can put them away when you are not supervising so they will not get eaten!

Toddlers Age between 2-3 Years

Two-year-old is becoming such a big girl! She can now say her own name and knows the difference between the words "you" and "me". She can respond to two step directions such as "Go get your socks and shoes". She can tell you what she is doing and she is learning new words daily. She has become aware of the words in a book and she chooses books to look at by herself. She can sort objects by size, shape, color, or use. She can use objects as tools to perform a task. She understands the functions of many objects. She has begun to engage in symbolic play (that is, she uses objects to represent other objects). She may use two blocks to represent different animals. She is trying very hard to master the use of her fork and spoon. She learns by observing and imitating adults. She likes to have you remind her of the events of the day before she goes to sleep. You will often hear her talking to herself in bed.

Activities

1. Give her objects to sort.
2. Use concept words in your daily conversations (near-far, up-down, in-out, empty-full, above-below, in front of-behind, etc.).
3. Repeat a simple nursery rhyme daily with your child until she can say it.
4. Each morning talk about what day it is and what you plan to do that day.
5. Read to child daily. Some of your books should be predictable books.
6. Ask for child's opinion sometimes.
7. Let her create with crayons and then ask her to tell you about her picture.
8. Begin counting objects with her.
9. Let her begin to do simple chores like setting the table. She will feel good about helping, and the two of you can count the silverware and napkins as you set them out.
10. Let her stack rings on a peg and get her a few simple puzzles with knobs.

Activities with Two-Year-Olds

Counting: Begin to count with our playful Animals. Don't worry if child doesn't count very high to begin with. Take time. Have fun talking about the animals. Talk about size, color, and the sounds they make, too.

Pre-schoolers Age between 3-5 Years

Three-Year-Olds: She constructs her own understanding of concepts, number, and cause and effect. Three-year-old will begin to use logical reasoning. She likes to reflect on experiences in order to make sense of them. She can still only focus on one dimension at a time (she believes that a tall, thin glass holds more than a short, wide one). She can classify familiar objects by use. She can rote count to 10 (1, 2, 3, 4, 5,) but she may get the numbers out of sequence. She can recall a two step direction such as, "Go find the ball and bring it to me." You will notice some improvement in her memory skills.

Four-Year-Olds

She can classify objects by size, shape, and use. She can name the 8 common colors. Her number skills are improving. She can count meaningfully to 5 (if you place 5 apples on the table and ask her to count them, she will be able to count those 5 apples). Her long-term memory is expanding. She engages in symbolic thought. She makes plans before acting because she can now see the consequences in advance. She engages in more make believe play which in turn helps develop reasoning and creativity.

She still engages in magical thinking (inanimate objects are alive). She can use one-to-one correspondence. She can describe objects by their appearance. She understands many concepts but still has trouble with time and space. She can sort by 2 attributes (size and shape). She can recall and execute a three step direction.

Activities

1. Make a game out of sorting blocks when it's time to put them up.

2. Make or purchase simple lotto games (matching board games for children). To make your own, mount different colored construction paper onto cardboard, cover it with clear contact paper, and cut it into playing card size. Have at least four colors of each card.
3. Get duplicate catalogs from companies such as car dealers, and cut up catalogs, mounting four similar car pictures on each set of four cards.
4. *Make collection-sorting games:* Collect a variety of different objects such as large paper clips, buttons, beads, washers, keys. Ask your child to sort the objects.
5. *Cook with child:* You can make a picture recipe for her with each step in the process numbered and illustrated in sequence. You can use drawn outlines of measuring cups and spoons or mount actual three-dimensional plastic utensils (cut in half) on cardboard. Discuss each step with the children as they do it. Ask them which comes next and then what.
6. *Make or purchase sequence cards:* For example, you can take a series of pictures of child building a block house, standing by the completed house, and knocking it down. Cover the photos with clear contact paper. Ask child to put the pictures in the sequence in which they occurred.
7. *Read a book:* The traditional fairy tales contain the concept of smallest to biggest. 1, 2, 3. To the Zoo, and are books that show number concepts.
8. Sing or play chants such as "One little, two little, three little ducks. . . "
9. Ask your child to help you set the table. Giving each family member a napkin, fork, and plate helps her with one-to-one correspondence.

10. *Build with blocks:* This gives child experiences with the concept of space.

Role and Need of Nutrition in Child Development

Good, Healthy Foods can Help Child a Good, Healthy Life

Good nutrition is key to your child's growth and development at every age—as a baby, a toddler, a school-aged child, and even as a teenager. The foods you choose to give your child help him grow and develop physically. But, good nutrition is just as important to social-emotional, cognitive, and language development.

Role of Nutrition

Even before birth, a child's brain is busily taking in information and creating paths to a storage area for each bit of information. This process uses a large amount of energy. Energy is provided by the nutrition the child receives. It is vitally important to cognitive development for her to be receiving appropriate amounts of nutrients. Protein is especially important to brain development both before and after birth. The "wiring" of the brain that is taking place at a furious pace during the early years will affect child for the rest of her life.

Nutrition for Cognitive Development

Cognitive development is your child's development of the thinking and organizing systems of her brain. Even as a baby, her brain is already taking in and storing information. This is a constant process, and one that takes a lot of energy-energy that's provided by good nutrition. When you consider that brain development at this stage will affect your child for the rest of her life, you can see why good nutrition is essential.

Piaget's Stages of Cognitive Development

Cognitive Development in Children

Probably the most cited theory in the cognitive development in children is Jean Piaget (1896-1980). As with all stage theories, *Piaget's Theory of Cognitive Development* maintains that children go through specific stages as their intellect and ability to see relationships matures. These stages are completed in a fixed order with all children, even those in other countries. The age range, however can vary from child to child.

Sensory Motor Stage. This stage occurs between the ages of birth and two years of age, as infants begin to understand the information entering their sense and their ability to interact with the world. During this stage, the child learns to manipulate objects although they fail to understand the permanency of these objects if they are not within their current sensory perception. In other words, once an object is removed from the child's view, he or she is unable to understand that the object still exists.

The major achievement during this stage is that of Object Permanency, or the ability to understand that these objects do in fact continue to exist. This includes his ability to understand that when mom leaves the room, she will eventually return, resulting in an increased sense of safety and security. Object Permanency occurs during the end of this stage and represents the child's ability to maintain a mental image of the object (or person) without the actual perception.

The Pre-operational Period (2-7 Years)

Pre-operational Stage: The second stage begins after Object Permanency is achieved and occurs between the ages of two to seven years of age. During this stage, the development of language occurs at a rapid pace. Children learn how to interact with their environment in a more complex manner through the use of words and images. This stage is marked by Egocentrism, or the child's belief that everyone sees the world the same way that she does. The fail to understand the differences in perception and believe that inanimate objects have the same perceptions they do, such as seeing things, feeling, hearing and their sense of touch.

A second important factor in this stage is that of Conservation, which is the ability to understand that quantity does not change if the shape changes. In other words, if a short and wide glass of water is poured into a tall and thin glass. Children in this stage will perceive the taller glass as having more water due only because of it's height. This is due to the children's inability to understand *reversibility* and to focus on only one aspect of a stimulus (called cent ration), such as height, as opposed to understanding other aspects, such as glass width.

Period of Concrete Operations (7-11 Years)

Concrete Operations Stage: Occurring between ages 7 and about 12, the third stage of cognitive development is marked by a gradual decrease in centristic thought and the increased ability to focus on more than one aspect of a stimulus. They can understand the concept of grouping, knowing that a small dog and a large dog are still both dogs, or that pennies, quarters, and dollar bills are part of the bigger concept of money.

They can only apply this new understanding to concrete objects (those they have actually experienced). In other words, imagined objects or those they have not seen, heard, or touched, continue to remain somewhat mystical to these children, and abstract thinking has yet to develop.

Period of Formal Operations (11-15 Years)

Formal Operations Stage: In the final stage of cognitive development (from age 12 and beyond), children begin to develop a more abstract view of the world. They are able to apply reversibility and conservation to both real and imagined situations. They also develop an increased understanding of the world and the idea of cause and effect. By the teenage years, they are able to develop their own theories about the world. This stage is achieved by most children, although failure to do so has been associated with lower intelligence.

Stages of Cognitive Development

Ages 4 to 7 Months: Cognitive Development

During your baby's first four months, did you have doubts that she really understood much that was happening around her? This parental reaction is not surprising. After all, although you knew when she was comfortable and uncomfortable, she probably showed few signs of actually thinking. Now, as her memory and attention span increase, you'll start to see evidence that she's not only absorbing information but also applying it to her day-to-day activities.

Discovering Cause and Effect

During this period, one of the most important concepts she'll refine is the principle of cause and effect. She'll probably stumble upon this notion by accident somewhere between 4 and 5 months. Perhaps while kicking her mattress, she'll notice the crib shaking. Or maybe she'll realize that her rattle makes a noise when she hits or waves it. Once she understands that she can cause these interesting reactions, she'll continue to experiment with other ways to make things happen.

Baby will quickly discover that some things, like bells and keys, make interesting sounds when moved or shaken. When she bangs certain things on the table or drops them on the floor, she'll start a chain of responses from her audience, including funny faces, groans, and other reactions that may lead to the reappearance or disappearance of the object. Before long, she'll begin intentionally dropping things to see you pick them up. As annoying as this may be at times, it's one important way for her to learn about cause and effect and her personal ability to influence her environment.

It's important that you give child the objects she needs for these experiments and encourage her to test her "theories." But make sure that everything you give her to play with is unbreakable, lightweight and large enough that she can't possibly swallow it. If you run out of the usual toys or she loses interest in them, plastic or wooden spoons, unbreakable cups, and jar or bowl lids and boxes are endlessly entertaining and inexpensive.

Discovering Object Permanence

Another major discovery that your baby will make during this period is that objects continue to exist when they're out of her sight, a principle called object permanence. During her first few months, she assumed that the world consisted only of things that she could see. When you left her room, she assumed you vanished; when you returned, you were a whole new person to her. In much the same way, when you hid a toy under a cloth or a box, she thought it was gone for good and wouldn't bother looking for it. But sometime after 4 months she'll begin to realize that the world is more permanent than she thought. You're the same person who greets her every morning. Her teddy bear on the floor is the same one that was in bed with her the night before. The block that you hid under the can did not actually vanish after all. By playing hiding games and observing the comings and goings of people and things around her, baby will continue to learn about object permanence for many months to come.

Age 2 to 3 Years: Cognitive Development

Think back to child's infancy and the early toddler months. That was a time when he learned about the world by touching, looking, manipulating and listening. Now the learning process has become more thoughtful. His grasp of language is increasing and he's beginning to form mental images for things, actions and concepts. He also can solve some problems in his head, performing mental trial-and-error instead of having to manipulate objects physically. And as his memory and intellectual abilities develop, he'll begin to understand simple time concepts, such as "You can play after you finish eating."

Toddler also is starting to understand the relationship between objects. For instance, he'll be able to match similar shapes when you give him shape-sorting toys and simple jigsaw puzzles. He'll begin to recognize the purpose of numbers in counting objects, especially the number 2. And as his understanding of cause and effect develops, he'll become much more interested in winding up toys and turning lights and appliances on and off.

If we were to single out the major intellectual limitation at this age, it would be child's feeling that everything that happens in his world is the result of something he has done. With a belief like this, it becomes very difficult for him to understand correctly such concepts as death, divorce or illness without feeling that he played some role in it. So if parents separate or a family member gets sick, children often feel responsible.

Reasoning, 2-year-old is often difficult. After all, he views everything in extremely simple terms. He still often confuses fantasy with reality unless he's actively playing make-believe." Therefore, during this stage, be sure to choose your own words carefully. Comments that you think are funny or playful, such as "If you eat more ice cream, you'll explode," may actually panic him because he won't know you're joking.

Age 3 to 4 Years: Cognitive Development

3-year-old will spend most of her waking hours questioning everything that happens around her. She loves to ask, "Why do I have to. . . ?" and she'll pay close attention to your answers as long as they're simple and to the point. Don't feel that you have to explain your rules fully; she can't yet understand such reasoning and isn't interested in it anyway. If you try to have this kind of "serious" conversation, you'll quickly see her stare into space or turn her attention to more entertaining matters, like a toy across the room or a truck passing outside the window. Instead, telling her to do something "because it's good for you" or "so you don't get hurt" will make more sense to her than a detailed explanation.

Answering "Why "Questions

Child's more abstract "why" questions may be more difficult, partly because there may be hundreds of them each day, and also because some of them have no answers or none that you know. If the question is "Why does the sun shine?" or "Why can't the dog talk to me?" you can answer that you don't know, or invite her to look into the question further by finding a book about the sun or about dogs. Be sure to take these questions seriously. As you do, you help broaden child's knowledge, feed her curiosity, and teach her to think more clearly.

3-year-old is faced with specific learning challenges, you'll find her reasoning still rather one-sided. She can't yet see an issue from two angles, nor can she solve problems that require her to look at more than one factor at the same time. For example, if you take two equal cups of water and pour one into a short, fat container and the other into a tall, skinny one, she'll probably say the tall container holds more water than the short. Even if she sees the two equal cups to start with and watches you pour, she'll come up with the same answer. By her logic, the taller container is "bigger" and therefore must hold more. At around age 7, children finally understand that they have to look at multiple aspects of a problem before arriving at an answer.

Sense of Time

At about 3 years of age, child's sense of time will become much clearer. She'll now know her own daily routine and will try hard to figure out the routines of others. For example, she may eagerly watch for the mail carrier who arrives every day but be perplexed that the garbage man comes only one day out of seven. She'll understand that certain special events, such as holidays and birthdays, occur every once in a while, but even if she can tell you how old she is, she'll have no real sense of the length of a year.

Developmental Evaluations

Although it's almost human nature to try to measure child's intellectual progress, beware of over or under-estimating her reasoning or thinking ability without formal testing. It's easy to convince yourself that your friendly, happy, highly verbal 3-year-old is brilliant, while the quieter, more laid-back youngster playing next to her is not as bright. This may or may not be true, but the only way to know for sure is to have the child evaluated professionally. All pediatricians are familiar with these developmental evaluations, and some actually conduct formal assessments themselves. Many pediatricians prefer to refer children to testing specialists. So, if you believe your child is either gifted or lagging behind, ask your doctor about such testing. If your suspicions prove true, you may want to enter her in a special program geared to her individual needs and abilities.

Brain Growth During the Third Year

- Encourage playing with blocks and soft toys, which helps child develop eye-hand coordination, fine-motor skills and a sense of competence.
- Give consistent warm, physical contact-hugging, skin-to-skin, body-to-body contact to establish your toddler's sense of security and well-being.
- Be attentive to your child's rhythms and moods. Respond to her when she is upset as well as when she is happy. Be encouraging and supportive, with firm discipline as appropriate, but without yelling or hitting. Provide consistent guidelines.
- Talk or sing to child during dressing, bathing, feeding, playing, walking and driving, using adult talk. Speak slowly and give child time to respond. Try not to reply with "uh-huh" because child will recognize when you're not listening; instead, expand upon child's phrases.

- Be predictable; establish a pattern for mealtimes, naps and bedtime.
- Develop word associations by giving word labels to everyday objects and activities.
- Read to child every day. Choose books that encourage touching and pointing to objects, and read rhymes, jingles and nursery stories.
- If you speak a foreign language, use it at home.
- Play calm and melodic music for child
- Listen to and answer child's questions. Also, ask questions to stimulate decision-making processes.
- Begin to explain "safety" in simple terms. For example, feeling the heat from the stove teaches the meaning and danger of hot objects.
- Make sure other people who provide care and supervision for baby understand the importance of forming a loving and comforting relationship with child.
- Encourage child to look at books and to draw.
- Help child use words to describe emotions and to express feelings, such as happiness, joy, anger and fear.
- Spend time on the floor playing with child every day.
- Choose quality child care that is affectionate, responsive, educational and safe. Visit your child-care provider frequently and share the ideas about positive care giving.

Age 4 to 5 Years: Cognitive Development

By age 4, the child is beginning to explore many basic concepts that will be taught in greater detail in school. For example, she now understands that the day is divided into morning, afternoon and night, and that there are different seasons. By the time she enters kindergarten she may know some days of the week, and that each day is measured in hours and minutes. She also may comprehend the essential ideas of counting, the alphabet, size relationships (big versus small) and the names of geometric shapes.

There are many good children's books that illustrate these concepts, but don't feel compelled to rush things. There's no advantage to her learning them this early, and if she feels pressured to perform now, she may actually resist learning when she gets to school.

The best approach is to offer the child a wide range of learning opportunities. For instance, this is the perfect age to introduce her to zoos and museums, if you haven't already. Many museums have special sections designed for children, where she can actively experience the learning process.

Encouraging Interests

Respect her special interests and talents. If the child seems very artistic, take her to art museums and galleries or let her try a preschool art class. Also, if you know an artist, take her for a visit so she can see what a studio is like. On the other hand, if she's most interested in machines and dinosaurs take her to the natural history museum, help her learn to build models, and provide her with construction kits that allow her to create her own machines. Whatever her interests, you can use books to help answer her questions and open her horizons even further. At this age, then, your child should be discovering the joy of learning so that she will be self-motivated when her formal education begins.

Bibliography

Baldwin, A.L. (1955), *Behaviour and Development in Childhood*, New York.

Bayley, N. (1975) *On the Growth of Intelligence*, American Psychologist, .

Bereiter, C. and Engleman S., (1966) *Teaching Disadvantage Children in the Pre-School.*

Loom, B. (1964) *Stability and change in Human Characteristics*, New York.

Bowlby, J. (1951), *Maternal Care and Child Health.*

Ericson, E. (1950), *Childhood and Society*, New York.

Hurlock, E. (1972), *Child Development*, Tokyo.

Kohlberg, L. (1964), *Development of Moral Character and Moral Ideology*, New York.

Kohlberg, L. (1968), *Early Education, a Cognitive Development View, Child Development.*

Kohlberg, L. (1974), *Moral Development and Faith.*

Lenneberg, E.H. (1967), *Biological Function of Language.*

Panda, K.C. (1978), *Elements of Child Development.*

Piaget, J. (1932), *The Moral Judgment of the Child*, London.

Piaget, J. (1952), *The Origins of Intelligence in Children*, New York.

Piaget, J. (1968), *Six Psychological Study*, London.

Smith, J.O, (1963), *Group Language Development for Educable Mentally Retardates.*

Taylor, C.W. (1964), *Creativity: Progress and Potential*, New York.

Terman, L.M. (1925), *Genetic Study of Genius.*

Throndike, E.L. (1927), *Measurement of Intelligence*, New York.

Torrance, E.P. (1962), *Guiding Creative Talents.*

Index

A

Academic training, 122
Active play, 126
Activity level, 229
Activity of cognitive development, 272
Activity of intellectual development, 160
Adaptability, 231
Adult motor development, 60
Anal stage, 236
Argument, 104
Articulation, 212
Articulation problem, 212
Assessment, 219
Athletic games, 114
Autonomy versus shame, 244

B

Baby communication, 198
Baby cubbies, 22
Barriers to creativity, 171
Bilateral coordination, 40
Bilingual homes, 197
Bodily kimesthetic, 143
Body proportion, 33
Body weight, 33
Bouncing rides, 92
Brain growth, 286
Brilliant, 131
Bronfenbrenner's theory, 253

C

Caring by parents, 66
Caring for infants, 66
Causes and effect, 282
Causes of articulation, 213
Causes of language disorder, 194
Changes in height, 33
Changes in toys, 98
Characteristics of childhood emotions, 84
Characteristics of creative children, 173
Characteristics of language development, 210
Chart of language development, 182
Child behaviour, 119
Child development, 11
Child pronounce, 214
Child's personality, 232
Childhood behaviour problems, 86
Childhood emotional pattern, 85
Children at risk, 216
Children's literacy development, 170
Choices and limits, 70
Classification of motor development, 60
Cluttering, 195
Cognitive development, 271
Communication pattern, 203
Communication problem, 204
Communication, 198
Community, 28
Concept of child development, 11
Concept of intelligence, 136
Concept of moral development, 263

Concept of personality development, 223
Concept of social and emotional development, 63
Concept of play, 89
Concrete operational period, 281
Concrete operational stage, 158
Constructive play, 128
Conventional morality, 252
Cooperation versus competition, 73
Cooperative play, 126
Creative activity, 165
Creative play, 98, 126, 177
Creative thinking and writing, 174
Creativity among children, 174
Creativity development through art, 172
Creativity development, 165
Croquet, 120
Crying, 29
Cuddling, 90

D

Daily diets of child, 25
Dealing with feeling, 69
Defective speech, 194
Definition of intelligence, 136
Definition of speech disorder, 210
Developmental changes in catching, 59
Developmental delay, 45
Developmental evaluation, 285
Diet for intellectual development, 163
Differing chairs, 43
Difficulties of temperament, 231
Direct personality, 227
Distractibility, 218, 229
Dramatic play, 126

E

Educational implication, 211
Ego centric judgement, 254
Ego defense mechanism, 240
Ego psychology, 243
Ego versus despair, 246
Elevator, 92
Embryonic, 120
Emotional health, 69, 71
Emotional need, 75
Empathy, 72
Encourage creativity, 169
Enhancement of creativity, 177
Enhancement of motor development, 57
Erickson psychosocial theory, 242
Essential attribute of play, 115
Exchange stage, 251

F

Fairness, 73
Family relationship, 196
Fantasy play, 128
Fine motor skills, 32, 38
First baby learn, 89
Five senses, 32
Food painting, 94
Formal operational period, 159, 281
Fostering the creative process, 166
Frued psychosexual development, 236
Functional articulation, 214
Fusion, 111
Fussing, 93

G

Garden's theory, 139
General intelligence, 137
Generativity versus stagnation, 245
Genital stage, 237
Getting along together, 71
Global delay, 46
Goals and priorities, 136

Growing independence, 54
Guidelines for policy, 124

H

Health, 196
Hereditary factor, 224
Hide and seek, 94
Home, 29
Hypertonia, 44

I

I.Q. test, 132
Ideas and interest, 147
Illness and infection, 32
Imaginary situation, 108
Immediate impulse, 115
Implications for education, 162
Importance of creative development, 165
Importance of trust, 69
Incidence, 210
Industry versus inferiority, 245
Infancy and childhood, 37
Initiative versus guilt, 244
Inner directed personality, 227
Intellectual capability, 154
Intellectual development, 153
Intellectual growth, 162
Intelligence development, 131
Intelligence theory, 147
Intelligence, 196
Intelligent, 131
Intense feeling, 30
Intensity, 230
Interests, 287
Internal processes, 114
Interpersonal, 143
Intimacy versus isolation, 245
Intra personal, 144

J

Jean Piaget intellectual development, 155

K

Kangaroo hop, 43
Kohlberg theory, 248

L

Language and speech, 209
Language development, 181
Language disorder, 193
Language pathologist, 218
Language problem, 216
Language teaching—principles, 192
Large muscle, 15
Large muscle skill, 23
Latency stage, 237
Law and order, 255
Learn all sounds, 214
Learning activity, 26
Learning disability, 215
Learning milestones, 92
Learning play, 91
Learning through play, 97
Linguistic, 144
Lisping, 194
Logical mathematical, 145

M

Malnutrition, 163
Manipulative play, 127
Meaning of action, 117
Methods of teaching, 175
Modal personality, 227
Modelling behaviour, 72
Mood, 231
Moral behaviour, 247
Moral development theory, 250
Moral development, 247
Moral realism, 109
Motor development, 33, 35
Multiple intelligence, 134, 139
Musical, 146
Myelin, 36

N

Naturalist intelligence, 146
Nature and Nurture, 249
Nature of intelligence, 136
Nervous system, 33
Nutrition in child development, 278
Nutritional need, 25

O

Obedience orientation, 255
Object permanence, 282
Opportunity for creativity, 166
Oral stage, 236

P

Pacifier, 48
Parents communication, 202
Parents role, 203, 235
Peakaboo, 94
Persistance, 231
Personality development, 223
Phallic stage, 237
Phases of motor development, 58
Physical and motor play, 128
Physical growth, 32
Physical need, 75
Piaget theory, 162, 257, 279
Piaget's approach, 135
Play and its role, 100
Play development, 89
Play time, 98
Positive manifold, 137
Positive role, 15, 74, 271
Post conventional morality, 252
Postural locomotor development, 33
Pre-conventional morality, 251
Prehension development, 34
Pre-operational stage, 157, 280
Pre-schematic stage, 167
Preschool child, 22
Pretend, 83
Prevention, 219
Programme in child development, 28
Prone reaction, 44
Prototype, 116
Pseudo naturalistic, 168

Q

Quiet play, 127

R

Reaching and grasping, 39
Reaction time, 137
Reading and writing, 190
Realistic stage, 168
Reality behind creativity, 170
Realm of spontaneity, 116
Regularity, 230
Remedy of articulation, 215
Reward and punishment, 251
Role of nutrition, 74, 279
Role of parents, 172
Routine care, 29

S

Safe exploration, 30
Schematic stage, 167
School age, 55
School readiness, 55
Self exploration, 68
Sense of time, 285
Sensory motor stage, 156, 279
Sensory threshold, 230
Simple motor activity, 42
Situational constraint, 110
Slurring, 195
Small muscle skill, 16, 24
Social and emotional development, 63
Social competence, 71
Social contract, 252
Social development, 86
Social play, 128

Spatial, 147
Stage theory, 37
Stages of cognitive development, 281
Stages of language development, 181
Stages of moral development, 254
Stages of motor development, 47, 58
Stages of physical development, 11
Stages of play, 89
Stammering, 195
Stamford Binet test, 132
Sternburg's theory, 140
Story staters, 191
Structural model, 238
Study of motor development, 56
Stuttering, 195
Superficially, 121

T

Talking with infants, 30
Talking with infants, 67
Techniques to improve language development, 197
Temperament traits, 229
Temperament, 227-28
Theory of intelligence, 141
Theory [illegible]d emotional dev[illegible]3
Tips of c[illegible]73
Toddlers[illegible]
Topograp[illegible]l, 239
Tradition[illegible] personality, 227
Treatmen[illegible]
Trust vers[illegible]st, 244
Twins, 197
Types of pe[illegible], 225
Types of pla[illegible]
Types of sou[illegible], 213

Under nouris[illegible]4
Universal pri[illegible] 261

Variety of expe[illegible], 166

Wheel barrier, [illegible]
Withdrawal, 23[illegible]

Z

Zones and model[illegible]3